TELEVISION AND COMMON KNOWLEDGE

In today's world television is the primary source of 'common knowledge', the widely-shared pool of information and perspectives from which people create their understanding of self, world and citizenship. Democracy is based on the idea that every citizen is well informed and thus able to determine how they participate in political, social and cultural processes. How, and how well, does television contribute to a realization of this ideal?

Television and Common Knowledge is a collection of new essays examining television as a vehicle for informed citizenship. First, the contributors examine how knowledge is produced and circulated within public spheres and across the social and cultural borderlines of modern society, then they investigate the broader social and cultural functions which television has for its audiences. Later chapters concentrate on specific tv genres such as news, documentary, political discussions and popular science programmes, considering the changing ways in which they attempt to inform and entertain, and how they are perceived by viewers.

Drawing on a wide range of theoretical approaches, and covering topics as diverse as popular science programmes, the therapeutic functions of television and the joys of 'zapping' in a multi-channel environment, *Television and Common Knowledge* provides original insights into the social role of television as well as significant contributions to media theory.

Contributors: Suzanne de Cheveigné, John Corner, Daniel Dayan, John Ellis, Jostein Gripsrud, Klaus Bruhn Jensen, Anders Johansen, Peter Larsen, Sonia Livingstone, David Morley, Graham Murdock, Roger Silverstone.

Jostein Gripsrud is Professor of Media Studies at the University of Bergen, Norway.

COMEDIA SERIES
Edited by David Morley

Other Comedia titles available from Routledge:

ADVERTISING INTERNATIONAL
The Privatisation of Public Space
Armand Mettelart (translated by Michael Channan)

BLACK BRITISH CULTURE AND SOCIETY
A Reader
Edited by Kwesi Owusu

THE CONSUMERIST MANIFESTO
Advertising in Postmodern Times
Martin Davidson

CULTURAL SNIPING
The Art of Transgression
Jo Spence

CULTURES OF CONSUMPTION
Masculinities and Social Space in Late
Twentieth-century Britain
Frank Mort

CUT 'N' MIX
Culture, Identity and Caribbean Music
Dick Hebdige

THE DYNASTY YEARS
Hollywood Television and Critical Media
Studies
Jostein Gripsrud

FAMILY TELEVISION
Cultural Power and Domestic Leisure
David Morley

HIDING IN THE LIGHT
On Images and Things
Dick Hebdige

THE KNOWN WORLD OF BROADCAST
NEWS
Stanley Baran and Roger Wallis

MIGRANCY, CULTURE, IDENTITY
Iain Chambers

THE PHOTOGRAPHIC IMAGE IN DIGITAL
CULTURE
Edited by Martin Lister

SPECTACULAR BODIES
Gender, Genre and the Action Cinema
Yvonne Tasker

STUART HALL
Critical Dialogues in Cultural Studies
Edited by Kuan-Hsing Chen and David Morley

TEACHING THE MEDIA
Len Masterman

TELEVISION AND COMMON
KNOWLEDGE
Edited by Jostein Gripsrud

TELEVISION AUDIENCES AND CULTURAL
STUDIES
David Morley

TELEVISION, ETHNICITY AND
CULTURAL CHANGE
Marie Gillespie

TELEVISION MYTHOLOGIES
Len Masterman

TO BE CONTINUED...
Soap Opera Around the World
Edited by Robert C. Allen

TRANSNATIONAL CONNECTIONS
Culture, People, Places
Ulf Hannerz

VIDEO PLAYTIME
The Gendering of a Leisure Technology
Ann Gray

TELEVISION AND COMMON KNOWLEDGE

Edited by Jostein Gripsrud

London and New York

First published 1999
by Routledge
11 New Fetter Lane, London EC4P 4EE

Simultaneously published in the USA and Canada
by Routledge
29 West 35th Street, New York, NY 10001

Typeset in Joanna and Bembo by Routledge
Printed and bound in Great Britain by
Biddles Ltd, Guildford and King's Lynn

British Library Cataloguing in Publication Data
A catalogue record for this book is available from the British Library

Library of Congress Cataloging in Publication Data
Television and common knowledge / edited by Jostein Gripsrud.
p.cm.
Includes bibliographical references and index.
1. Television–Social aspects. 2. Knowledge, Sociology of. 3. Popular
culture–History–20th century. I Gripsrud, Jostein
PN1992.6 T379   1999
302.23'45–dc21   98–34504
CIP

ISBN 0–415–18928–4 (hbk)
ISBN 0–415–18929–2 (pbk)

CONTENTS

List of contributors   *x*

Television and common knowledge: an introduction   **1**

PART I
Public sphere(s)   **5**

1 **Rights and representations: public discourse and cultural
   citizenship**   **7**
   GRAHAM MURDOCK

   A tale of two narratives 7
   From simple to complex citizenship 8
   Underwriting rights 10
   Defining cultural rights 11
   Questions of representation 13
   Discourse/image/form 13
   The political economy of populism 14
   Public space and public discourse 15
   References 17

2 **Media and diasporas**   **18**
   DANIEL DAYAN

   Fragile communities, particularistic media 18
   The context of globalization 19
   Identity as process: production, confrontation, adoption 20
   Medias and diasporas 22
   Conclusions 28
   Acknowledgement 31
   References 31

3 Scholars, journalism, television: notes on some conditions
   for mediation and intervention   34

   JOSTEIN GRIPSRUD

   Introduction 34
   Television, knowledge and postmodernism 35
   Enlightenment, the public sphere and broadcast television 37
   Journalism and academia as social fields 39
   Journalistic v. academic habitus 41
   Scholars mingling with the media: motives and consequences 42
   Television, stereotypes and audience perceptions of academics 45
   Television's priorities and the hierarchies of scholarly disciplines 48
   The conditions for acting as public intellectuals 49
   References 52

PART II
Sociocultural functions   53

4 Television as working-through   55

   JOHN ELLIS

   Introduction 55
   Soaps 60
   Documentaries 61
   In praise of uncertainty 64
   Sport 64
   Narrative forms 66
   In praise of discontinuity 67
   Conclusion 68
   Notes 69
   References 70

5 Rhetoric, play, performance: revisiting a study of the making
   of a BBC documentary   71

   ROGER SILVERSTONE

   Introduction 71
   The nature of a return 71
   Discursive spaces 74
   Rhetoric 76
   Play 79

Performance 82
Conclusion 85
Notes 86
References 88

6 **Mediated knowledge: recognition of the familiar, discovery
   of the new**   **91**
   SONIA LIVINGSTONE

   Mediated knowledge and active audiences 91
   Towards a research agenda for mediated knowledge 93
   Theorizing knowledgeable audiences 95
   Recognition of the familiar, discovery of the new 96
   Knowledge, space and time 98
   Mediated and non-mediated knowledge 100
   Implications for audience-reception research 101
   Notes 103
   References 105

7 **Imaginary spaces: television, technology and everyday
   consciousness**   **108**
   PETER LARSEN

   You press the button, we do the rest 108
   Bearings 109
   Places and spaces, maps and tours 110
   An institutional story 112
   Travel stories 113
   Tour guides 114
   In the flow 115
   Screen: opening, window pane, borderline 116
   Mapping 117
   Acknowledgement 120
   Notes 120
   References 120

PART III

Genres   **123**

8 **Knowledge as received: a project on audience uses of
   television news in world cultures**   **125**
   KLAUS BRUHN JENSEN

   Introduction 125
   The flow of international news 126
   News of the World: project outline 129
   Preliminary findings 131
   Implications for theory and policy 133
   Acknowledgement 134
   References 135

9 **Finding out about the world from television news: some
   difficulties**   **136**
   DAVID MORLEY

   Introduction 136
   Decoding the television news 140
   The world and the television world 141
   Evaluating things you do not know about 143
   Media dependency theory: real confusions 144
   The sitcom and the vice-president: paradoxes of the real 147
   Polysemy, ambiguity and contradiction 151
   Postscript 155
   References 156

10 **Credibility and media development**   **159**
   ANDERS JOHANSEN

   References 171

11 **Documentary: the transformation of a social aesthetic**   **173**
   JOHN CORNER

   Introduction 173
   Public television in the 1990s 174
   Documentary: a flawed genre? 175
   Documentary modality: four primary ingredients 177
   Four trends in recent British documentary 179

Acknowledgement 183
Notes 183
References 184

12 **Science on TV: forms and reception of science programmes on
French television** **185**
SUZANNE DE CHEVEIGNÉ

Introduction 185
Identifying the forms 186
Two essential variables 187
The intellectual reading 188
The beneficiary reading 189
Disappointed beneficiaries 190
The intimistic reading 191
The excluded position 195
Conclusion 196
Notes 197
References 197

Index 199

CONTRIBUTORS

Suzanne de Cheveigné is Research Fellow at the CNRS, Laboratoire Communication et Politique, Paris.

John Corner is Reader in the School of Politics and Communication Studies at the University of Liverpool.

Daniel Dayan is Research Fellow at the CNRS, Laboratoire d'Anthropologie des Institutions et Organisations Sociales, Paris and Professor II in the Department of Media and Communication at the University of Oslo.

John Ellis is Professor of Moving Image Studies in the Department of Media Production at Bournemouth University and Professor II in the Department of Media Studies at the University of Bergen.

Jostein Gripsrud is Professor in the Department of Media Studies at the University of Bergen.

Klaus Bruhn Jensen is Associate Professor in the Department of Film and Media Studies at Copenhagen University.

Anders Johansen is Professor in the Department of Media Studies at the University of Bergen.

Peter Larsen is Professor in the Department of Media Studies at the University of Bergen.

Sonia Livingstone is Senior Lecturer in the Department of Social Psychology at the London School of Economics and Political Science.

David Morley is Professor of Communications in the Department of Media and Communications, Goldsmiths College, University of London.

Graham Murdock is Reader in the Sociology of Culture, Loughborough University and Professor II in the Department of Media Studies at the University of Bergen.

Roger Silverstone is Professor of Media and Communication at the London School of Economics and Political Science.

TELEVISION AND COMMON KNOWLEDGE

An introduction

This book comes out of a research project at the University of Bergen, Norway, entitled Rhetoric, Knowledge, Mediation. The project, which was funded by the Norwegian Research Council through the programme Research on the Mediation of Culture and Tradition (KULT), was a cross- and multidisciplinary project intended to explore a number of interrelated problem areas linked to the project title's three terms:

- *The interrelatedness of language and knowledge*: What are the characteristics of the typical 'linguistic' forms and rhetorical devices of research and the sciences, and how is the knowledge produced determined by these 'linguistic' features? Are other forms of knowledge imaginable, produced in other kinds of language?
- *Mass media as mediators and producers of knowledge and culture*: What are the characteristics of rhetorical devices commonly employed by broadly oriented mass media, and how is that which they communicate or mediate determined by these features? What are the social conditions of the media's own production of knowledge and their mediating activities? What does a mediation or 'translation' between the languages of research and the languages of the media imply?
- *Rhetorical theory and its current status*: To what extent and in which sense is classical rhetoric, originally developed with a view to oral communication (speech), relevant to modern print, visual and electronic media?

This book is, then, obviously primarily related to the second of these problem areas, even if both inspiration from rhetorical theory and attention to (widely conceived) rhetorical problems mark most contributions. The very expression 'common knowledge' may be seen as a reference to classical rhetorical theory, since 'common knowledge' in one sense or another provided the basis for all effective rhetoric in the days of Aristotle, Cicero and Quintilian. In our time, and specifically in this context, 'common' may, besides the meaning 'commonly shared', also connote the low status of the medium under scrutiny. The crux of the matter(s) discussed in this book is in a sense that the central medium for the production and mediation of knowledge in advanced, late-modern democracies is also a medium which is routinely regarded with contempt by those presumably most knowledgeable.

All articles, with the exception of those written by Peter Larsen, David Morley and myself, come out of a colloquium at the University of Bergen in the autumn of 1995, devoted to the production and distribution of knowledge in and through the medium of television. The event turned out to be one of those deplorably rare academic occasions where one can sense that some really imaginative thinking is presented and further developed through lively discussions. The papers, some of them slightly revised, therefore deserve to be presented to a wider audience, in the hope that they may stimulate further exploratory thinking and research. The added papers by Peter Larsen and David Morley, both invited to the colloquium but, like me, the convenor, unable to attend at the time, are written in the same spirit as the others and included for the same reasons.

An investigation of television's role as a producer and mediator of knowledge in today's world must evidently employ a wide-ranging set of approaches. Even if we maintain a focus on TV as a primary contributor to *common knowledge*, to the widely shared pool of information and perspectives from which people shape their conceptions of self, world and citizenship, the complexity of this role is almost overwhelming. Anything from the medium's social organization, its technological features, its specific forms of textuality to, not least, its kaleidoscopic patterns of reception is relevant to studies in this area. The contributions in this volume cover many of these aspects, in ways which open up, rather than foreclose, further work in many directions.

In Part I, 'Public sphere(s)', Graham Murdock (Chapter 1) discusses the role of television in the context of democratic processes, and the ways in which television relates – and *should* relate – to the distribution of resources for active and informed citizenship. His argument is clearly tied to classic Enlightenment ideas and a Habermasian conception of the public sphere. Daniel Dayan (Chapter 2) then both complements and to a degree problematizes Murdock's views by pointing to the increasing importance of various, not least ethnically deemed, diasporic, communities that to some extent form semi-autonomous spheres of communication within modern societies. It is, however, also pointed out by Dayan that these specific 'micro' public spheres also are – and increasingly over time – embedded in and in constant interaction with the public sphere at large. In the editor's own contribution the main idea is to have a closer look at the social and cultural relationships between two key groups in the public sphere, and in the processes of production and mediation of knowledge – scholars and journalists. Starting from a brief defence of the validity of a notion of knowledge in so-called postmodern times, the chapter analyses the changing relations of power between scholars and journalists, drawing on Pierre Bourdieu's conception of 'social fields', and also discusses how factors such as cultural stereotypes of 'the academic' may influence the position of scholars in television and other mass media.

Part II, 'Sociocultural functions', consists of four contributions which in different ways speak of the general sociocultural functions of television, perceived as they relate to notions of 'knowledge' and to various dimensions of the processes and elements of audience reception. John Ellis (Chapter 4) suggests a view of television as a 'vast mechanism for processing the raw data of news-reality into more narrativized, explained forms'. He compares this to the psychoanalytic notion of 'working-through', a process where psychic material is 'worried over until it is exhausted' rather than turned into some finished product. A number of central television genres are discussed in the light of this metaphor, from the general starting point that we live in 'an age that has, because of television itself to a large degree, far too much information and too little explanation'. Roger Silverstone (Chapter 5), after presenting some critical afterthoughts on his 1985 study of the making of a television science documentary, takes another look at the relationship between text and audience, or, rather, 'the *discursive* spaces that contain both text and audience'. Rejecting theorizations of television as an undifferentiated medium, Silverstone proposes that one can identify three different but non-discrete discursive spaces suggested by the televisual texts themselves. Each of these has different implications both for the forms of knowledge at stake and for the forms of audience engagement suggested.

In her contribution, Sonia Livingstone (Chapter 6) discusses the mediation of knowledge as it relates to broader problems now faced by empirical studies of audience reception. In what amounts to an overview of theoretical and empirical work on reception, Livingstone deconstructs the opposition between 'transmission' and 'ritual' models of communication, arguing that we need both in order to understand the processes of mediating/mediated knowledge. These processes involve both the transmission of new ideas and knowledge to audiences and the 'digestion' of these 'inputs' in more or less local communities. She questions the assumption of much reception research that audiences encounter media texts with a set of interpretative resources that are essentially unrelated to the media, and consequently at least partly also deconstructs the opposition between 'audience' and '(media) texts'. Relations between people can be 'facilitated, managed or reconstituted by the media', and we need to understand these communicative relationships between people if we wish to understand the mediation of different kinds of knowledge.

The fourth and final contribution to Part II is Peter Larsen's phenomenologically inflected essay on the experience of zapping in a transnational, multi-channel environment (Chapter 7). More precisely, he analyses the ways in which viewers speak of this experience. Starting with Michel de Certeau's distinction between 'place' and 'space', Larsen moves through various dimensions of the zapping experience, regarding it as 'travels' between various 'places', thus turning them into practised spaces. The essay is thus a contribution to an understanding of common knowledge about television itself: how we learn to relate to the technologically advanced medium of television in our everyday lives, how we establish practical knowledge about its functions and possibilities, and how all of this is revealed in everyday talk about our uses of the medium.

The book's third and final part, 'Genres', contains five articles dealing, in different ways, with key television genres central to questions of mediated knowledge – documentary, news, political discussions and popular science programmes. Klaus Bruhn Jensen (Chapter 8) presents an international study of television newscasts which takes a closer look at the relationships between the global flow of TV news on the one hand and local audiences on the other. What especially interested the participating researchers was the 'potential uses of television news by viewers as a resource for citizenship – locally, regionally, nationally and, in principle, transnationally', and the preliminary results presented have important implications both theoretically and politically. David Morley's discussion of the news genre (Chapter 9) definitely has a local starting point – namely, his own relationship to TV news – but branches out in various directions in an attempt to explore the ways in which, and the conditions under which, the genre may appear meaningful to viewers given today's sociocultural situation and television's peculiar role in it. Morley ends his discussion by pointing to the effect the election of a Labour government in Britain seems to have had on many people's interest in the news. Labour's victory after eighteen years of Tory rule indicated that some sort of change was possible after all, and that politics and related staple items of newscasts are consequently not altogether meaningless.

Anders Johansen (Chapter 10) then looks into a particular aspect of television's presentation of political matters, in studio discussions, interviews and speeches. It is a study of how television presents particular rhetorical conditions for those who appear there, and how the most effective forms of *ethos* in our day and age are forms particularly suited to – and in a sense produced by – the broadcast media, and especially television. John Corner (Chapter 11) writes about the current status of television documentary, relating recent developments in the styles and formats of factual programming to the changed institutional matrix of (primarily) British and European broadcast TV, on the one hand, and the epistemological claims and forms of address traditionally associated with documentary as a genre, on the other.

Finally, Suzanne de Cheveigné (Chapter 12) analyses the reception of popular science programmes on French television, convincingly demonstrating how complex and difficult it is to address broadly composed audiences with knowledge produced within the natural sciences – or, most probably, any other scholarly discipline. Importantly, however, she also argues that the pattern is not completely confusing; the number of different types of 'readings' of the programmes is limited, not endlessly varied.

This is, in other words, not a book which delivers final solutions to any of the problems it covers. Rather, it opens ways of thinking about and concretely investigating how television is positioned within the processes whereby various forms of knowledge are produced and distributed in our late-modern societies. It is the hope of the editor and contributors that others will follow up the work initiated here, critically and constructively. Ultimately, the forms and mediation of 'common knowledge' in and through television concern the basis for and the future of democracy.

Part I

PUBLIC SPHERE(S)

1

RIGHTS AND
REPRESENTATIONS
Public discourse and cultural citizenship

Graham Murdock

A TALE OF TWO NARRATIVES

One of the most seductive themes running through debates around postmodernity is the story of the collapse of grand narratives and their totalizing projects. This tale finds its most dramatic moment in the dynamiting of the Pruitt-Igoe housing development in St Louis in 1972. This demolition is widely presented as marking the moment when modern architecture 'died' (Jencks 1984: 9) and the clean, austere machines for living in gave way to the plural, personalized styles of suburbia and the playfulness and excess of Las Vegas. The prisoners in modernity's Bastilles of the imagination are freed from their incarceration. The general yields to the local, the standardized to the customized. Identities proliferate. The repressed return. As Jean-François Lyotard argued in 1985, 'the grand narratives that characterise western modernity...[were] concerned precisely with the overstepping/ surpassing of particular cultural identity towards a universal civic identity' (quoted in Kahn 1995: 8). Now there is only the endless play of difference.

It is narrative set in a landscape of affluence. If he had looked 'beyond the confines of the prosperous European Union' to societies about to enter a period of dissolution and reconstitution he would have seen questions of civic identity being pushed to the centre of debate (Bulmer and Rees 1996: 281) – by the crowds that tore down the Berlin Wall, by the solitary student who stood in front of a row of tanks on their way to crush the pro-democracy movement in central Beijing and by Nelson Mandela on the day of his release from prison, walking alone down the road that led away from apartheid towards the new democracy in South Africa. They were laying claim to the Enlightenment's most potent political legacy – the ideal of full and equal citizenship and its extension to the general notion of human rights.

The claim to citizenship found enduring expression in the French Revolution's militant demand for liberty, equality and fraternity, but because the relations between these terms were never properly defined they have generated continual disputes. When the French philosopher Alexis de Tocqueville journeyed around America, the other modern 'revolutionary' republic, in the 1830s he was struck by the tension between the integrating qualities of empathy and mutuality – the 'habits of the heart' as he called them – fostered by the rich network of civil institutions and the spirit of competitive individualism that increasingly separated citizens from one another. This balance, or imbalance, has been an abiding concern in American political philosophy ever since. It finds its most recent expression in the battle between liberals – who emphasize personal autonomy and the right to individual choice – and communitarians, who stress the need for shared ties of loyalty and reciprocity (see Mulhall and Swift 1992).

It is no accident that the revival of philosophical debate about the proper relationship between liberty and fraternity has coincided with the rise of neoliberal economic and social policies in America and a number of other Western democracies. The New Right's progressive reduction of citizenship to questions of individual choice in the marketplace created by the enterprise economy has led 'radical liberals' like Ralf Dahrendorf to insist that 'the social entitlements of citizenship are as important a condition of progress as the opportunities for choice which require entrepreneurial initiative and an innovative spirit' (Dahrendorf 1990: 38). As a riposte, conservatives argue that the promotion of 'the civic or social virtues ("the caring virtues", as they are sometimes called)' may well 'undermine the "vigorous virtues" associated with the free market – self-reliance, self-sufficiency, entrepreneurship, ambition' – and so weaken the essential conditions of personal freedom (Himmelfarb 1996: 13).

The fact that the relationships between liberties and loyalties, rights and responsibilities are matters of continuing contest makes the organization of television central to the constitution of contemporary citizenship. Because it is a pivotal 'theatre of discourse...that enters the life of the entire public', society has an obvious stake 'in which speakers have the opportunity to take their turn on this platform of public narrative', who they speak for, whose experiences, viewpoints and arguments they articulate, and which questions they ask (Price 1995: 75). Before exploring the shifting relationship between citizenship and television in more detail, however, we need to specify the dimensions of citizenship a little more carefully.

FROM SIMPLE TO COMPLEX CITIZENSHIP

In general terms we can define the basic entitlement of citizenship as *the right to participate fully in social life with dignity and without fear, and to help formulate the forms it might take in the future*. Definitions of what specific rights need to be guaranteed in order to underwrite this ideal have not remained static, however. Rights have been progressively extended to new spheres of social action and to new social groupings (such as children), and the nature and distribution of the resources required to render them substantial rather than simply nominal have been matters of continual argument, as have the forms of social responsibility that accompany rights. As a consequence, conceptions of citizenship have moved from the relatively simple to the increasingly complex.

The original definition grew out of debates about the relationship between two major social domains of modernity – the state and government, on the one hand, and civil society, on the other. This produced claims to two major sets of rights.

Rights in relation to the state revolved around the right to protection from the arbitrary use of force by either the state and its agencies (as in detention without trial or torture) or other citizens. Securing this second condition nourished the idea of the state as a 'night-watchman' guaranteeing the personal safety of citizens through appropriate levels of policing and military defence coupled with prohibitions against the unauthorized personal use of force (through duelling, vendettas or vigilante action, for example). Disputes between citizens and between citizens and the state were to be resolved by the rule of law. Every citizen claimed the right to equal, non-discriminatory treatment before the law, the right to participate in selecting representatives to those forums that decided on new laws and revoked old ones (most typically through universal adult franchise), and the right to participate in the practical application of law to specific cases through the jury system.

These rights were instituted as core components of liberal democracies only after bitter and extended struggles, and even now there are a number of unresolved issues. For example, is capital punishment an unacceptable exercise of state power? What are the proper limits to the state's right to maintain surveillance of its citizens in the interests of internal security? There is even less consensus over the responsibilities that accompany these rights, or on how best to secure them. Should there be a legal requirement to vote, with penalties for non-compliance (as in Australia), for example?

At first sight, rights in relation to civil society appear less disputable. Certainly there is general agreement that in democracies citizens' rights must include freedom of conscience and belief, freedom of association and freedom of expression. But there are difficulties. Rights of expression involve the rights of listeners as well as of speakers. The proliferation of identities within contemporary cultures poses particular problems. The argument that everyone should enjoy the 'freedom to belong to an identity and to contribute to its definition' (Melucci 1988: 258) and the freedom 'to withdraw from belonging in order to create new meanings' (Melucci 1989: 173) is central to the idea that contemporary politics is increasingly centred on the politics of identity – the struggle over forms of belonging, loyalty and solidarity. This, in turn, 'requires the conditions which enable individuals and social groups to be recognised for what they are or wish to be' (ibid.: 172). But what if the construction of one identity requires the dismissal or denial of others? What if the repressed exercise their own forms of repression? What are the limits to 'free' speech in the major arenas of public discourse? As the principal stock exchange of public discourse, television has to negotiate the politics of difference on a daily basis, looking to balance assertion against injury.

One seductive solution to this dilemma is to avoid confrontations by parcelling out differences into specially demarcated 'minority' programmes or streamed channels – to move from broadcasting addressed to everyone to 'narrowcasting' serving self-defining groups. But this immediately raises another problem. It makes it impossible to create a shared cultural space which combines respect for difference with a commitment to developing a workable contemporary conception of the 'common good'. Achieving this requires the recognition of solidarities as well as separations, the renegotiation of communality as well as difference. It depends on bringing diverse experiences, identities and positions together in the same symbolic arena, exploring their interplay, and balancing recognition and respect for particular identities against the renewal of a culture held in common. As Stuart Hall has argued, in today's conditions of fracture and fragmentation it is more necessary than ever that we 'create…enough of a shared culture to mean that we can exist in the same space without eating one another' (Hall quoted in Sanders 1994: 18).

In response, many of those working in television would argue that they are helping to create a 'shared culture' on a daily basis. They are, but it is a culture more and more based around the figure of the consumer and the ideology of consumerism; the notion that identity and fulfilment can be purchased in the marketplace, and that the good life is to be found through total immersion in the world of goods, postmodernity's new baptism. This development undermines citizenship in two ways. First, it privileges personal spending over social and political participation, and addresses viewers as shoppers rather than as members of intersecting moral communities. Second, by equating social differences with variations in choice and style it negates any attempt to arrive at a conception of the 'common good' based on the negotiation of differences in their full complexity.

UNDERWRITING RIGHTS

The tensions between 'consumers' and 'citizens' are part of a problematic general relationship between the requirements of democracy and the dynamics of capitalism. As originally conceived, civil society was a comfortably copious, baggy concept. Because it covered all institutions and associations that were not part of the state, it included the nascent organizations of capitalism as well as the dense network of voluntary and community groups and social movements. However, as the nineteenth century wore on and corporate ownership became more concentrated, it became increasingly clear that the activities and aims of the major capitalist companies were antithetical to the extension of citizenship.

If people were to become full citizens they had to have access to the material and symbolic resources that secured social inclusion and facilitated participation. Rights had to be publicly underwritten. This required that the state abandon its minimalist night-watchman role and intervene in the workings of market capitalism. Many of these initiatives were aimed at protecting citizens as workers and consumers from the arbitrary use of corporate power and ensuring a minimal basis for social participation. They included interventions in areas such as minimum wages, health and safety, holiday and sick-leave entitlements, and trade union rights. Despite over a century of struggle, arrangements in these areas are far from settled. Rights are always precarious. They can be weakened or reversed. They are continually contested by corporations arguing for greater 'flexibility'. These moves are met, in return, with resistance and counter-claims for new rights in areas such as equal opportunities, positive discrimination and corporate responsibility for environmental pollution or the health hazards of smoking.

Alongside attempts to curb corporate power in the public interest, positive initiatives were launched to compensate for market failures by publicly funded core resources for citizenship that the market could not or would not provide. The material basis necessary to underwrite social participation with dignity – a life-long basic income, a reasonable level of health care, safe domestic and public space – became the business of the welfare system. It was a practical strategy for securing inclusion, based on the assumption that 'In a good society there cannot, must not, be a deprived and excluded underclass' and that those 'who heretofore have made it up must become fully a part of the larger social community' (Galbraith 1994: 15).

But it was clear that, in addition to guaranteeing basic material conditions for participation, full citizenship also required access to relevant symbolic resources and the competences to use them effectively. Efforts to secure full cultural rights centred on the development of an array of public institutions – the education system, museums and galleries, public libraries and public broadcasting. They were to be paid for out of taxes and to be equally open to all. Judging how well they have succeeded in delivering cultural rights, however, depends on how these rights are defined.

DEFINING CULTURAL RIGHTS

We can begin by outlining four basic sets of cultural rights:

1   *Rights to information.* Citizens have rights of access to the widest possible range of relevant information about the conditions that structure their range of choices, and about the actions, motivations and strategies of significant social, political and economic actors, particularly those with significant power over people's lives. These would include state agencies, the government, corporations, opposition parties and social movements, and transnational agencies and organizations.

2   *Rights to experience.* Citizens have rights of access to the greatest possible diversity of representations of personal and social experience. Whereas in

11

television information has been primarily the preserve of actuality programmes – news, current affairs and documentary – the exploration of experience has been mainly accomplished through fiction. As John Mepham (1990) has argued, sharing stories is an essential resource for fostering the capacities and reciprocities of full citizenship. They offer:

> A form of inquiry to which people can turn in their efforts to answer questions which invariably spring up in their lives. What is possible for me, who can I be, what can my life consist of, how can I bring these things about? What is it like to be someone else, to be particular kinds of other people? How does it come about that people can be like that? We have to make an unending effort to answer questions like this so that we can…make imaginatively informed choices and responses to other people.…These questions and these capacities and skills are basic to having a sense of self, an identity, and to fair dealing with others within a system of social relationships.
>
> (Mepham 1990: 60)

3   *Rights to knowledge.* Access to information and experience offers 'thick descriptions' of the world, and 'structures of feeling' based on empathy and the capacity to view the world through other people's eyes, but it does not provide explanations. It does not reveal how particular events and lives have been shaped by deep-seated processes of inertia and change, how biographies are anchored in history. Connecting the particular to the general, the micro to the macro, requires access to frameworks of interpretation that point to links, patterns and processes, and suggest explanations. They translate information and experience into knowledge. By explaining the forces shaping the present and tracing its links to the past, they open up ways of formulating strategies for change.

At the same time, the postmodernists are right to insist that the contemporary intellectual field is more fractured and contested than ever before. Knowledge is no longer a gift, carefully wrapped by experts. It is the stake in a continual contest of positions. Consequently, cultural rights in the contemporary situation must guarantee access to the key debates and arguments in this contest, but what kind of access?

4   *Rights to participation.* Traditionally, public broadcasting has constructed its audiences as listeners rather than speakers, spectators rather than image-makers. Over the last fifteen years or so, however, these asymmetric relationships have been progressively challenged by viewers demanding the right to speak about their own lives and aspirations in their own voice, and to picture the things that matter to them in ways they have chosen. These claims to participation in the making of public meaning raise difficult issues of representation.

QUESTIONS OF REPRESENTATION

In thinking about representation we need to hold on firmly to the two major senses that the term carries in English. Questions of representation are, first, questions about social delegation, about who is entitled to speak for or about others, and what responsibilities they owe to the constituencies whose views and hopes they claim to articulate. But they are also questions about cultural forms and genres, about ways in which the raw materials of language and imagery are combined in particular expressive forms – documentaries, episodes of soap operas, single plays – and about how well these contribute to the resources of information, experience, interpretation and explanation required for the exercise of full citizenship.

In both these senses, the organization of representation within television has undergone something of a sea change in recent years.

DISCOURSE/IMAGE/FORM

The ways in which television addresses itself to matters of public concern, debate and value are inextricably tied up with questions of how programmes are put together as combinations of pictures and speech (Corner 1995). As John Ellis points out in his contribution to this symposium (Chapter 4), forms and genres play a pivotal role in this process. They are devices for converting the fluid, conflictual flow of social discourse and resonant imagery into structured and accessible modes of knowing. They may address the field of relevant discourse in a relatively 'open' or a relatively 'closed' way. We can assess a programme's degree of openness by asking two basic questions. First, how much space does the programme provide for the range of competing discourses? How far is it organized around the official or prevailing discourse, and how far is it hospitable to alternative and oppositional positions. Second, how is the contest of discourses organized? Is one perspective preferred and given particular privileges in terms of space and legitimacy? Or are competing ways of talking and looking treated in a more even-handed way? Does the programme leave the outcome indeterminate and invite the viewer to judge, or does it close around a particular conclusion?

Posed in this way, the conclusion would seem to be that complex citizenship is best served by open programmes that offer a diversity of positions and require the engaged participation of viewers. As John Ellis argues, open programmes work through debates and dilemmas to the point of exhaustion rather than the point of conclusion or resolution (see Chapter 4). They launch speculations, take imaginative walks and offer only provisional endings. This would apply not only to certain forms of documentary and current affairs productions, but also to serial fiction that addresses the problems and contingencies of everyday life. Because they are based on never-ending, continually unfolding narratives, they offer extended spaces in which to view particular events from a variety of vantage points and to recognize the precariousness of any accommodation.

This celebration of open forms rules out programmes that are organized around a particular discourse. But are there no circumstances in which a tendency to closure might serve the needs of complex citizenship? Is there no place for investigation and advocacy that deconstructs the prevailing discourses of officialdom, asks awkward questions and offers counter-accounts? From the point of view of rights to information and knowledge, clearly there must be.

The problem of using television to present knowledge, rather than information or experience, is compounded by the fact that it is a visual as well as an oral medium. Our established models of the public sphere are deeply rooted in a commitment to rational argument. But images do not walk in straight lines. They do not wait to take turns. They work by association, detonating a collision of connotations. They argue by simultaneity, not sequence. This sets up a permanent tension between the pleasures of the image, and the ripples of memory and identity it activates, and the search for explanations that offer a purchase on circumstance and power.

In exploring these dilemmas we need to think about the problems of representation not simply in relation to the structure of particular programmes but in relation to the organization of the overall schedule, as an arena of symbolic forms and social relations.

THE POLITICAL ECONOMY OF POPULISM

It is impossible to engage with these questions now without taking account of the television system's rapid movement towards more populist forms of organization.

The tradition of public-service broadcasting was informed by an ethos of paternalism. It assumed that experts knew more than the man and woman in the street, and that 'authors' (whether writers or programme makers) engaged with contemporary reality and experience in deeper, more wide-ranging ways, that they saw beyond the immediate and the obvious, and that it was the duty of broadcasting to bring these insights and ways of looking to the widest possible public. Although it produced programmes that underwrote citizens' rights to information, experience and knowledge, this project was based on a contradiction. It aimed to foster 'ordinary people's' participation and inclusiveness within the body politic by excluding them from its own processes of production.

This easy dismissal fuelled the mounting demands for greater access from the mid-1970s onwards. More and more groups demanded the right to speak on their own behalf. In current affairs we see the rise of new styles of talk show in which members of the public speak at length about their lives and preoccupations. The dialogue of expertise is replaced by the raw testimonies of experience. In the field of documentary we see the shift from investigative programmes with a 'voice-of-God' commentary explaining what is being shown and said, to video diaries compiled by viewers detailing the circumstances, enthusiasms and dilemmas at the centre of their lives. These movements have added new forms to the array of representations, engaged with issues left off the standard list of social problems and installed vernacular discourses in the centre of the public domain. But they have also weakened television's ability to underwrite rights to knowledge.

They have replaced paternalism's hierarchies of capacity and insight with the open horizons of a populism, which celebrates common sense as the only sense worth having and presents audience size as the only valid criterion of communicative success. This aggressive promotion of ordinariness fits snugly with the political economy of the new commercialism. The rapid proliferation of channels and fragmentation of viewer loyalties places an ever higher premium on delivering predictable pleasures by working with rather than against prevailing tastes and mental maps. This applies to both mass and niche audiences. The result is that citizenship is undermined on two fronts. Groups on the social and political periphery according to the official charts are offered clearly demarcated channels or channel segments on cable or multi-channel systems, or programmes within established broadcast systems (almost always at unsocial hours), thereby confirming their marginal status. 'Here, access takes on another meaning, embracing techniques that allow the marginalised to speak to the marginalised, improving internal communication networks for those who are otherwise disenfranchised' (Price 1995: 80). This exclusion/inclusion allows the major mass channels of public communication to evade the problems of orchestrating encounters and debates across proliferating and cross-cutting identities, and to concentrate on assembling audiences around affiliations and ways of looking that already occupy the cultural centre. In the process the project of constructing a shared culture based on recognition and respect for difference coupled with a commitment to renegotiating a workable conception of the common good slips steadily down the list of priorities.

This problem is compounded rather than resolved by rise of new digital forms of television: 'The new technologies, redolent with addressability (the capacity of producers to reach individual households rather than the mass) and complex interactivity (the capacity for senders and receivers to communicate)' are based on re-routing speech now in the public domain and converting it into commodities to be purchased by viewer subscriptions (Price 1995: 79). In these conditions the multiplication of channels means less diversity of representation in the public domain.

PUBLIC SPACE AND PUBLIC DISCOURSE

If there is to be any chance of pursuing the unfinished project of citizenship in the era of privatization we need to defend the basic principles of public communicative activity more vigorously than ever. Four conditions are essential:

1   It must provide a relatively open arena of representation. This requires strong barriers against the exercise of undue influence and co-option by the two

major centres of discursive power – state and government and the corporate world. Limiting the incursions of all forms of commercial speech – from spot advertising to public relations puffs and corporate sponsorship – has acquired even greater importance in a cultural system increasingly commandeered by promotion.

2   It must demolish the accepted divisions between mass and minority, mainstream and margins, and develop forms of representation, participation and scheduling that promote encounters and debates between the widest possible range of identities and positions. It must draw continuously on the domains of advocacy developed by particular social groups and movements, and bring 'dialogic, contesting voices' into the centre of the common domain (Dahlgren 1995: 156).

3   It must balance the promotion of diversity of information and experience against citizens' rights of access to frameworks of knowledge, and to the principles that allow them to be evaluated and challenged.

4   It must ensure that the full range of its services remains equally available to all. It must defend their status as public goods and resist their conversion into commodities.

In the current circumstances, remaking public broadcasting and struggling to construct a viable public domain within the emerging moving image industries constitute a titanic task. But it is a necessary one if there is to be any hope of defending and extending the rights of complex citizenship. The odds call for a creative response. We can begin by thinking about the kinds of programmes that would provide pleasure and promote the core capacities of citizenship, and then work backwards to the organizational, financial and political conditions that would be required to support and develop them.

Critics of 'actually existing' public broadcasting (among whom I include myself) and enthusiasts of 'free' markets in representations will certainly ask why we should model the future on an institutional ideal that has so often failed to live up to its promises in the past. The answer is simple. Restructured and re-imagined, it still offers the most open, flexible and inclusive solution to the problem of underwriting the cultural rights of citizenship. Convincing sceptics of this, however, will require a great deal of hard work across the boundaries of political philosophy, discourse and rhetoric studies, textual analysis, audience research and political economy. And we will need to practise what we advocate. We will need to respect these differences of perspective and intellectual identity. But we will also need to move beyond them to construct a new shared framework that knits together the economic, social and aesthetic life of contemporary communication.

REFERENCES

Bulmer, Martin and Rees, Anthony M. (1996) 'Conclusion: citizenship in the twenty-first century', in Martin Bulmer and Anthony M. Rees (eds) *Citizenship Today: The Contemporary Relevance of T. H. Marshall*, London: UCL Press.

Corner, John (1995) *Television Form and Public Address*, London: Edward Arnold.

Dahlgren, Peter (1995) *Television and the Public Sphere: Citizenship, Democracy and the Media*, London: Sage Publications.

Dahrendorf, Ralf (1990) *Reflections on the Revolution in Europe*, London: Chatto & Windus.

Galbraith, John Kenneth (1994) 'The good life beckons', *New Statesman and Society*, 28 January: 14–16.

Himmelfarb, Gertrude (1996) 'The unravelled fabric – and how to knit it up', *Times Literary Supplement* 4859, 17 May: 12–13

Jencks, Charles (1984) *The Language of Post-modern Architecture*, 4th edition, London: Academy Editions.

Kahn, Joel S. (1995) *Culture, Multiculture, Postculture*, London: Sage Publications.

Melucci, Alberto (1988) 'Social movements and the democratisation of everyday life', in John Keane (ed.) *Civil Society and the State: New European Perspectives*, London: Verso.

—— (1989) *Nomads of the Present: Social Movements and Individual Needs in Contemporary Society*, London: Hutchinson Radius.

Mepham, John (1990) 'The ethics in quality television', in Geoff Mulgan (ed.) *The Question of Quality*, London: BFI Publishing.

Mulhall, Stephen and Swift, Adam (1992) *Liberals and Communitarians*, Oxford: Basil Blackwell.

Price, Monroe E (1995) 'Free expression and digital dreams: the open and closed terrain of speech', *Critical Inquiry* 22(1), autumn: 64–89.

Sanders, Claire (1994) 'A leading indicator', *Times Higher Educational Supplement*, 13 May: 17–18.

2

MEDIA AND DIASPORAS

Daniel Dayan

FRAGILE COMMUNITIES, PARTICULARISTIC MEDIA

There is a long tradition in communication studies that is concerned with the role of the media in creating new, usually wider and ultimately political communities. This project is concerned with another role that can be imparted to the mass media, that of reconstructing or maintaining in existence already established but somehow fragile or imperilled communities – minority groups, immigrants, exiles, diasporas.

The media seem here to play a role that is both internally cohesive and secessive vis-à-vis society at large. They tend to be particularist or particularizing, eliciting a number of questions: how do they fulfil their particularistic role? Is the process of community construction accompanied by a parallel process of mediatic innovation? Does this particularistic vocation entail a necessary rejection of universalistic values? Is it at odds with a normative view of the public sphere?

With reference to political sociology, and to the vast range of studies that link media, identity and territory, this presentation wishes to point to the differences between the goals of a study on particularistic media and those of the research traditions that have addressed the role of the media in the formation of communities. It also attempts to situate the performance of particularistic media in an historical context characterized by economic globalization, fear of cultural homogenization, and the rise of movements that reject universalism. But, fundamentally, it focuses on three sorts of questions:

1   What is the particular type of knowledge mobilized in the construction of a group's identity? How do particularistic media contribute to the construction, mediation and adoption of this identity?
2   What are the problems raised by the development of media capable of connecting to each other different segments of diasporas?
3   Particularistic media may offer competing versions of a group's identity. In what circumstances can they stop being mere clusters of media and lead to the emergence of micro public spheres?

THE CONTEXT OF GLOBALIZATION

Redefining the local

The vast literature currently being developed on the interaction between local and globalizing processes sounds curiously familiar to media specialists. When geographers and economists deal with globalization, they re-enact debates that often took place long ago in communication research. These are the debates between hypodermic-needle paradigms, theories of powerful effects, theories of limited effects, theories stressing media users and their gratifications, theories of reception and resistance. Such a parallelism is understandable. In both cases the problematic of effects, impacts or influences is linked to a topography of centres and peripheries, and in both cases mass communication systems happen to be central actors. Such a parallelism becomes manifest with the abandonment of the early conceptualizations of the global–local relationship. This relationship is no longer seen as simply one of homogenization. The image of a dominating centre and a dominated periphery is abandoned (Racine 1995). The local is not merely the site of an endorsement or rejection of initiatives taken elsewhere. The local is not only made of victims. It is also made of actors (Laidi *et al.* 1997; Laidi 1998).

This autonomy of local processes is visible in the cultural sphere. In the manifesto that opens the first issue of the journal *Public Culture*, Arjun Appadurai and Carole Breckenridge (1988a) stress that transnational flows are much less homogenizing than was previously believed. The local is no longer the end of the road, the final and lowly destination of messages emanating from a lofty centre. The local has become cosmopolitan in its own way. Cosmopolitanism comes in different guises and forms. Diasporas of migrant workers develop their own in reference to the host cultures, to the traditions of their respective groups, to the reconstruction of such traditions by their elites. These elites are no longer exclusive relays towards the global and the masses are no longer confined to the local. They are themselves in motion; they are made of tourists, of television watchers, of *Gastarbeiter* (ibid.).

As a result of this interpenetration, globalization should interest anthropologists as well as economists. Anthropologists cannot avoid noticing the territorial shadows projected by globalization; they have to account for the metamorphoses occurring at the local level.

Particularistic movements: resisting homogenization or universality

Central to this project are some specific responses to globalization. These responses take the form of stressing particularism, of reconstructing endangered identities. Are such responses laudable or dangerous?

Identity processes in the late twentieth century are characterized by a powerful return of nationalist themes, by the hasty, almost incessant emergence of new nations. Often expressed in the language of ethnicity, the politics of these new nations gives a bad name to particularist politics. However, particularism may perhaps adopt forms that are not doomed to become horrible. Should we automatically stigmatize the maintenance of diversity in the face of homogenization? Are particularistic media involved in an active rejection of universality?

There is no doubt that the maintenance of diversity may involve a rejection of universalism. It may lead to the secessionism model that Todd Gitlin condemns in his *Twilight of Common Dreams* (Gitlin 1995). It may foster the decline of that universalist model of the nation-state that Dominique Schnapper rightly describes as a product of enlightenment: a territory in which nationalism has been superseded by the legal principle of a community based on citizenship (Schnapper 1994). When people no longer believe in a progress-oriented history, particularism might open the road towards regressions, romantic infatuations, mass graves.

Yet particularistic motives are not doomed from the beginning. They can involve a rejection of universalism, but they need not. In fact the discourse of particularism is far from monolithic. The media that ensure the continued survival of certain groups tend to offer these groups competing versions of their identity. Some are lethal. Some are not. There are many sorts of particularist rhetorics and many ways of mediating the knowledge required for community construction. Constructing identities, maintaining identities involves various processes. Processes of what sort?

IDENTITY AS PROCESS: PRODUCTION, CONFRONTATION, ADOPTION

Maintaining or producing identity

Particularistic media complement the role of institutions in charge of the custody and transmission of filiation and memory. Described, among others, by Lucette Valensi (1992) and Nicole Lapierre (1989), such institutions include universities, museums and schools; they involve the intervention of various actors; they often enter into dialogue with social enterprises (in Victor Turner's sense) or with social movements. But in fragile communities the question of identity is no longer one of routine maintenance and such institutions are mostly absent. In such communities maintaining a group's identity requires complex strategies. Two sorts of problems must be addressed.

The problem of autonomy: What are we? Who are we? Who says so?

Problems of the first sort emerge in those situations in which the concerned community is a minority submitted to the decisions of a majority and surrounded by 'generalist' media whose messages are conceived for that majority. In such contexts it is necessary to distinguish between those constructions of identity that are independent and autonomous, and those that are produced either within the majority or under its influence. Take the example of a group dispersed on the territories of several nation-states. Are the respective versions of that group's identity always independent of the pressures exerted by those states?

Following a suggestion made by Elihu Katz (1993), one could imagine a systematic description of identity-producing discourses in intercultural contexts. Such a description would delineate a number of discursive possibilities, by distinguishing between constructions that are (1) about, by or for (2) a minority or the majority. Among the numerous possibilities included in such a discursive matrix, some are doomed to confront each other, leading to potentially explosive situations. At the heart of the confrontation is the conflict between the heteronomy of a 'What are you?' and the autonomous 'Who are we?' (Leca, in Badie and Wolton 1996). But, as is suggested by the same matrix, there are many nuanced positions between these two extremes.

Choosing among identity proposals: identities in contest

Problems of a second type have to do with choosing among proposed identities. As in any other society, different versions of the identity of the same group will be constructed. These versions will confront each other in the forums that Appadurai and Breckenridge equate with their notion of a public culture and whose existence often depends on that of particularistic media. Debates, contests and sometimes social dramas can be expected to erupt around issues of identity. But these debates (such as those that have surrounded a number of films or photographic exhibits on minorities in various countries) represent only a first stage of reception. They do not tell us how identities are adopted, how they become internalized or altogether indistinguishable from those who have adopted them. In other words, the process of identity construction remains insufficiently analysed if one describes only what takes place in the public sphere, if the analysis only deals with the level of the offer. In order to find out about the internalization of identity one has to take a second step and move into the private sphere.

Adopting identity: from public sphere to private sphere

This second step aims at identifying those discourses that have actually served as bases for decision-making, those images that helped individuals to make crucial decisions. Originally made at a personal level, individual choices end up acquiring historical dimensions. Take the example of a minority group to whom one of the identities proposed was that of a symbiotic fusion with the surrounding majority. It is relevant to the history of that group that so many of its members chose emigration, thus rejecting the symbiotic model in favour of other constructions. Such constructions do play an essential part in the life of individuals. They confer historical intelligibility, explain momentous decisions such as that of leaving a given country, of speaking a given language, of being called by a given name. They are the subject of intense debates between siblings, between parents and children, between husbands and wives. They provide some of the insights usually found in literary genres, in particular in the *Bildungsroman*. In the absence of works of fiction, oral histories will provide a privileged access to constructions of this type and to those situations where the intimate meets the historical.

MEDIAS AND DIASPORAS

Dispersed groups

The study of particularistic media seems particularly relevant when media are instruments of survival for endangered cultures, when their presence ensures the maintenance of links within geographically dispersed groups. Among a growing number of such groups, one can mention the Jewish, Armenian, Palestinian and Kurdish diasporas; Iranian exile groups in the US; North African migrant communities in continental Europe; Pakistani and Indian communities in Britain.

Though they do form small-scale communities locally – neighbourhoods, 'street-corner' or 'housing-project' societies – such groups often do not share a common space. Typically, they are spread over the territories of many nation-states and their members are exposed to an unusually vast range of potential identities. Of course a nationalistic perspective is not always absent from the identities elaborated by/for these groups. Indeed most of the communities that concern themselves with particularistic media also refer to some 'national' centre. But this centre is not necessarily political. Often it is no more than a founding myth enshrined in collective memory.

The range of interdiasporic media

It seems unproductive to limit the definition of diasporic communication to the range of organizations conventionally defined as 'media'. Thus, instead of exclusively dealing with radio, cinema, television or journalism, one should try to account for other – for example smaller – 'media', and to focus on the various practices, institutions and organizations that link the different segments of diasporic ensembles to each other. Many of such practices (pilgrimages, religious occasions, family rituals, etc.) can be described as 'traditional'. They would be better described as 'neotraditional'. They are not reminiscences of another age but contemporary reconstructions – conscious redemptions or reflexive rephrasings of folk cultures. They include:

1   Production and circulation of newsletters, audio and video cassettes, holy icons and small media in general. (Specialized shops sell 'ethnic' videos in the

immigrant neighbourhoods of most large European cities, between stalls of imported foods and spices.)

2　Exchange of letters, photographs, home videos and travellers. This last point is particularly important. Diasporas mobilize huge amounts of back-and-forth travelling. They entail the creation of specialized organizations or agencies, they are 'charter-flight societies'. The dominant form of travel is linked to 'family' tourism. But travelling also includes prospective tourism (preparing the ground for emigration) or a tourism of pilgrimage, usually marking the end of the acculturation process and the moment of rediscovery (or reinvention) of neglected traditions. Unsurprisingly, the ranks of the pilgrims include historiographers and sociologists of diasporas.

3　Constitution of religious communities or cultural associations by individuals of similar origins attracted by the nature of worship or style of interaction.

4　Creation of interdiasporic networks (and circulation of directives, slogans, sermons, preachings, etc.) by religious or political organizations with specific agendas. Diasporic communities are increasingly used as auxiliary constituencies and mobilized for ideological or financial purposes.

Of course, diasporic communication also relies on conventional media. Sometimes it does so indirectly; sometimes quite explicitly. Let us mention the following:

1　Styles of reception of mainstream programmes that include regular news or soap operas. Responding to topics that are often unrelated to the diasporic experience, these reception practices illustrate what Michel de Certeau described as the tactics of the powerless. They are part of a 'culture of consumption' (Gillespie 1995) whose definition owes many of its traits to Tamar Liebes and Elihu Katz.

2　Community-oriented genres made available on mainstream television. The Sunday morning programmes offered in France by Antenne II are conceived in strictly religious terms, offering in turn Moslem, Jewish, Orthodox and Protestant liturgies and commentaries. Yet they are often experienced as nostalgic reminders of the old country, evocations of home, links to faraway experiences.

3　Openly communitarian media such as daily, weekly or monthly newspapers; regular radio broadcasts; television programmes on specialist cable or satellite channels. Consider Tamil Ozhi ('The Tamil light'), an interesting example of a channel with unequivocal diasporic ambitions:

Broadcasting by satellite (Eutelsat), from a building in La Courneuve in Paris' northern suburbs, Tamil Ozhi is the first Tamil television channel in Europe.…Part of the MCM group of channels…it will offer 8 hours of daily broadcasting covering the whole of Europe. The daily diet of Tamil Ozhi includes an evening film or musical of about 150 minutes (on subscription). Images are provided by SUN TV (the Indian Tamil TV-channel). Plans for the remaining part of the 8 hours include linguistic programs (initiations to Tamil, French, English and German) and a daily newscast of about 30 minutes.

(*Libération*, 25 June 1997)

One can wonder where the financing of the channel comes from (the Sri Lankan government? the independence movements?) and whose version of the Tamil diaspora is offered in it. Clearly, one should acknowledge – with Hamid Naficy (1993) – that the notion of 'diasporic' television encompasses realities that can be not only diverse but contradictory. But, before elaborating on this point, let us note that, far from excluding each other, the various media mentioned here interact with each other. They enter into all sorts of combinations. The texture of these combinations, their moving hierarchies, the clusters they form, are quite relevant to the cultural analyst. So are the units, the communicative practices to be found in such clusters. Three of these practices – involving conventional media, domestic media and neotraditional activities – seem particularly significant. Two emanate from the private sphere: the circulation of home videos and the multiplication of diasporic pilgrimages. The third concerns a public phenomenon: the evolution of 'minority' or 'community' television towards genres that are differentiated by ideology and constituency.

Home videos

Describing the 'web of connections' between Punjabis on the Indian subcontinent, in various parts of Britain, in Germany and in the USA, Mary Gillespie points out that such 'connections are not limited to symbolic links between viewers of the same blockbuster Bombay movies' (Gillespie 1995). More direct links between kin and friends are established. They take the form of 'video letters and home videos of weddings and other rites of passage, especially coming-of-age celebrations' (ibid.: 7). Such videos, adds Gillespie, 'serve a range of social, cultural and political functions. They enable families to maintain contact with distant kin; they may be used to introduce eligible marriage partners and their families to each other; they may familiarize Punjabi families in, say, Yucca valley, Calif, with the life of their kin in Southall and vice versa', or they may illustrate 'the lives and works of a sikh *sant* (holy man),…circulated across the globe, to be used in religious worship and instruction' (ibid.: 7).

Gillespie also adds that they may serve to disseminate propaganda for Khalistan…a separate, sovereign Sikh nation in the Punjab' (ibid.: 7). At this point the videos she describes clearly move out of the private domain and enter the public sphere – or try to create one. They display a phenomenon already encountered in the context of Tamil television, an uneasy mixture of nostalgia and propaganda, of mobilization and elegy.

24

Genres of minority television

This paradoxical combination is precisely what characterizes an emerging genre that could be called 'minority television', a genre that Hamid Naficy illustrates by his systematic study of Iranian television in Los Angeles. Naficy's work is immensely useful in neatly distinguishing between types of television seemingly intended for the same populations yet radically different in their time orientation, in their political ambitions, in the historical projects they propose.

In southern California minority broadcasts are regrouped in the equivalent of a television ghetto, a specialist Los Angeles network created in the early 1990s by KSCI-TV. 'The *International Channel Network*, [is] the nation's first and only twenty-four hour, seven day a week, multilingual network, offering programs by satellite in sixteen different languages' (Naficy 1993: 6). But, while they share the KSCI 'niche', while they are 'nested' into a flow of 'otherness', while they are submitted to random schedulings and frequent reschedulings, minority programmes have little in common beyond their marginal status. In fact, suggests Naficy, the menu of minority television should be divided in three categories: ethnic, transnational and exilic television:

- *Ethnic television* refers to television programmes primarily produced in the host country by long-established indigenous minorities. Black entertainment television (BET) is the primary example of this category; much of its programming originates in and centres on life and times in the United States. The homeland for these programmes is ultimately located here and now, not over there and then.
- *Transnational television* is fed mostly by products imported from the homeland or those produced by American and multinational media concerns. The Korean-language broadcasts, for example, are produced by Korean Broadcasting Service in South Korea, and imported and distributed in the United States by the government-owned 'Korean Television Enterprises'.
- *Exilic television* is, by definition, produced in the host country as a response to, and in parallel with, the exiles' own transitional and provisional status. Television programmes produced by Iranians, Arabs and Armenians fall within this classification. Such programmes are often produced by small-time individual producers, not by media conglomerates of the home or host societies. Their tendency is to stress 'collective and individual struggles for authenticity and identity...Thus, almost...all Iranian programs aired in the...Los Angeles...area are produced outside Iran by entrepreneurs who oppose the Islamic government there' (Naficy 1993: 62).

While each of Naficy's categories illustrates the notion of a diasporic media discourse, it is clear that they are heterogeneous, if not altogether antagonistic. Transnational television relays the world view of an existing (or potential) centre. It is an instrument of control, displaying highly polished products at privileged times. Exilic television offers an improvised and often messy rite of passage to stranded members of a dispersed group, to survivors attempting to support each other during the difficult process of acculturation. Affectively, exilic television functions as a 'transitional object', as a link between a world that has vanished and the immigrants' new surroundings. Formally, it is dominated by an emblematic genre – the magazine, a programme that includes a little bit of everything, from news to fiction to music videos to advertisements, and whose shapelessness evokes the huge bundles and bursting suitcases carried by immigrants. Ethnic television either escapes the diasporic situation (it is not necessarily linked to exile) or takes over when acculturation is done. Either there is no regretted 'centre' to turn to or this centre has been forgotten. The distinction between the three discourses easily lends itself to a distinction inspired by that of Katz (1993, Section 3). Exilic television is made by immigrants, for immigrants, but about the home country. It is a discourse of survival. Transnational television is made by the home country, about the home country, but for the diaspora. It is a call for loyalty. Ethnic television may concern immigrants and be intended for immigrants, but it is a discourse about the host country. Nostalgia has lost its grip.

Time for pilgrimage

The moment when nostalgia loses its grip, the moment when it can be openly expressed, when it can be spoken without pain, is also the moment of visits to old homes and former countries, of immersions in earlier languages, of encounters with untranslated versions of self. It is the moment of pilgrimages, a need encountered by all those who have lived in diaspora, the need to check both that 'all is still there' and that 'it is all over', the need to have been right in leaving and to be proved wrong. 'At a certain moment in my life', writes Michael Arlen, 'I decided to take a trip in order to find out what being Armenian meant to me' (Arlen 1977: 7). 'It is April 1959,' writes the Polish-Canadian essayist Eva Hoffman. 'I am standing at the railing of the Batory's upper deck, and I feel that my life is ending. I'm looking out at the crowd that has gathered on the shore to see the ship's departure...a crowd that, all of a sudden, is irrevocably on the other side' (Hoffman 1989: 3). This type of experience should be described with the tools of ethnography. For the moment all we have are excerpts from a few films (those of Isa Genini, for example) and those curious passages in which sociologists, historians and other explorers of diasporas switch to first-person narratives. For example, Hamid Naficy:

> As I stepped out of the plane and into the ramp – the last person to get off – I encountered this incredibly warm air, so thick and so warm that it had become a material thing into which I stepped. Ghosts of other planes seemed to silently float in that dark thickness like grey whales in water. I was remarkably calm....My sister Nahid...had asked me to talk into a tape recorder for them. After relating a few jokes and childhood

anecdotes, I broke into singing Rumi's famous poem 'Song of the reed'. I began hesitatingly, but my voice gradually gained confidence...I closed my eyes and abandoned myself to the exilic lament of the poem....At a few points I forgot the lines and paused, but my father who was sitting near me quickly fed them to me.

(Naficy 1993: 126)

Finally, here is my own version of the same pilgrimage, the version that started me on this paper:

Casablanca was the city I knew, except that it used to be empty and sleepy, like a narrative by Marguerite Duras, and, all of a sudden, it was swarming with people. I had invited my mother to come to Morocco. I took her to the high school she had attended, then to the classroom in which she had taken her exams to become a teacher and, finally, to the street where our former house stood. People kept looking at us. Then I was identified. A young grocer pointed at me and said: 'I know you. This house is yours'. Then, incongruously, he greeted me in Hebrew. (He had been taught Hebrew instead of Arabic because the only school that had some room for him was a Hebrew school. 'So, I thought, better learn Hebrew than nothing at all!') Of course this grocer could not remember me. He must have been a child when I left, myself a skinny teenager. But he had probably remembered my father. He had collapsed two generations into one person. He proceeded then to alert the whole street. Moments later 'my' house – or what was left of it – was wide open, and a party was given in the honour of 'those who did not forget us and returned'. The historical winners of independence behaved graciously towards the members of the group that had lost. They acted as if they had missed us all that time, all those thirty years. They behaved as if the house was still ours, as if they themselves were just guests, passing by. I was astonished by this almost Chinese politeness. I was moved and at the same time disoriented. My only way of describing what I felt is that I was a ghost. Not only the ghost of my father, but one whom the new owners of the land had to pacify, so that he would quietly return to the limbo from which he had suddenly stepped out. Offerings were made. I was a potentially evil, vengeful spirit. I had to be cajoled until I left with a blessing and not a curse....

(Dayan 1996, oral presentation at the Van Leer Institute, Jerusalem)

Pilgrimages are moments of ambivalence.

CONCLUSIONS

Four major questions came out during this presentation. They relate, respectively, to notions developed by Peter Dahlgren, Benedict Anderson, Michael Schudson and Arjun Appadurai. Each will be summarized, then followed by brief comments.

1   Is it possible for clusters of particularistic media to be transformed into embryonic public spheres, thus serving as paradoxical vehicles for universalistic values?
2   Is the maintenance of diasporic communities a technical problem only? Can it really be distinguished from the construction or imagination of the community?
3   Can one fully address the question of identity formation by simply analysing the ideological constructions offered in the public sphere?
4   Can one speak of a new object for ethnographies, of the passage from descriptions centred on territory to descriptions focused on networks?

The reference to Dahlgren: media clusters or micro public spheres

Many studies have already been devoted to particularistic media, including Hamid Naficy's essays on the Iranian diaspora in California and the making of an exile culture (Naficy 1993); Larry Gross's remarkable analysis of the gay press in the US (Gross 1993); and Annabelle Sreberny Mohammadi's (1994) description of the mobilization of small media in the context of the Iranian revolution. Susan Herbst's remarks on the role played by the press in the brief emergence of a black public sphere in Chicago are particularly suggestive in the connection they make between particularistic media and the question of the public sphere (Herbst 1994). This connection should be further explored here.

We know that the transmission of identity constructions mobilizes a very wide range of media – 'big' and 'small', modern and traditional. The diversity of such media is matched by that of their audiences. Some media tend exclusively to be the media of a given group. Some are shared with the rest of the population. The coexistence of all these media seems to involve more than a simple contiguity. Thus one may raise the question of the relationship between particularistic media and the surrounding national public sphere, that of the continuities between minority and majority media.

But the emergence of clusters of media addressing given communities may lead to specific consequences inside such communities. These media clusters are expected to play a role of differentiation. They are meant to be particularizing. Yet – and this is one of the hypotheses guiding this project – they might induce the constitution of what Peter Dahlgren (1994b) would characterize as micro public spheres. If so – and despite professed particularistic ambitions – one can hardly imagine how such micro public spheres would manage to remain sealed to the public sphere at large, how they would prevent issues and behavioural models from circulating back and forth. Sooner or later one can expect the smaller sphere to become infiltrated by the values and procedural models that prevail in the larger one. Sooner or later, one can expect traditional groups to be exposed to practices that include free argumentation and open debate. Sooner or later, a process of homogenization might take place, affecting the internal organization of the community and leading to new sites of power, to new modes of legitimation, to new internal strategies.

Naficy (1993) was already pointing to an irony of this type when he showed that, far from exclusively protecting traditional lifestyles, the construction of exile cultures served as a rite of passage into – and an instrument of acculturation to – the host society. Particularistic media are not always instruments of a secession.

The reference to Anderson: diasporas imagined by whom?

The role of the media in constructing communities has been addressed in a number of influential studies, including those by Walter Ong (1967), James Carey (1992), Elizabeth Eisenstein (1979), Benedict Anderson (1983), Philip Schlesinger (1991a), Pierre Sorlin (1992). In many cases such studies are historical. In practically every instance they explore the societal impact of technological innovation. Some of the crucial questions they ask are as follows:

- What distinguishes a collective entity called an audience – or a public – from other social groupings or communities (be they ideological, religious, cultural, national, etc.)?
- What is the nature of the processes that may turn audiences into communities or communities into audiences?

The latter is, in particular, the question asked by Benedict Anderson, when he explores the formidable impact of the press (and printed literature) in terms of the following:

- reorganizing as continuous geographic spaces what were formerly perceived as distinct;
- offering a shared experience of time to groups that lived by different clocks;
- homogenizing various dialects into standard languages.

By reinforcing each other, such transformations lead to the emergence of national communities. National communities are not only 'imagined communities', but also communities that often started as audiences.

In contrast to this literature and to the work of Anderson, the question raised here is not that of the construction of new communities. This project does not mean to describe the part played by the media in the contagious dynamics that leads to the delineation of constantly enlarged sociations. On the contrary, it focuses on media whose vocation is not globalizing but particularistic, media whose aim is not to create new identities but to prevent the death of existing ones.

Yet this particularistic vocation is studied in reference to diasporas, and the very existence of diasporas calls for a question inspired by Anderson. Instead of being unproblematic – given, merely 'factual' – a diaspora is always an intellectual construction tied to a given narrative. Like other types of communities, but more so than most, diasporas are incarnations of existing discourses, enactments of such discourses, echoes or anticipations of historical projects. They are 'imagined communities' par excellence, and they can be imagined in a number of – sometimes conflicting – ways. Thus their maintenance, far from being a technical problem, involves a constant activity of reinvention.

The reference to Schudson: the 'resonance' of proposed identities

Another point that should be stressed concerning this project is the decision not to examine processes of identity construction exclusively at the level of the offer. Instead, there is a strong focus on the reception, adoption or rejection of identity models.

Of course, an important aspect of the construction of identities takes place in the public sphere. But in order to avoid a reductive approach to a complex phenomenon one must also examine the ways in which identity constructions, once proposed in public, are received in the private realm. How do community members behave vis-à-vis the proposed constructions? Why do they adopt them or not adopt them, and when? Some events call for momentous personal decisions. Are they also decisive turning points in identity formation?

Quite helpful in this context is Michael Schudson's (1988) delineation of the various dimensions involved in the 'power' of cultural objects. Defining 'cultural objects' in a manner general enough to permit the inclusion of extremely different texts or practices (e.g. poems, telegrams, biblical narratives, television shows), Schudson distinguishes between their reach, rhetorical force, institutional retention and resolution, on the one hand, and the difficult question of their 'resonance', on the other. While most sociological studies on the construction of identities have tended to deal with Schudson's first four dimensions, this project is also concerned with the fifth.

The reference to Appadurai: the changing site of ethnographies

Finally, in contrast with an ideal practice of ethnography, the communities whose study is proposed here are quite problematic. Their borders are unstable. Their territories are uncertain. They are constantly restructured in response to the presence of media.

Yet the traditional loci of anthropological fieldwork are progressively disappearing. Culture can no longer be studied in small, stable societies, in societies with precise borders. It has to be described in the context of societies increasingly characterized by their heterogeneity, by their connection to world economies, by the exportation of their members (Appadurai and Breckenridge 1988a).

In such a context diasporic groups are no longer infrequent or exceptional. When the cultural identity of an increasing number of such groups tends to become dissociated from any direct territorial inscription one can expect ethnographers to shift their attention away from their traditional objects (spatially circumscribed communities) and to start studying those communication devices that keep dispersed groups alive by linking peripheries to centres and connecting presents to pasts.

In other words, ethnography can no longer afford to ignore media research. On the contrary, studies on the media and the groups that use them might become a new ethnographic field. Beyond its normative dimension, the notion of a public sphere might then turn into a descriptive instrument.

ACKNOWLEDGEMENT

This chapter develops a text in Curran, James and Liebes, Tamer (eds) *Media, Ritual, Identity*, London: Routledge, 1998. Many thanks to the editors for granting reprint permission.

REFERENCES

Abdi, Nidam (1997) 'Lumière: la télé des Tamouls d'Europe', *Libération*, 4 June.

Abélès, Marc (1995) 'Pour une antropologie des institutions', *L'Homme* 135, Juillet–Septembre.

Anderson, Benedict (1983) *Imagined Communities: Reflections on the Origins and Spread of Nationalism*, London: Verso.

Appadurai, Arjun (1990) 'Disjuncture and difference in the global cultural economy', in M. Featherstone (ed.) *Global Culture: Nationalism, Globalization, Modernity*, London: Sage.

—— (1993) 'Patriotism and its futures', *Public Culture* 5.

Appadurai, Arjun and Carole Breckenridge (1988a) 'Editors' comments', *Public Culture* I(1), fall.

—— (1988b) 'Why public culture?', *Public Culture* I(1), fall.

—— (1992) 'Museums are good to think: heritage on view in India', in I. Karp and S. D. Lavine (eds) *Museums and Communities: The Politics of Public Culture*, Washington, DC: Smithsonian Institute.

Arlen, Michael (1977) *Embarquement pour Ararat*, Paris: Gallimard.

Badie, Bertrand and Wolton, Dominique (1996) *Identité et territoire*, a round table involving interventions by Jean Leca, Dominique Schnapper, Michel Foucher, Jean Robert Henry, Robert Toulemon, Olivier Dollfuss Paris, April, CNRS and Institut National de l'Audiovisuel.

Brody, Jeanne (1995) *Rue des Rosiers*, Paris: Autrement.

Carey, James (1992) *Communication as Culture: Essays on Media and Society*, London: Routledge.

Certeau, Michel de (1984) *The Practice of Everyday Life*, Berkeley: University of California Press.

Cohen, Robin (1995) 'Rethinking Babylon: iconoclastic conceptions of the diasporic experience', *New Community* 21(1), January.

Dahlgren, Peter (1994a) *Media and the Public Sphere*, London: Sage.

—— (1994b) 'La Sphère publique à l'âge des nouveaux medias', in D. Dayan and I. Veyrat-Masson (eds) *Espaces publics en images*, Hermès Series, vols 13 and 14, Paris: CNRS Press.

Dayan, Daniel (1996) 'Nations, networks and diasporas', oral presentation, Jerusalem Conference in honour of Elihu Katz: Media and the Flow of Communications, Academy of Sciences, Jerusalem, May.

—— (1997) 'L'Importance du local', in Zaki Laidi (ed.) *Le Temps mondial*, debate with Edgar Morin, Guy Hermet, Zaki Laidi, Bessarab Nicolescu, Paul Virilio, Paris: Éditions Complexe.

Eisenstein, Elizabeth (1979) *The Printing Press as an Agent of Change*, New York: Cambridge University Press.

Gillespie, Marie (1995) *Television, Ethnicity and Cultural Change*, London: Routledge.

Gilroy, Paul (1993) *The Black Atlantic: Modernity and Double Consciousness*, London and New York: Verso.

Giraud, Michel (1996) 'Les Populations caraibéennes en Amérique du Nord et en Europe', *MSH Informations* 73, Paris.

Gitlin, Todd (1995) *The Twilight of Common Dreams*, New York: Hall Metropolitan.

Gross, Larry (1993) *The Contested Closet: The Politics and Ethics of Outing*, London: University of Minnesota Press.

Habermas, J. (1991) *The Structural Transformation of the Public Sphere*, Cambridge, MA: MIT Press.

Halbwachs, Maurice (1968) *La Mémoire collective*, Paris: PUF.

Hall, Stuart (1988) 'New ethnicities', in K Mercer (ed.) *Black Film, British Cinema*, London: Institute for Contemporary Arts.

—— (1990) 'Cultural identity and diaspora', in J. Rutherford (ed.) *Identity, Community, Culture, Difference*, London: Lawrence & Wishart.

—— (1993) *Rethinking Ethnicities: Three Blind Mice (One Black, One White, One Hybrid)*, Inaugural Lecture, University of East London, New Ethnicities Unit.

Hannerz, Ulf (1990) 'Cosmopolitans and locals in world culture', in M. Featherstone (ed.) *Global Culture: Nationalism, Globalization, Modernity*, London: Sage.

Herbst, Susan (1994) ' "Race" domination, mass media and public experience', *Politics at the Margin: Historical Studies of Public Experience Outside the Mainstream: Chicago 1934–1960*, Cambridge University Press.

Hoffman, Eva (1989) *Lost in Translation*, London: Heinemann.

Katz, Elihu (1993) 'By, for and about', personal communication to Serge Proulx and Daniel Dayan, University of Pennsylvania–Annenberg School for Communication, Philadelphia.

Laidi, Zaki (1998) *A World Without Meaning*, London: Routledge.

Laidi, Zaki et al. (1997) *Le Temps mondiale*, Brussels: Éditions Complexe.

Lapierre, Nicole (1989) *Le Silence de la mémoire*, Paris: Plon.

Liebes, Tamar and Elihu Katz (1990) *The Export of Meaning*, Oxford: Oxford University Press.

Morley, David and Kevin Robins (1995) *Spaces of Identity: Global Media, Electronic Landscapes and Cultural Boundaries*, London: Routledge.

Naficy, Hamid (1993) *The Making of an Exile Culture*, London: University of Minnesota Press.

Ong, Walter (1967) *The Presence of the Word*, New Haven: Yale University Press.

Peters, J. D. (forthcoming) 'Exile, diaspora, nomadism: mobility in the Western canon', in Hamid Naficy (ed.) *House, Exile, Homeland: A Media Studies Reader*, London: Routledge.

Racine, Jean Luc (1995) 'Les Territoires de la globalisation i réseaux forts et espaces flous: décideurs et citoyens', unpublished paper, UNESCO MOST Programme, Paris Conference.

Robins, Kevin (1989) 'Re-imagined communities', *Cultural Studies* 3(2).

Rushdie, Salman (1991) *Imaginary Homelands*, London: Granta Books.

Schlesinger, Philip (1991a) *Media, State and Nation: Political Violence and Collective Identities*, London: Sage.

—— (1991b) 'Europeanness as new cultural battlefield', *Innovation* 5(1).

Schnapper, Dominique (1994) *La Communauté des citoyens*, Paris: Gallimard.

Schudson, Michael (1988) 'How culture works', *Critical Studies in Mass Communication*, Cambridge: Cambridge University Press.

—— (1994) 'Culture and the integration of national societies', *International Social Science Journal* 139, Blackwell/UNESCO.

Sorlin, Pierre (1992) 'Le mirage du public', *Revue d'histoire moderne et contemporaine* 39, Paris.

Sreberny Mohammadi, Annabelle and Mohammadi, Ali (1994) *Small Media Big Revolution: Communication Culture and the Iranian Revolution*, Minneapolis and London: University of Minnesota Press.

Turner, Victor (1974) *Dramas, Fields and Metaphors*, Ithaca: Cornell University Press.

Valensi, Lucette (1992) *Fables de la mémoire: la bataille des trois rois*, Paris: Hachette.

33

3

SCHOLARS, JOURNALISM, TELEVISION

Notes on some conditions for mediation and intervention

Jostein Gripsrud

INTRODUCTION

It is a central part of both the social legitimation of academic institutions and the ethos of scholarship that 'society at large' or 'people in general' should, sooner or later, in some way or other, benefit from the professional activities of scholars. Research is conducted either within universities, where the teaching of students is a primary mediating activity, or within institutions communicating directly with the particular financial or political interests outside academia that they serve. But there are also, perhaps increasingly, internal and external pressures to communicate scholarly activities and their results to wider audiences, 'the public', in various ways. Popularization – or, as the French put it, 'vulgarisation' – can take many forms, from speaking to a group of school teachers to writing books intended for wider audiences. In whatever form, however, popularization – not to mention political intervention – always means transgressing the boundaries of academic institutions, somehow leaving the specific languages and practices of academia behind in order to speak under different conditions, those of the general public sphere.

The central medium in today's public sphere is, without doubt, television, and that medium presents scholars with particular challenges. Some of these have to do with the more general differences and conflictual relationship between scholarship and journalism; others are more specific to the medium. The purpose of this article is to look into some of the factors that make the relationship between scholars and television deeply problematic, and, in the end, to suggest ways of thinking about relationships with journalism in general and television in particular which may be fruitful for those interested in how scholars can act as public intellectuals today. I should emphasize that I do not claim to have solutions to all problems I touch upon; the article is basically a preliminary report from work in progress.

An important source of inspiration for parts of the following is Pierre Bourdieu's sociological work. On the other hand, the article is also to some extent a response to Bourdieu's extremely critical view of journalism and television, as it is presented in his book *Sur la Télévision* (Bourdieu 1996). The book is not only an attack on current journalistic practices and on the ever stronger rule of people meters and sales figures. It is also an attack on academics who get involved with television journalism in certain ways, and it is consequently presenting those of us who may have a somewhat different or at least more nuanced perception of journalism, television and its professionals with a number of questions in need of answers.

But first we may want to ask whether it is worth the bother of trying to communicate scholarly knowledge to people outside academia. It seems to me that a 'yes' answer to this question presupposes that there is such a thing as 'knowledge' which scholars can claim is of relevance or even importance to other people. 'Knowledge' here means thoughts and information in perspective, in meaningful context(s). So before analysing the relations between scholars and television I will first briefly address the problem of knowledge as it appears in a certain influential theoretical formation.

TELEVISION, KNOWLEDGE AND POSTMODERNISM

The idea of regarding television as a medium suited to the mediation of serious knowledge may to many seem quite farfetched. It is not only that television appears to some, particularly in the US, to be primarily a medium of free-floating signifiers and drug-like entertainment threatening any serious public discourse on serious matters. Broadcast television is also the central medium in late-modern social formations where once-sanctified concepts like knowledge and truth have been the objects of fundamental doubt and even ridicule. In fact, television has been treated as the most prominent symptom of a sociocultural condition in which the terms knowledge and truth can only be used within inverted commas.

Perhaps the most consequent and well-known proponent of such a position is Jean Baudrillard, who just days before the Gulf War broke out proclaimed that no real war in the Gulf was going to take place, it was all a matter of (primarily televisual) *simulacra* (Baudrillard 1991). While obviously extreme, Baudrillard's way of thinking here could be regarded as a consequence of an epistemology characteristic of much writing and talking problematically referred to in *toto* as 'postmodernism'. Postmodernism's position as the predominant intellectual fashion of the 1980s and early 1990s was due not least to a report commissioned by the government of Quebec, Canada, and delivered by the French philosopher Jean-François Lyotard: *The Postmodern Condition* (1979, English edition 1984). The often forgotten subtitle of Lyotard's report was precisely *A Report on Knowledge*. Issues of epistemology, on the one hand, and of the social roles of knowledge, on the other, are central concerns of contemporary critical discourses in the humanities and social sciences.

The critiques of traditional Western epistemologies formulated by French scholars with a background in structuralism, such as Michel Foucault and Jacques Derrida, often somewhat uneasily combined with contributions from US pragmatists such as Richard Rorty, have been extremely influential. A sprawling body of work has developed in which the inherent instability of meaning in signs and texts, the fact that any construction of historical narratives is debatable and the inescapable partiality of anyone's speaking position were taken to mean that all claims to the existence of truth and knowledge as intersubjectively acceptable entities were not just obsolete but also politically deeply suspect. As the works and second-hand renditions of the postmodern master thinkers trickled downwards and outwards to thousands of practitioners in the various fields of scholarly inquiry, simplified and vulgarized versions acquired a status as axioms in some quarters, not least within media and cultural studies. In writings and in gatherings on and off campus one would often encounter general statements such as 'there is no such thing as truth' (a statement implicitly held to be absolutely true) or 'knowledge is only a question of power' (also, of course, universally true).

The simplistic conflation of truth and/or knowledge with a highly abstract and general notion of 'power', inspired by ideas put forward by Michel Foucault, actually makes it impossible to understand even the work of Foucault himself. This one-time journalist for the Italian newspaper *Corriere della sera* in Iran, where he went to 'get to know what was about to happen there' (Foucault 1979: 9), could never have conducted his extremely thorough and intellectually challenging historical studies if he had subscribed to a theoretical eradication of any notion of intersubjective truth and knowledge. Moreover, had his readership not (at least in practice) upheld elementary ideas about historical truth and knowledge, Foucault's work would not have been so convincing; nor would it have seemed so necessary to take it into account in various related fields. A fundamental respect for knowledge as something not entirely particularistic and relativistic underlies, for instance, the following thoughts, formulated by Foucault when he was trying to give reasons for preferring some writers to others:

> [I prefer] people for whom knowledge is not only an act in which one acquires an objective insight, but for whom knowledge is a spiritual adventure and a spiritual transformation. The one who knows does not only differ from the one who does not know by the simple fact that he knows of certain things, but by the fact that he is no longer the same, and that he ceased being the same from that moment on when he decided to get to know something. In other words: Knowledge is that which transforms the very subjectivity of the one who knows.
>
> (Foucault 1979: 7)

To Foucault, then, there *are* 'objective insights' in some sense, and there *is* an indisputable difference between having and not having knowledge of certain things; these are necessary preconditions for what interests him more (at least in this context), namely the ability of knowledge to transform the subjectivity of those who know. Foucault's linking of knowledge and subjectivity here — and his idea that knowledge is something desirable, something well worth having — is, *mutatis mutandis*, also at the core of Enlightenment ideas about desirable subjectivity and the corresponding democratic notions of *citizenship*.

And this is what the public communication or mediation of knowledge is most centrally about: providing resources for active citizenship. Such activities lose meaning if any claim to a degree of universality, of intersubjective validity, is given up.

ENLIGHTENMENT, THE PUBLIC SPHERE AND BROADCAST TELEVISION

Participation in the discourses of the liberal public sphere, as conceived in the eighteenth century, presupposed knowledge of the issues under discussion, knowledge ranging from matters of fact to matters of adequate perspectives and rhetorical strategies. Citizens of democracies were conceived as autonomous subjects in the sense that their reasoning and views were to be based on a judge-ment which in principle was independent, not forced upon them by way of social powers outside critical public discourse itself. No aristocrat, plutocrat or bureau-crat should, because of his social position, decide about truth, reason or political measures derived from them. Any citizen could make up his (or her, some hundred years later) own mind, employing universal mental faculties and freely available information and knowledge.

The ideals of the liberal public sphere still form the basis for notions of democracy — and for the ethical principles which are officially supposed to govern the functions of the media within democratic societies (see also Chapter 1). This is so even if these ideals may to a significant extent have become (false) ideology, as was once argued by Jürgen Habermas (1962/1989). The importance of Enlightenment ideas in the very conception of modern mass media can be illus-trated by the etymological origins of the term 'broadcasting', which originally referred to the activity of sowing seeds by hand, in the widest possible circles. The term that designates the predominant organizational and distributive form of radio and television is, in other words, an agricultural metaphor which evokes an optimistic modernist programme: there are centralized cultural resources (the bucket of seeds) which, given the widest possible distribution, may yield a rich harvest (see Gripsrud 1997).

The kind of centralization implied here is just one of several increasingly centralized structures in modern societies which, according to Raymond Williams's classic *Television: Technology and Cultural Form* (Williams 1975), provided one of two main social preconditions for broadcasting becoming the dominant social use of radio and, later, television technology. The other social feature of modernity which made broadcasting victorious as a form was what Williams called the 'mobile privatization' characteristic of people's lives – the radically increased geographical and social mobility of individuals, with the nuclear family as the dominant form of everyday community. In this situation of centralization on the one hand and mobile privatization on the other, broadcasting media qualified as the primary means of rapid, equal distribution of knowledge and information, and the production of social cohesion in the form of national or regional identity.

Within the tradition of European public-service broadcasting some version of the Enlightenment vision of the spreading of knowledge and other cultural resources has both legitimated public broadcasting monopolies, and to a considerable extent guided their operations. Public-service broadcasting in principle addresses its audiences primarily as citizens, not as consumers, and not just as pleasure-seeking zappers. Purely commercial television is simply in the business of selling audiences to advertisers and consequently only addresses audiences as citizens to a minimal extent, and rarely or never beyond the dictates of the people meters. This is not to say that, for instance, US television does not produce and distribute knowledge, only that it does so very differently from European public-service TV. As Raymond Williams (1975) has already documented, certain programme genres are simply more or less missing in US network television, genres vital to the distribution of knowledge useful for the practising of informed citizenship. The old Hollywood slogan 'if you want messages try Western Union' could be paralleled by network television's 'if you want serious knowledge try PBS and the Discovery Channel', channels that mostly serve well-educated minorities with a limited range of programming.

The kind of fracturing of the public sphere implied by a diversified broadcasting structure is, however, only one of several splits, differentiations and other structural changes that mark the development of public discourse since the 'classic' public sphere of the late eighteenth and early nineteenth centuries. Western societies are increasingly diversified in terms of cultures, ethnicities, lifestyles, etc., and the 'bucket of seeds' has, from this point of view, become harder to conceive of as the bucket relevant to all of us. While there are certainly good reasons to think about particular communities and their respective public spheres and forms of communication (see Chapter 2), this plurality of communicative contexts may also be seen as another good argument for the importance of maintaining a functioning, encompassing 'general' public sphere; all the diverse groups divided along various lines related to different identities are also in need of reciprocal insights into each others' worlds and views, for the simple reason that they depend on each other and share a number of economic, ecological, ethical and political concerns and interests. Broadcast television continues to be the medium most centrally placed for such exchanges of knowledge, perspectives and arguments.

While the media themselves are, of course, in important ways knowledge-producing institutions, it should be of particular interest to scholars how the knowledge produced in academic institutions may or may not circulate through media to a wider audience than that within academia. One of the earliest splits within the public sphere was that between scholars and publicists or journalists, core activists in 'classical' public discourse:

> an increasing specialization of intellectual labour lead to a growing split and struggle for intellectual hegemony between an increasingly industrialized and commercialized mass media and the traditional intelligentsia with their base in education and specialized cultural production for an elite.
>
> (Garnham 1995: 376)

The relations between these two professional categories are still vital to the processes of knowledge distribution.

JOURNALISM AND ACADEMIA AS SOCIAL FIELDS

Relations between academia and the dominant mass media – newspapers, radio and television – are normally considered problematic. There are a number of good reasons for this. Some of the more fundamental of these are tied to the different characteristics of the cultural production which goes on within the two social fields in question. Journalistic media will tend to work within constraints and pressures related to time and space, to deadlines and temporal or spatial frames for presentation, which are alien to normal academic research. As the very name of the profession indicates, most journalism is a day-to-day activity, while scholarly work is normally conducted within a perspective of years, decades and even generations. Moreover, as modern cultural industries, large-circulation newspapers, broadcast television and radio tend to strive for the widest possible audience reach, while publications of academic research will normally be addressing quite narrowly defined, more or less highly qualified, specialist audiences. Codes and formats employed in the textual products of the two fields will thus tend to be radically different. And, importantly, there are obvious limits to what can be done to change this.

Encounters between representatives of the two fields will consequently often have an element of conflicting interests, and outright confrontations may occur. But there is also an element of common ground in the relationship, stemming from a similarity in the professional ethos which in principle informs the activities and self-understanding of each of them. Both journalists and other media workers, on the one hand, and scholars, on the other, are in different ways engaged in producing and distributing forms of knowledge about various parts and dimensions of the world we inhabit, and this is in principle seriously intended business to both groups. Both professions are, then, as indicated above, historically and in their self-understanding tied to the Enlightenment project. The ethics of the journalistic crafts is comparable to that of scholarly disciplines in terms of shared values such as critical examination of available information, taking care in presenting an argued and/or reasonably adequate account of this information, some responsibility for the nature of public discourse, etc. Furthermore, the legitimation of the media as 'a tribune of the people, holding power to account', is clearly related to the critical role of the traditional intelligentsia (Garnham 1995: 377).

The fact that this commonality tends to be overlooked is due to several factors. One of them is, of course, that the ethics taught in journalism schools might be hard to stick to in the increasingly commercialized everyday of most media work. On the other hand, the ethos of the scholarly field may also at times appear to be ideological mumbo-jumbo suitable mostly for festive occasions when judged against the increasingly competitive, routinized and bureaucratized realities of universities and other research institutions. There is, however, another reason, which becomes visible if we take a further look at the term 'social field', which I have already employed above.

'Field' (*champ*) is a key term in the sociological theory of Pierre Bourdieu. He once defined it as 'a space in which a game takes place, a field of objective relations between individuals and institutions competing for the same stake' (Bourdieu 1984: 197, quoted in Moi 1991). Normally journalists and scholars are, so to speak, busy playing their own games on their own home grounds. What happens in a situation where scholars are to communicate in and through mass media is that players from different fields meet in the same arena – the general public sphere. This is quite a complex game, since both types of players (scholars and journalists) are out to gain (or at least keep) recognition both in their own primary, professional fields and in the field where the stake is the recognition of a more or less anonymous 'mass' audience.

Journalists here have the benefit of home ground since the general public sphere is where they normally present their work or appear in person, and so they do, of course, have the upper hand – in more than one way. While gaining recognition from their journalist peers is not necessarily the same as gaining it from the public – analytically speaking – in practice journalists who achieve popularity or celebrity can nowadays very often immediately change such recognition into the currency of professional recognition. In Bourdieu's terms, one could say that the role of *heteronomous* recognition, as opposed to the *autonomous* recognition within the field, in relation to the field's own norms, is radically more important in journalism than in academia. For scholars, the journalistic exchange rate between heteronomous and autonomous recognition is much harder to achieve. Gaining recognition from the public at large is not at all a guarantee that one will be gaining recognition within academia.

A central point for Bourdieu in his *Sur la Télévision* (1996) is that journalism's autonomy is now more than ever threatened by heteronomous influences stemming from increased market orientation, and the ever greater importance of people-meter figures as a measure of 'quality' and 'success' in journalism. This also aggravates the problem of 'the intrusion of journalistic criteria and values' in the scholarly field which he had already pointed out in *Homo Academicus* (Bourdieu

[1984] 1988: 112). It is no longer only a question of preferring, for instance, easier, short-term forms of production which are rewarded with immediate signs of some social recognition over the long-term, uncertain work on more ambitious projects. According to Bourdieu's *Sur la Télévision*, bending to the norms of journalism now represents a more thoroughgoing abandonment of scholarly virtues; it implies a near total immersion in the suspect machinery of publicity.

JOURNALISTIC V. ACADEMIC *HABITUS*

Corresponding to the differences between the journalistic and the academic fields, there are differences in the *habitus* regulating the activities of media professionals, on the one hand, and scholars, on the other. A *habitus* is, in Pierre Bourdieu's well-known usage of the term, a specific configuration of dispositions, i.e. socially (re)produced inclinations to perceive, understand and act in certain patterned ways in certain situations. *Habitus* is 'social life incorporated, and thus individuated', as it was once expressed by Bourdieu (1990: 31); it is, in other words, a notion which points to and includes the social production of what we might call conceptions of self in various social fields, and hence professions. It follows from this that journalists and researchers will tend to understand themselves and their professional activities in different ways, evaluate themselves and their respective performances on different grounds, and measure success and failure according to different parameters.

In Bourdieu's sociological thinking, *habitus* is central to the patterned sociocultural practices and preferences called lifestyles. The traditional academic ideal is a lifestyle marked by a certain (aristocratic) asceticism (see Bourdieu 1988: 223). This is in part related to the position of academics in the upper echelons of the social structure, somewhere between the bourgeoisie, whose position depends on its control of economic capital, and artists, whose position depends only on the amount of their cultural capital; they are not as poor as most artists but cannot match the spending of the wealthy bourgeoisie. But the aristocratic asceticism of traditional academics is also – and not least – dependent on the specific kinds of virtues necessary for success within the academic field itself, such as the ability to sacrifice worldly pleasures while investing all of one's energy in long-term, concentrated work which is primarily to receive the non-material rewards of satisfaction and appreciation by one's peers within the field.

In line with this (and classic bourgeois morality), the proper *homo academicus* will tend to emphasize and value 'interior' rather than 'exterior' qualities in a person. In fact, the 'person' does not in principle deserve interest at all, only the person's work or product. Façade or appearance is thus not only less important; it is in principle unimportant, and thus anything flamboyant or flashy is immediately suspect. The same goes for the intentional exposure of people or 'personalities' in any social setting, possibly outside intimate relationships. The proper academic prefers conservative, classic clothes, in earth tones or other

41

modest colours, and does not speak of his or her intimate pleasures or problems in public. There are here obvious links to Bourdieu's well-known distinction between 'pure' and 'barbaric' taste.

Journalists, on the other hand, will – since they are integrated, full-time, central actors in the contemporary public sphere – tend to conceive of the relations between the personal and the public, the interior and the façade, quite differently from proper academics. Their professional lives are deeply involved in promotional press conferences, cocktail parties with the rich and famous, socializing with public figures, including, not least, other journalists. It is part of their professional identity to be very sensitive about appearances and 'images', and they tend to think of themselves as 'representatives of ordinary people' when providing as intimate glimpses as possible of the 'real personality' of those appearing in public life. Journalists, and especially those working in television, will consequently also tend to be wary of their own appearance or image in public life, and a status as celebrity, as noted above, hardly jeopardizes either their status among their peers or their career opportunities. As celebrities, they normally give interviews about their personal lives, preferences and problems, just as any other stars, and do not seem to mind. The journalistic attention to the momentary, the here-and-now event, the heroes of the day, furthermore entails a validation of the excitement and dynamics of hectic, publicity-oriented public life which is alien to the proper academic *habitus*. What the journalistic profession thrives on, and to a large extent concentrates on, is, of course, in general despised by properly socialized academics.

SCHOLARS MINGLING WITH THE MEDIA: MOTIVES AND CONSEQUENCES

With the above points in mind, it is not surprising that academics who often appear on television, and, more generally, those who are frequently interviewed or otherwise referred to even in newspapers, may risk condemnation from their peers. A Norwegian survey in 1988 found that two-thirds of the social scientists responding agreed that condemnation would not just be a risk, but a matter of simple consequence (Ottosen 1988: 23).

On the other hand, academics will have to admit that television is, as indicated above, the absolutely central medium of communication in today's world. It is the central stage in the public sphere(s) of modern societies. Consequently, any academic who for some reason feels obliged to communicate, or is simply interested in communicating, knowledge or perspectives to a wider audience will have to consider some form of participation in television programmes of some sort. Such participation may be differently motivated and produce different results.

The main and still clearly valid motives are tied to a general, socially committed educational interest in the communication of new (or old) knowledge or, say, an interest in political intervention. But there also seems to be a growing feeling among scientists and researchers that media coverage in general is a good thing for more mundane reasons. 'Sociology has not had a good press', says, for instance, a former President of the British Sociological Association, Robert G. Burgess, and so the association 'has attempted to counter this [negative] image by appointing a press officer and making links with the media' (Burgess 1994: 21). Through various initiatives, the association and its president tried – with highly mixed results – to develop a 'professional image' beneficial to sociology's professionals and students by communicating through the media how useful sociology is and how popular the discipline is among students. Such an interest in 'good publicity' is just another example of the extent to which the modern public sphere has become a space for more or less manipulative, legitimating discourses, for public relations or marketing, rather than a forum for earnest, enlightened discussions (see Habermas [1962] 1989). The logic of publicity represents unavoidable premises for all kinds of public institutions and services, and consequently also for scholars and scholarly disciplines.

Not only is media coverage thought to contribute to the general political legitimacy of disciplines or universities and other research institutions; it is more specifically considered helpful in the struggle to finance the work of individual researchers or research groups (see Peters 1995: 32f; Ottosen 1988: 23). It may, moreover, also boost the sales of books and increase the chances of other additional income for financially strapped academics. Media exposure can, however, at times also provide scholars with esteem in the eyes of the general audience as compensation for lack of esteem within the academic field. Since funding institutions may be attentive to such public recognition, media exposure may result in easier access to funding and thus provide the scholars in question with some extra power within the academic field itself. But the exchange of general social recognition into academic recognition does not, of course, necessarily involve money at all; in certain circumstances intellectual celebrity may become 'a path to promotion within the institution itself' (Bourdieu [1984] 1988: 112). This possibility is, however, probably more important in some national and cultural contexts than in others. Private universities competing for donations will probably be more interested in hiring and promoting academic 'stars' than in institutions more or less totally relying on the allocation of tax money.

Whatever the motives or intentions, participation in television programmes holds a number of problems for any serious academic. One cannot simply count on the permission to use television for one's own purposes – as Bourdieu in fact did when he presented the lectures that make up his *Sur la Télévision* (1996) (see below). Rather, one can expect to be used for someone else's purposes – those of TV journalists, producers, programmers and (other) executives. Scholars interested in maintaining the seriousness of their contributions should therefore carefully consider the degree to which they are allowed to influence the conditions and context of their participation. A number of entertaining anecdotes can be told about serious researchers being used as a kind of prop in programmes that were entirely the making of more or less creative producers.

Anders Johansen, a contributor to this volume (Chapter 10), was once interviewed at length about the phenomenology of music and its relationship to
conceptions of time. In the actual programme minimal bits and pieces of the
interview appeared in between quite idiosyncratically associative footage and
highly violent extracts from *Tom and Jerry* cartoons. Another contributor to this
book, Graham Murdock (Chapter 1), was once asked to participate in a Channel 4
programme which was to argue 'that the links between violence on the screen and
real life violence were problematic and contestable'. His verbal contribution was
shot in a room where other people had far more significant things to do in visual
terms:

> The main participants were a professional stunt man and stunt arranger
> and a special effects expert. They were shown setting up a shooting and
> talking about their trade. When everything was ready, a woman burst
> through the French windows and shot the stunt man, spraying fake
> blood around from a series of vivid bullet holes across the chest. Clips of
> the meticulous process of fabricating violence were interspersed
> throughout the second half of the programme, leaving the final shooting
> to provide a dramatic ending and a visual reminder of the programme's
> basic argument.
>
> (Murdock 1994: 118)

Murdock was shown speaking to the camera, and this was interspersed with
sequences where the stunt arranger and the special effects expert were working
and talking, and was thus thoroughly associated with them both in terms of the
programme's space (location) and its syntax. The difference between Murdock as a
scholar and the professionals of screen violence was consequently minimized or
erased. Nor was there a voiceover commentary or any other (for instance graphic)
element which pointed out the difference.

While neither of these scholars is entirely negative about the programme he
appeared in, it is also clear that both found the directors' overwhelming emphasis
on the visually enticing elements quite problematic, to say the least. To an extreme
degree, they both experienced a significant loss of control of their 'message',
which is part of any attempt to communicate via someone else – and, obviously,
via modern mass media.

Bourdieu's book *Sur la Télévision* was, as indicated above, originally presented as
televised lectures. But they were distributed only on a particular Parisian cable
channel and most probably reached a quite limited audience. This form of distribution also explains why Bourdieu enjoyed a near total control of the conditions
of his appearance:

> Firstly, my time is not limited; secondly, the subject of my discourse has
> not been imposed upon me – I have chosen it freely and may still change
> it; thirdly, no one is here, as in ordinary programs, to call me to order, in

the name of technology, in the name of the 'public which is not going to understand', in the name of morality, good taste etc.

(Bourdieu 1996: 10).

The question is whether such *total control* is the only condition on which serious scholars are to accept invitations to appear on television. Is there no possibility of conditions which may be said to grant *sufficient* control, somewhere between the use of scholars as props or marionettes and the demand of total mastery of 'the means of production' (*ibid.*)?

Before returning to this question I would like to look at certain aspects of scholarly participation in television which are left out of Bourdieu's argument. They are about the rhetorical conditions presented by an audiovisual mass medium, conditions that regardless of journalistic practices are operative whenever professors or other scholars try to address 'the masses' through such a medium.

TELEVISION, STEREOTYPES AND AUDIENCE PERCEPTIONS OF ACADEMICS

The characteristics of the proper academic *habitus* described above immediately constitute an adversary relationship with current popular culture in general and the medium of television in particular. Jürgen Habermas suggested as early as the start of the 1960s that rational public discourse has been transformed into stage(d) entertainment in modern, commercialized media, and the medium of television was seen as a primary example of this general tendency. In his *The Fall of Public Man* (1977), Richard Sennett arrived at similarly pessimistic conclusions from a somewhat different angle, concentrating on the 'tyranny of intimacy' which has tended to make personal features (the 'personality', morals, feelings, etc.) of those who appear in public the main subject of public discourse.

In a strikingly less pessimistic fashion, Joshua Meyrowitz, in his *No Sense of Place* (1985), identified the medium of television as a driving force behind the collapse of the formerly rigid boundaries between the public and the private realms – and between various other social categories – thus directly affecting the social distribution of various kinds of knowledge: Children now know more about the world of adults than ever before, boys and men have a much more intimate knowledge of the world of girls and women, and the world of politics literally looks a lot different now than it used to do just a few decades ago. Television daily presents leading politicians and other authorities in close-up, revealing every twitch of an eyelid, every drop of sweat, and demonstrates again and again in various ways that politicians are basically 'just people, like you and me'. Consequently, the distinction between what Erving Goffman (1959) once called 'front stage' and 'back stage' has more or less withered away, and the public sphere has become dominated by what Meyrowitz calls 'middle-stage' behaviour (a 'deep back stage' still normally remains hidden from the public).

The new portrayal of politicians and other authorities may mean that rational public discourse will tend to be distorted in certain psychologistic ways (see Chapter 10). On the other hand, one may, as Meyrowitz does, also point out a certain anti-authoritarian, liberalizing tendency here. Television's audiences will tend to apply everyday codes of face-to-face communication not only when judging physical attractiveness but also when judging the trustworthiness and respectability of anyone who appears on the screen. This should then imply that less authority will be given simply by the formal social position occupied by those speaking on television; the degree to which they adhere to certain everyday codes of appearance and conduct has become more important. The category 'conduct' will here, of course, include the degree to which the people in question are saying things that appear to be worth listening to.

Consequently, scholars or other intellectuals who appear on television to talk about or present various more or less scholarly issues will necessarily be subjected to the kinds of evaluations of screen 'personalities' which audiences routinely produce when watching TV. They will be categorized as more or less sympathetic, more or less credible, more or less interesting, etc. on the basis of widespread everyday codes or 'schemata'. In the language of classical rhetoric, then, television and its insistent close-ups thus present both new conditions for and possibly a new emphasis on the mediator's *ethos*, i.e. his or her ability to convey *phronesis* ('sound judgement'), *areté* ('good human character traits') and *eunoia* ('goodwill/good intentions in relation to the audience'). There are reasons to believe that many scholars will find it hard to accept that their appearance as speakers in close-up should influence the ways in which their 'message' is perceived and/or understood. They are trained to suspect and unmask 'surfaces' and 'appearances' of all kinds, to look for what is 'underneath' and 'behind'. Scholars tend to think that people may appear as they like, that it is *only* what they actually *say* that matters. (Even if there *are* operative codes of conduct, clothing, hairstyles, etc. also within academia.) The impression that personal style might reduce the attention to what is said may be enough for many to turn down invitations to participate in TV programmes at all.

But maybe 'personal style' is less the issue than 'styles' that are socially produced and hence possible to categorize and analyse as social phenomena? It is simply so-called common knowledge that different social groups vary in terms of behaviour and, even more generally, in 'looks'. A philosopher friend of mine said of another philosopher that this latter person's background in the countryside could easily be seen from his walk: he lifts his feet so high when walking that it is obvious he grew up wading through grass. We all know, not least through a zillion parodies, the stereotypical appearances of aristocratic upper-class people, 'feminine' gay men, cowboys (real and imagined), etc. 'Stereotypes' may be a somewhat old-fashioned term but is still important here. Even if frequently contradicted by experience, stereotypes or social clichés still tend to function as ready-made tools for sorting out impressions of people in an often confusing modern world full of strangers. Academics who go on television speak to audiences with such clichés or prejudices in their heads, both stereotypes of a general kind and a spectre of stereotypes specifically related to 'academics', 'intellectuals', etc.

As listings of the terms by which these educated groups are referred to in a number of different countries demonstrate (see the journal *Liber* nos. 25 and 26, 1996), these stereotypes are overwhelmingly of a negative or sarcastic kind (eggheads, bookworms, etc.). Studies of how, for instance, teachers (at all levels of education) are portrayed in US and other Western popular culture have pointed out that both female and male representatives of this profession tend to be power-less and sexless (see Gerbner 1974). Even if more recent Hollywood movies in the *Stand and Deliver* genre may modify this, the abundance of nutty professors, mean scientists and weak do-gooders still represent the main tradition.

This does not mean, however, that popular culture is consistently negative in its imagery of knowledge or those who possess it. Technical or physical skills are normally treasured, and the same seems to be the case with knowledge produced through experience, as opposed to knowledge gathered from books and formal education. In line with centuries of (masculinist?) tradition, knowledge that stems from 'personal experience' appears as wisdom, and wisdom lends authority to whoever has it. Those who represent wisdom are, however, normally at least middle-aged, so they can be considered past their obvious reproductive period, and hence confirm that knowledge and sex do not go well together. But they may well be powerful and are definitely worth listening to.

The centuries (if not millenia)-old opposition between the stereotypes of 'the bookworm' and 'the experienced person' is then worth keeping in mind when looking at how academics and other intellectuals appear on television. Such stereotypes are condensations of a number of more specific character traits, which in this case could be grouped in oppositional pairs such as weak v. strong, femi-nine v. masculine, timid v. self-confident, humourless v. humorous, lifeless v. vital, unsensual v. sensual, rigid v. relaxed. It is not difficult to imagine how physical appearance and body language may be used to categorize many traditional academics and intellectuals as representing the first of the terms in these opposi-tions. In a sense, then, it is an empirical question whether it is possible to be a serious scholar and still in one's televised persona qualify as representing wisdom, 'human warmth' or other currently attractive forms of ethos.

I do not, of course, propose that TV audiences will simply place any academic or intellectual appearing on the screen in one of two boxes and respond with attention in one case and with rejection in the other. Obviously, what remains most important of all is what those appearing on TV are actually *saying*. Most viewers are also aware that people are more complicated than stereotypes, and consequently allow some space for individual specificity. Nuances may be added by how the TV programme in question provides a context for the individual(s) that appear in it. Still, television's visual rendering of the person speaking presents a set of unavoidable and historically relatively new rhetorical conditions for speaking convincingly directly to a widely composed audience. And these conditions do not necessarily favour the traditionally socialized scholar, although the space for individual variations is considerable.

TELEVISION'S PRIORITIES AND THE HIERARCHIES OF SCHOLARLY DISCIPLINES

Scholarly disciplines differ in terms of the likelihood of their getting media attention at all, and also in terms of the roles they are offered in the media. Odontologists cannot expect to have their own TV show or frequently appear as experts in the news. The social sciences are, on the other hand, very often represented in the press and in broadcast media in news and current affairs formats, both through reports on recent research and in commentary. But there are so far very few examples, if indeed there are any (to my knowledge), of social scientists hosting TV series about their fields of expertise. This format or genre seems to me to be the near exclusive domain of people from the natural sciences, on the one hand, and people from the arts, on the other.

These disciplines quite frequently also appear in the ways and forms typical of social scientists (commenting on ecological issues, natural disasters, technological advances; or on historical issues, exhibitions, literary and other high-art events). But their near total dominance of the 'hosted series' genre may be seen as an indication of their special status. It seems evident that this status is related to the role of these disciplines as managers of ideological – here meaning epistemological and cultural – cornerstones of modern societies. The social sciences (including economics) are, on the other hand, more directly associated with the immediate administrative and political agenda of the modern, technocratic state, i.e. the business of running society on a day-to-day basis. For viewers of newscasts and current affairs programmes, social scientists may appear hard to separate from the bureaucrats in government agencies, large corporations or influential organizations. With the possible exception of certain kinds of sociologists, who may appear to be closely related to the bookworms and eggheads in fields at a greater distance from political and economic power, social scientists are probably not as clearly conceived as living in a strange world of their own as are natural scientists and people from the humanities.

These (partly hypothetical) differentiated social perceptions of scholarly fields which television in various ways (re)presents are culturally and historically variable. Studies of how disciplines are presented in various national and historical contexts can thus provide insights into the ideological make-up of specific nation-states and historical periods. For example, in the 1960s Norwegian television had two distinct roles for literary scholars and people from the natural sciences when employed as hosts of programme series. A leading senior literary historian (Francis Bull) would be presented sitting in a high-backed, throne-like chair, speaking in carefully formed, if also vivid, sentences about the founding fathers of the country's national literature. There are obvious links between these and similarly styled presentations of literary subjects in television and the fact that practically all Norwegian krone bills, and all the most valuable ones, had pictures of writers on them. Writers were simply the most prominent icons of national cultural identity. Natural scientists, on the other hand, appeared on TV as clown-like, playful characters, fooling around with more or less dangerous experiments and slimy creatures. While both categories of programmes actually enjoyed widespread popularity, the natural scientists were popular in a different way – even if slightly twisted, they were folksy, not aloof, and spoke of concrete matters, not of the solemn, the abstract and the there and then.

At present one may only wonder whether similar differences have occurred in other countries, although Suzanne de Cheveigné's contribution to this volume (Chapter 12) touches on this issue in a French context. One might ask, for instance, whether British series such as Kenneth Clark's *Civilisation*, produced in the late 1960s, and John Berger's *Ways of Seeing*, from the early 1970s, a kind of critical 'reply' to Clark, could be made today – and why (not). And why is it that probably the most memorable of US contributions in this area is Carl Sagan's *Cosmos* from the late 1970s, i.e. a series about astronomy or astrophysics?

'Educational television' sounds boring. But it has not always been boring, and consequently need not always be. In fact, various forms of educational TV used to be popular with large audiences in many European countries, and were for decades, and certain subspecies of such programming are still considered popular material by both commercial and public-service broadcasters. But programmes intended to present knowledge produced by academic institutions of one kind or another, hosted by either scholars or well-educated television journalists, are now both different from what they used to be and normally much more marginal in the competitive programming of all broadcasters. The kinds of educational series I and other Europeans remember from television in, say, the 1960s, are hardly imaginable today. But creative efforts may be able to demonstrate that other meaningful forms, adequate today, are possible.

THE CONDITIONS FOR ACTING AS PUBLIC INTELLECTUALS

Directly educational television is hardly the only imaginable way to mediate critical knowledge through television. I asked above whether there are possibilities somewhere between the roles of marionettes for producers and the demand for total control of the means of production. I think there are. The all-or-nothing sorts of dichotomies that tend to dominate the ways intellectuals imagine their sociopolitical potentials are misleading.

Sartre's (1972) famous distinction between 'intellectuals' and 'technicians of knowledge' is one of these dichotomies. He defined 'intellectuals' as people with cultural resources who intervene publicly far outside their area of professional or scholarly knowledge, as when professors of philosophy or poets air their opinions on the storage of nuclear waste. 'Technicians of knowledge', on the other hand, remain completely within the confines of their area of professional or scholarly expertise and rarely intervene publicly at all. It seems to me that this dichotomy is not able to grasp the most widespread of scholarly or other intellectual public interventions. Such interventions normally appear as *extensions* of scholarly or professional expertise into areas of immediate political interest, i.e. they are based in specialist knowledge but stretch or move beyond the purely scholarly into suggestions of concrete applications of specialist knowledge in areas where political struggles are going on.

A more recent dichotomy of a similar kind is that proposed by Zygmunt Bauman (1989) between intellectuals as 'legislators' and 'interpreters'. The 'legislator' role – also referred to as a 'strategy for intellectual work' which Bauman regards as typically 'modern' – consists in

> making authoritative statements which arbitrate in controversies of opinions and which select those opinions which, having been selected, become correct and binding. The authority to arbitrate is in this case legitimized by superior (objective) knowledge to which intellectuals have a better access than the non-intellectual part of society. Access to such knowledge is better thanks to procedural rules which assure the attainment of truth, the arrival at valid moral judgement, and the selection of proper artistic taste. Such procedural rules have a universal validity, as do the products of their application....Like the knowledge they produce, intellectuals are not bound by localized, communal traditions. They are, together with their knowledge, extra-territorial. This gives them the right and the duty to validate (or invalidate) beliefs that may be held in various sections of society.
>
> (Bauman 1989: 5)

The 'interpreter' role or strategy, regarded as 'postmodern', on the other hand, consists in

> translating statements, made within one communally based tradition, so that they can be understood within the system of knowledge based on another tradition. Instead of being orientated towards selecting the best social order, this strategy is aimed at facilitating communication between autonomous (sovereign) participants. It is concerned with preventing the distortion of meaning in the process of communication.
>
> (*ibid.*: 5)

Bauman hastens to emphasize that the 'postmodern' role is not to replace the 'modern' – 'I do not believe that modernity, as a type of intellectual mode, has been conclusively superseded by the advent of post-modernity, or that the latter has refuted the validity of the first (if one can refute anything taking a consistently post-modern stance)' (*ibid.*: 6). Still, what his dichotomy suggests is precisely a choice between one old-fashioned, authoritarian strategy ultimately aimed at legislation and regulation, and the self-effacing, non-judgemental oiler of the wheels of communication between different but obviously in principle equal 'systems of knowledge'.

In other words, Bauman presents us with a choice which, just as Sartre's, does not allow for the kinds of intellectual interventions that are closest at hand to most scholars – those extensions of scholarly knowledge (not necessarily produced in the positivist tradition) into the terrain of practical politics, in the forms of factual information, commentaries, suggestions and recommendations. Such interventions presuppose both solid knowledge of the field or issues in question *and* some political or ethical *engagement* on the side of the scholar. In the same way as any other citizen, scholars and other traditional intellectuals are allowed to hold opinions in their fields of interest and to act as citizens in public discourse. This public discourse is, moreover, probably more demanding than ever in terms of arguments – now, more than ever before, opinions need to be qualified by solid, knowledge-based arguments. This is so even if the performative aspects of argumentation, as indicated in the above sections on television, may also be more important than before, besides being different.

The more general educational or enlightening mediation of scholarly produced knowledge, understood as 'information in perspective', could of course partly facilitate communication between cultures, i.e. be part of what Bauman would call a 'postmodern' intellectual strategy. But it is certainly also about making 'authoritative statements' which can 'arbitrate in controversies of opinion'. In a number of current public debates (say, on immigration, on ecology, on the state of health services or public libraries or education or whatever) there is certainly a need for grounded information and knowledge-based arguments. Scholars and other intellectuals are (luckily) not the ones to make the final decisions in such matters, in the form of new legislation. Our task is simply – to the best of our ability, by way of our privileges in diverse fields of knowledge – to contribute to well-informed democratic decisions.

A wide range of media and forums must be used for this purpose, from the classroom and the scholarly article to the op-ed piece, the newspaper interview and the television appearance. Television is probably the most difficult of all media to handle meaningfully, and there is no reason why all scholars or other intellectuals should always feel obliged to participate there. It simply takes special skills and probably talent to make the most of ten seconds on the news, thirty seconds in a current affairs programme, etc. (Personally, I will never again spend four hours waiting for my chance to utter two sentences in a five-minute debate.)

While struggling to maintain, for instance, public-service television and formats within it which allow space and time for thoughts, the most promising of strategies here is one which aims to forge some kind of alliance between the intellectuals within education and research, on the one hand, and the newer class of media intellectuals (journalists etc.), on the other, based on the commonalities of ethos which I touched on above. For scholars in various brands of media and communication studies, but also in some other fields, it is worth thinking about the fact that very many of these media intellectuals are our own former students. Even if forms of direct cooperation may not be easy to find, starting a seriously intended dialogue should not be impossible.

REFERENCES

Baudrillard, Jean (1991) 'The reality Gulf', *Guardian*, 11 January.

Bauman, Zygmunt (1989) *Legislators and Interpreters: On Modernity, Post-modernity and Intellectuals*, Cambridge: Polity Press.

Bourdieu, Pierre (1984) *Questions de sociologie*, Paris: Éditions de Minuit.

—— ([1984]1988) *Homo Academicus*, Cambridge: Polity Press.

—— (1990) *In Other Words: Essays Towards a Reflexive Sociology*, Cambridge: Polity Press.

—— (1996) *Sur la Télévision and L'Emprise du journalisme*, Paris: Liber Éditions.

Burgess, Robert G. (1994) 'If you want publicity…call an estate agent?', in C. Haslam and A. Bryman (eds) *Social Scientists Meet the Media*, London and New York: Routledge.

Foucault, Michel (1979) 'Samtal med Michel Foucault. Paris 12.12.78', interview conducted by Stig Larsson and Åle Sandgren, *Kris* 11–12: 6–9.

Garnham, Nicholas (1995) 'The media and narratives of the intellectual', in *Media, Culture and Society* 17(3), July: 359–84.

Gerbner, George (1974) 'Teacher image in mass culture: symbolic functions of the "hidden curriculum"', in D. R. Olson (ed.) *Media and Symbols: The Forms of Expression, Communication and Education*, Chicago, IL: University of Chicago Press.

Goffman, Erving (1959) *The Presentation of Self in Everyday Life*, New York: Anchor.

Gripsrud, Jostein (1997) 'Television, broadcasting, flow: key metaphors in TV theory', in C. Geraghty and D. Lusted (eds) *The Television Studies Book*, London: Edward Arnold.

Habermas, Jürgen ([1962]1989) *The Structural Transformation of the Public Sphere*, Cambridge, MA: MIT Press.

Lyotard, Jean-François ([1979]1984) *The Postmodern Condition: A Report on Knowledge*, Minneapolis, MN: University of Minnesota Press.

Meyrowitz, Joshua (1985) *No Sense of Place: The Impact of Electronic Media on Social Behavior*, New York and Oxford: Oxford University Press.

Moi, Toril (1991) 'Appropriating Bourdieu: feminist theory and Pierre Bourdieu's sociology of culture', *New Literary History* 22: 1017–49.

Murdock, Graham (1994) 'Tales of expertise and experience: sociological reasoning and popular representation', in C. Haslam and A. Bryman (eds) *Social Scientists Meet the Media*, London and New York: Routledge.

Ottosen, Rune (1988) *Forskningsformidling og journalistikk*, Norsk Journalisthøgskole, Forskningsrapport no. 4.

Peters, Hans Peter (1995) 'The interaction of journalists and scientific experts: co-operation and conflict between two professional cultures', in *Media, Culture and Society* 17(1), January: 31–48.

Sartre, Jean-Paul (1972) *Plaidoyer pour les Intellectuels*, Paris: Éditions Gallimard.

Sennett, Richard (1977) *The Fall of Public Man*, London and Boston, MA: Faber & Faber.

Williams, Raymond (1975) *Television: Technology and Cultural Form*, New York: Schocken Books.

Part II

SOCIOCULTURAL FUNCTIONS

4

TELEVISION AS WORKING-THROUGH

John Ellis

INTRODUCTION

I think it is time again to ask the big question: 'What actually is television?' We are reaching the point where new models of television as a process seem to be required. So here, in a contingent form, is a model that I happen to be working on, a model that has particular relevance for the definition of documentary, and for the relationship of television to knowledge in general.

Pierre Sorlin, in a conference paper pointing out the relative rarity of the close-up in cinema compared to its massive presence in television, suggested that television can be seen as a process of steadying the image (Sorlin 1998). Television news, he suggested, brings in images that are barely visible and often inadequate. They are badly framed, wrongly lit, unstable, totally contingent. He then presented television's activity as a process of stabilization of that image material carried out through documentary and soap, and ending at the near-cinema of television fiction. This seems to me to be an extraordinarily suggestive notion, which need not be confined to the realm of the visual on television.

Indeed, television can be seen as a vast mechanism for processing the raw data of news reality into more narrativized, explained forms. This can be likened to the process of 'working-through' described by psychoanalysis, a process whereby material is not so much processed into a finished product as continually worried over until it is exhausted.[1] Television attempts to define, tries out explanations, creates narratives, talks over, makes intelligible, tries to marginalize, harnesses speculation, tries to make fit and, very occasionally, anathematizes.

So this is not a straight-through process that takes in the bleeding hunks of meat at the news end and parcels them out as sausages at the other. It is a far more multifaceted and leaky process than that. For this is an important role in an age that has, because of television itself to a large degree, far too much information and far too little explanation. Television does not provide any overall explanation; nor does it necessarily ignore or trivialize. Television itself, just like its soap operas, comes to no conclusions. Its process of working-through is more complex and inconclusive than that.

Television news ranges the world (or at least the world it knows) in search of things that are happening now. News has two criteria: immediacy and importance. The relative importance of the events that news can cover is gauged by criteria of power and distance. The more an event affects the structures of power in a particular society, the more prominence it may gain. The closer the event is to that society, the more coverage it may get. Neville Chamberlain's formula 'a faraway country of which we know little' summarizes how these criteria tend to work even today.[2] Of course, spectacular disasters in remote areas for which there is available footage tend to find their way into television news; they qualify because of the criteria of immediacy. Television news technology has been driven by the demand that it should provide ever more instantaneous material, to the extent that flexible digital video formats plus satellite technology are moving us towards an era of 'real-time' news in which we can see events more or less as they happen.

All other criteria are secondary so far as news is concerned. So the quality of the footage is hardly relevant; news will accept poor-quality images and poor-quality speakers if the immediacy and the importance of the events will justify them. We are all used to the unaesthetic framings, the action caught halfway through by a sudden pan shot, the dubious quality of the sound, the dropout, the barely lit images, the images shot against bright light. This is wild footage from a wild world. News bulletins are constructed (with a great degree of uniformity the world over it seems) from these hasty, contingent, poor-quality images, on the one hand, and, on the other, their direct antithesis: the controlled image of the news anchorperson (whose title here is surely significant), plus the highly contrived graphics that accompany the explanatory material provided by the anchorperson. News is a dialectic between these two extremes of disorder and control.[3]

Television then sets to work to resolve the antagonism between these two poles, as they clearly constitute an inadequate way of perceiving the world. Television works through the material from the news in two linked ways. It uses words, providing forms of explanation and understanding, further information and the kinds of psychological perspectives that are impossible within the news format. Television also works through by providing increasing stability to the images of disorder: it reframes and focuses; it narrativizes and adds production values. The crisis of the news bulletin can eventually become the made-for-TV movie. This is the closest that television will come to the meat-to-sausage model of working-through, yet even then, as we shall see, the movie's conclusions tend not to be as cut and dried as those of cinema fiction. Usually the process of working-through is very diverse, involving chat, soap, documentary and, relatively rarely, the devices of the fiction movie.

Chat begins as soon as a story has broken. The first wave of chat comes from commentators in long-form news-based programmes, together with interested parties such as politicians or the representatives of pressure groups. They provide immediate reactions and particular interpretations which serve simply to contain the raw events in some kind of temporary bandage of words. Just occasionally they can go further, as the chairman of British Midland did when one of his planes crashed on a motorway at Kegworth. He eliminated any 'spokespeople' (the usual procedure of damage limitation) and went on TV himself to express his evidently sincere anguish.[4]

Daytime TV the next morning provides a place where discussion of issues or stories from the news can take place. Here the range of voices is far wider. Television has begun the verbal aspect of its working-through. Psychological explanations, random bits of information, stories of personal experience, cries for help all pass through the daytime TV talk shows like *Kilroy* in a relatively open and unstructured form, at least when compared to the news. The tendency is for the chat to concentrate on personal experience and psychological explanations; in part, this is a response to the 'public' or official agenda of the news (see, for instance, Livingstone and Lunt 1994; Mehl 1996).

From then on, the talk agendas proliferate. Differing explanations are offered, but not all with equal force. Some individuals act as more effective spokespeople than others; some programmes have agendas of their own. But the chat arena, though dominated by psychological explanations, is dense and conflictual. The chat arena constitutes a continual process of speculation on human behaviour and motives. Everything that was in the news will pass through this process in some way or another; connections are made between discrete and separate news items. Stories from the news arena are misremembered and misinterpreted, bringing forward the subterranean preoccupations of the individual speaker or of segments of the audience. This definition of chat, of course, is not confined to television; it is a fact of the whole audiovisual sphere and encompasses the activity of newspaper columnists as well.

The news promises 'stories'. News practice refers to 'breaking news stories'. However, all that news provides is bits of stories, and it certainly offers no endings that can make sense of what went before. It is 'news' precisely because it cannot offer such completeness. It operates in the same contemporary and uncertain moment as is inhabited by its audience. So chat provides, or attempts to provide, some of the narrative content that the news cannot. Television talk presents speculation about the possible narratives that the events might follow. In the television news and current affairs arena we hear (because speculation is a phenomenon of talk) constant musings on what may have happened, on what may be about to happen, on what would be the result if what may happen actually happens, and then on what could possibly happen as a result. All of this is bolstered by information on all the participating parties in the event, or participants who could enter into the narrative if events took a certain turn. At moments of crisis, like the Gulf War, television gives itself over to huge amounts of such speculation. The Gulf War provided very few actual television events; the cameras were deliberately kept away from the action. Instead, talk proliferated about possible activity and how to interpret the few clues that did emerge. All of this is born out of a frustration with narrative. Media and audience alike are desperate to know the end of the story and not to have to wait for events to unfold at their own pace. From this frustration comes the welter of detail and the unstoppable flood of speculation.

Most news stories are ongoing rather than in a convenient form like the Gulf War. During the siege of Sarajevo and the battle for Kabul there was no clear end in sight. Nor is there for the fight against inflation or global warming, however much we might wish for one. Speculation about these stories continues within the news media and especially on live television, but it is more muted in form. Immediately a possible end lurches into view the pace and quantity of speculation increases. The story moves up the news agenda, not because it is a crisis, but because it promises a resolution.

The first stage of television's working-through is this proliferation of possible explanations and narratives which takes place in talk. Such talk offers possibilities of understanding, and plays them against each other. Everyone involved in television talk about news offers their attractive options and their little nugget of information. No one has a privileged point of view, in the crucial sense that they cannot see into the future. This initial talk does not totalize. It offers explanations of the present by the dozen and speculations about the future by the score, but it can offer no conclusions.

Such a process of non-totalizing speculation is a crucial activity in an information-rich environment. During the twentieth century industrial society has embarked on a course that provides us, as its citizens, with more and more information about events that have no direct bearing on our own lives but which have an emotional effect on us simply by the fact of their representation. The fact that the representation on the news is necessarily skimpy and inadequate, snatched from the living event, makes our role as viewers all the more difficult. The events cannot be poignant because they are radically incomplete; they exist in almost the same moment as we do when we see them. They demand explanation, they incite curiosity, revulsion and the usually frustrated or passing desire for action. We need, in other words, to work them through. We need to carry out exactly that process of repression upon these representations that psychoanalysis describes; a process that does not eradicate but places them elsewhere, a process necessary for civilized life to remain possible.

After all, we have come a long way in a short time. Two centuries ago our fore-bears in Europe were watching public hangings and enjoying them; nowadays we watch executions in Bosnia on television and experience very different emotions. We have effected a fundamental change in so doing, but we do not really understand what the nature of that change might be. And we are only just beginning to know how to deal with these nightly spectacles of older forms of conflict resolution. We know far more than we need to know in order to function as citizens, perhaps more than we need to know in order to function as fulfilled human beings, but we have very little idea how to come to terms with what we know. Television's process of working-through is currently one of the principle ways of coming to terms with what we know.

Television's working-through is an open process; it has relevance to the problem of information overload and empathy fatigue only if it is an open process. Each programme certainly comes to its conclusion, or at least an ending of some kind; each presenter sums up, even if only to note the continuing nature of the controversy; each speaker encapsulates his or her view, well or badly; but television as a system does not totalize. This is an open arena, where issues, questions or worries are paraded for a time, within slots that are regular. The programme will be recognizably the same, day after day, week after week, for its seasonal run. The issues and people fed through it will be diverse and changing. This is another balance of stability (the show) and instability (the issues and the emotions around them). Instead of the anchoring stability of the news presentation, however, the chat arena multiplies views on any topic that is fed through its voracious machine.

Chat is a large arena, encompassing serious discussions of current events like *Newsnight*, as well as *Kilroy*, *Oprah* and *Geraldo*. Many of its topics will not relate directly to the news. Many are generated from entirely other agendas, those of the programmes themselves, or those set by the press, by the publicity machinery for people or products (especially books and television programmes) with a controversial message. This, too, adds diversity to the chat process. Chat lures in more of the world than the news bulletins of the previous few days, and in so doing it brings in a more personal, psychological perspective than news can ever provide. The chat arena is largely an arena of subjective reactions. It deals with problems of sex, of weight, of dealing with children, of tooth decay and bowel disorder, of make-up and romantic dilemmas. These perspectives cross with news material and cross-fertilization occurs. Through chat, the world of news begins to gain a psychological perspective.

The television spectacle of chat needs a wide diversity of experience and explanation in order to function. This tendency towards diversity is inherent in the conditions of competition between television programmes. Each seeks to differentiate itself from other programmes of a similar genre or in the same time slot. Nevertheless, there are inherent limits in the system. The function of celebrities is central to the chat arena. Celebrities are vaguely familiar figures, distinct from experts on a particular topic, whose views are nevertheless sought on a range of social issues that stop short of items of current political controversy. Many varieties of chat programmes use celebrities. Some are entirely celebrity-based. Celebrities are brought on to shows by 'celebrity bookers', who are usually negotiating televisions' way through the thicket of agents and public relations people attempting to promote the celebrity or their current product.

Chat-show celebrities are frequently people who are already television performers. The launch of a new television drama series is incomplete without the participation of one or more of its stars in the chat arena. There they discuss the thematic material of the series, the psychology of their particular character and feelings or events in their own personal lives that have some resonance with the theme of the programme. Soap operas, too, parade their stars on chat shows at times that suit the particular publicity needs of their show.

Here chat comes full circle. This is not an 'incestuous' process so much as a necessary adjunct to television's process of working-through. For soap operas, current affairs and documentary are the next stage of this working-through. In contrast to chat, where psychological frameworks of understanding are tried out, these diverse forms employ narrative processes of understanding. Where, for example, chat speculates about the motives of destructive housebreakers and feelings of their victims, the soap opera that incorporates such a narrative strand will show the event taking place in a particular context, involving individuals known to some extent to the audience. The event unrolls in the soap in a narrative time that is not dissimilar to that of the audience's lived time. It can go in various directions: the housebreakers could be the offspring of other characters who need to be dealt with; they could be disruptive outsiders; their actions will cause a moral dilemma of some kind for the characters. We see the feelings of those familiar characters whose house is broken into and vandalized, but we also see the actions that they take and the consequences of their actions. Narrative supplies a structure of cause and effect which complicates the emotional perspectives that chat has begun to supply. More complexity results, and more contradictions.

SOAPS

Soaps in Britain are particularly adept at incorporating social issues of current public concern. This is what distinguishes them from their Australian or American counterparts, for which public issues are more difficult. Social issues, like my example of the vandalizing housebreakers, could be found in *Neighbours*, *Brookside* or *Guiding Light* alike. By the standards of a Brazilian novella, the housebreaking would be a very mundane, even marginal event. In each case the storyline will have clear resonances with the constant public debates and official initiatives about crime, the decline of society and social disorder. In this sense the soap opera works through news issues – not slavishly, item by item, issue by issue, but by providing narratives with resonance to the everyday experience or the prevalent thinking of their viewing publics. So the regional differences between soap operas, though real enough, do not affect the core of the genre, its reason for existence in the televisual world. Soaps narrativize, in the same time of experience as the lived time of the audience, the moral dilemmas in the lives of their characters.

Soap operas multiply incidents around a core set of characters that is itself in a state of continual but slow-burn change. Soaps themselves explicitly offer no final resolution. In Ramsay Street or Coronation Street there will always be another day, and the axing of a failing soap from the schedules produces some kind of catastrophe that destroys the community for ever. The power of the soap is the fact that it appears that its characters are perpetually living in the same present as their audiences. The strength of this impression can be gauged when crossing national or regional boundaries and meeting people who are at a different stage in the development of the series. English fans of *Neighbours* or *Home and Away* have frustrating problems in discussing their characters with Australian counterparts; and this recalls the local British problems caused with *Crossroads* when the producing ITV regional company was six months ahead of the London region, whose schedulers were unwilling to run quite as many episodes each week. Eventually, London had to run to catch up.

Soaps have a particular constituency in teenagers. Soaps like *Neighbours* or *Brookside* offer modern society's 'apprentice adults' a wide range of narrativized dilemmas, combined with a considerable degree of psychological speculation offered by other characters. Soaps therefore offer teenagers a privileged vehicle for gaining an understanding of human relationships within a predominantly domestic and everyday context. It is possible to gain a degree of understanding through the slow-motion narrative resolutions of a soap. It is unlikely that this provides sufficient understanding to get through a real-life crisis. The soap scenarios open up major emotional questions to scrutiny; that is all. Soaps do so through the combination of the empathy that comes with narrative and a large degree of discussion of any situation by the whole range of the soap's characters. Such a combination is possible because of the regular and slow-moving nature of the form.

DOCUMENTARIES

Documentaries on television have a peculiar status. They are a protected species, yet, in Britain at least, they remain popular with audiences. John Corner demonstrates very effectively that documentaries retain an important place within the public discourse of television, defining, implicitly if not explicitly, a wide range of social problems and social attitudes. Documentaries present us with material garnered from everyday life, material which is distinctively different from that of fiction, or that of news (see Chapter 11; Corner 1995).

In Britain we have seen the development of a strong documentary tradition which, some say, has been powered by a terroristic anthropology practised upon the working class by the bourgeoisie, or by those with substantial cultural capital upon those with meagre cultural resources. Current criticism of the television documentary in Britain focuses on three problems: the use of reconstruction, the excessively intrusive activities of film-makers and the use of too many devices of narration. Suffice it to say that such criticisms, though seemingly new, recur throughout the history of the genre. Documentary is built on sand; it is based on an epistemologically unstable foundation. So the genre is perpetually shifting to take account of its own impossibility. Constituted on the basis of a fallacy and as the result of a desire, documentary is an inherently unstable genre. The desire that it answers need not necessarily be answered by the documentary as we know it (see Nichols 1994).

Documentary and the wider desire for factually based programming occupy a particular place within the universe of television. They provide material with some of the characteristics of news (particularly in the occasional technical deficiencies that come with reality filming), but offer the potential of a complete narrative rather than news's 'today's fragment' of a story.

Documentary genres are defined partly by a number of refusals; it is not news, but neither is it simply fiction. Documentary distinguishes itself from fiction by refusing to use some of the devices of fiction, vaunting its relative lack of scopic mobility (which is nevertheless still considerable). Documentaries have a provisional feel to their camerawork, demonstrating that events have been caught as they happen rather than constructed for the camera, although, of course, such techniques can be imitated in fiction – witness *NYPD Blue*. Documentaries do not create an inner life for characters; what you see and hear is what you get, and what you have to judge. Fiction usually provides more. Documentary also refuses to show some of the activities of its subjects (for instance, in Britain at least, their sex life), activities which would be quite at home in a fiction about similar characters.

Documentary, too, refuses some of the devices of narration and some of the project of the fiction narration. Documentaries have narratives (witness the slot designations *True Stories* and *Short Stories*), but they do not have the narrative drive of fiction; there is more that is contingent and less that is elegant. Documentary material is not organized, as a classic fiction tends to be, to deliver the ending of the narrative. Often incomplete or lacking in final closure, documentaries explicitly aim to show how life is, rather than how stories are. This refusal, too, is one of the central ways in which documentary can distinguish itself from fiction. Such refusals are essentially tactical, defined in relation to what fiction is doing at any historical point. These refusals constitute the ground upon which documentary works and substantiate its claim to be depicting reality. The gamble is that documentary will appear more real because it is less fictional.

Besides this series of refusals, documentary defines its own internal practices. John Corner has produced an elegant typology for the current subgenres of documentary: the observational, the testimonial, the combinatory and the visually associative. These types exist within a highly signalled genre; they are trailed, publicized and announced as 'documentary' in that overeager way that television has of making sure that its audience knows what it is that they are about to get.

Current affairs and documentary, to use the peculiar terms specific to British television, carry out a similar function of narrativization to that of the soap. Documentaries of the observational kind, to follow Corner's typology, set up a distinctive regime of attention. To watch an observational documentary is to see events unfolding which have not specifically been staged for the camera, though they may well have been incited by the camera's presence and certainly include a dimension of performance. Though the presence of filming is widely accepted now to have an ill-defined influence on the events being filmed, the situation itself has an existence independent of the filming; often it is a public institution like a school, London Zoo, a Royal Navy ship, a National Health Service hospital, or a private institution like a family, a business or a psychotherapy session.

Observational documentary seems to allow access to real interactions, distinguishable from both the chat arena and the soap universe because the quality of performance differs. People in documentaries may be playing themselves, but it is themselves that they are *playing*, and sometimes not very well. Part of the interest of observational documentaries lies in the waywardness of their characters. The hesitancies of their real speech, the uncertainties of their actions and the inadequacies of their to-camera justifications of their behaviour provide space for speculation among viewers about their 'real' motives. Armed with the psychological knowledge which informs chat-show debates and floats around in soap operas, viewers of documentaries can bring their own analytic frameworks to bear on the characters of documentary.

Sometimes this has surprising results. Paul Watson is one of the more up-front observational documentary-makers, and his careful casting of documentary subjects has created several situations in which these characters have attracted formal as well as informal speculation about their behaviour. Whether it be the dominant matriarchs of *The Family* and *Sylvania Waters* or the anachronistic toffs of *The Fishing Party*, Watson's characters have been surprised (and sometimes outraged) by the level of public debate that has taken place about their values and behaviours. Watson's extreme use of the 'observation' technique has produced extreme results – speculation in the public sphere about the psychology of documentary characters. Such speculation exists, however, in a more muted form around many documentary characters.

Observational documentaries encourage speculation about character and motive within powerfully defined situations. Observation film-making is fond of institutions because they provide a context for actions and character. More clearly than chat or soap, documentary provides situated psychologies. Even so, however concretely the situation of the characters is painted, this is not necessarily a means of criticizing those circumstances, or even of asserting the primacy of nurture over nature. The observational documentary form was widely adopted by British television during the 1980s as a response to a hostile government; if sad people were shown in desperate circumstances it seemed that their plight needed no comment. All too often, however, the effect tended to be that of confirming either the hopelessness of the situation or the feckless nature of the characters.

Explanation and comparison are the tools that documentary uses to remedy this problem with the open form of observational documentary. By assembling fragments of evidence from the world, from observations of actions to the testimonies of witnesses and the commentaries of experts, the combinatory documentary attempts to organize a coherent explanatory or investigative structure. Often, though, even with good casting of interviewees, the qualities of the real speech of these witnesses or experts tend to betray other perspectives. The waywardness of the viewing situation leaves the best-organized combinatory documentary adrift on a sea of doubt and contingency. Its attempts at closure are not thwarted by this, but they can be compromised.

IN PRAISE OF UNCERTAINTY

This is not to assert that viewers make their own meanings in a Fiskean process of voluntarist wish-fulfilment.[5] It is altogether less presumptive. I am simply asserting the primacy of uncertainty over certainty in the process of television meaning-making. The forms that television uses tend towards the certainty of closure – narrative forms which posit a resolution, explanatory forms that offer material graded and organized towards a particular conclusion. But television as a form itself tends towards the opposite, towards uncertainty and openness. This I believe to be television's distinctive contribution to the modern age – a relatively safe area in which uncertainty can be entertained (and can be entertaining). As our age is more uncertain than most – or at least more uncertain than that in which I grew up – it seems that television's contribution to our ability to live with uncertainty is crucial.[6]

However, the process of working-through, as I am describing it, requires a lack of finality for its effective operation. Televisual working-through seems to be a process of reconciliation based on familiarity and repetition-in-difference. Television's very use of narrative forms pushes them towards an openness that in many other media would seem intolerable, or at least inept. The narrative organization of soap operas is complex because of the number of different narrative strands that are in play in any one episode. The narrative organization of drama series contains one or more strands that reach a conclusion within one episode, but many more that recur in different ways over the life of the series. The dilemmas of the central characters in a drama series are resolved over the life of the series; the storylines associated with the week's incident or incidents are the ones which are generally resolved within one episode. Hence the sense of ending is relatively muted; both soap and series drama depend for their continued audiences upon their success in conveying an impression that the life of the central characters continues week on week. In documentaries, too, the narrative may cover a coherent incident and may be structured to provide a sense of ending, but there is always more to be said. The characters will continue their lives; the institution will continue its constant adaptations to the demands of the world outside.

SPORT

Sport on television demonstrates particularly clearly this aspect of narrative on television. It appears to offer a clear-cut narrative, yet sport also has some of the characteristics of news. Sports events take place in the wild world that news covers, but, unlike news events, sport promises that the events it shows will yield a definite ending. Sport gains its key value on television from being live, from showing the audience an event as it happens. A peculiarly touching example of this value has been at work on British television. Because of a deal with Sky TV between 1993 and 1996, the BBC broadcasts a midweek football match later on in the evening in which it is played, after the main 9 p.m. news. Since this news reports the results of all matches played that evening, the newsreader warns the audience that he or she is about to give the result of the match that the audience is about to see. So, after the words 'If you don't want to see the result, look away now', the evening's results are displayed in vision only.

Sport, like news, depends on the suspense of not knowing how things will work out. Sporting events, like news, take place in the same lived time as that of their audiences. But, unlike news, sport guarantees that there will be a resolution, an ending, within a clear and predetermined time-frame. Sport provides live narratives, full of conflict and uncertainty, that promise an ending. Television's presence, with its expectations of resolution, has pushed football further into the realm of increasing the tension in a drawn game; the penalty shootout has begun to replace the replay in crucial games. Sport works on television because it has a powerful sense of co-presence with its audience, which lives through the sporting event as it happens. Television sport, like television news, is a live form, and in this sense sport has an important role in television's aesthetic development by maintaining and renewing television's powerful impression of co-presence with its audience.

Sport promises a live narrative, a developing conflict or competition which will reach an ending in a predetermined period of time. Sport is a fascinating television form because it predetermines the time when the resolution will arrive, but no one can possibly know what that resolution will be. Just like a soap opera or a news story, the television sport event does not know what its ending will be; all that it knows is that there will be one at a given point in the future. Neither news nor soap opera makes such a promise. Sport is distinct in that it does, but it shares with soap and the news the fact that the particular result is not predetermined. Sports coverage, therefore, generates its own sub-industry of chat and speculation.

Even in the clear-cut narrative universe of sporting conflict, television still sees the need for a limited amount of working-through. The result, the victory, is analysed. The relative performances of teams and individuals are assessed and reassessed. The dubious decisions of judges and referees are re-examined, with all the electronic devices that television can provide. All of this serves to situate the sporting event within a continuum of sporting events. Other performances by the same teams or individuals are brought in as evidence that on this particular day they were not giving of their best or had found something extra. Then sports chat turns to the future, to the effects on the competitive league, or the national team, or the future of the particular athlete concerned.

Television sport generates its own chat in an effort to dull the sharpness of the conflict that is a competitive sporting event. Sport on television provides a classic narrative resolution, a conflict with winners and losers, but television as a cultural form seems almost uncomfortable with the starkness of the result. Sports talk serves to knit the event back into the fabric of ongoing existence by providing relativizing perspectives and emphasizing the longer-term narratives in which the single event is but an incident.

Television sport shows us much about the distinctive nature of television narration. The pleasure of watching sport on television lies in its special relation to narrative resolution. So sports events do not need the further narrativization that many other of our everyday or news-related concerns tend to require if they are to be worked through.

NARRATIVE FORMS

Other narrative television forms, be they narrative documentaries, drama series, situation comedies or made-for-TV films, offer a further element. Dramatic narratives on television offer a full working-out of particular narrative options which have been foreshadowed in the chat arena. In the schedule, alongside speculative chat, they offer full scenarios in which the audience can experience dilemmas from the inside. In dramatizing situations they invite the audience to use the psychological understandings that they may have gained from discussions in the chat arena. In dramatic narratives on television empathy replaces speculative understanding; one narrative possibility is followed through rather than several being offered.

Television offers many different narrative forms, each with their own attitude to narrative closure and the multiplication of incident rather than the ruthless push of plot. Series drama functions a little like a discontinuous soap, in that its characters can return for a further series, even though the main themes of the series narrative do achieve resolution at the end of the four, six, ten, or twenty episodes of the series. Often series are based in an institution which provides a handy flow of individual incidents around and through which the core characters live their particular problems. Hospitals and the police have been staple television institutions. BBC1's highly popular Saturday night series *Casualty* offers a stark and effective example in which accident victims parade their particular problems through the casualty unit and disappear at the end of the episode, never to be seen again. *Casualty*'s strength lies in its ability to include short narratives which show how the accident came about. American series like *ER* or *St Elsewhere* do not; their focus is entirely within the hospital, but this allows the series to have patients whose stories recur over episodes, even appearing sporadically throughout the run of series. In both cases the central (medical) characters, and perhaps the fate of the hospital itself, provide the overarching dilemmas which are resolved by the end of the series run.

The television serial is a more tightly knit narrative that does not have its eye on its own return. Television economics dictate that the serial is more a feature of European television than American, where its place is taken, fitfully, by the mini-series. The serial aims to resolve its narrative dilemmas within its limited run of episodes, and that resolution can encompass a dissolution of the core of the narrative. The main character can be killed; the central couple divorce; the warring parties resolve their differences and so offer meagre opportunities for further dramatic conflict. Even so, the television serial multiplies incident and marginal characters in a way that marks it as distinct from the cinema's more ruthlessly direct modes of telling a story.

Television narratives in general have a contingent and co-present quality about them; they offer themselves as narratives that are evolving. In this, television narratives are distinct from more cinematic (or novelistic) forms, which are constructed retrospectively, in the sense that they are organized to reach an ending which is known in advance. Such is the essence of the historic mode of narration which cinema and the novel have developed. The narrative is a tight organization of actions and themes in a pattern of crisis, innovation and repetition that is orchestrated to a particular resolution. In the classical narrative everything is there to move towards (or to delay the move towards) a resolution, which the narrative itself (but not necessarily the reader) knows in advance. So strong is this model that any extraneous matter, any digression, tends to find itself interpreted in some way as a contribution to this onward movement.[7]

Of course, television both transmits and makes stories that conform to this model. A significant amount of television output consists of cinema films whose mode of narration is overwhelmingly in the historic mode. Television, equally, makes single fictions which conform to this mode, be they made-for-TV movies or various kinds of single-episode or short-run dramas. But even in these cases the narrative impulse seems to relax a little in favour of introducing incidents which amplify the plot moment rather than move it on. With American television, made-for-TV movies often feature real-life dramas, and these stories are usually told in a form where fidelity to the vagaries of the original events assumes a great importance. The ruthless search for narrative tensions that leads Hollywood scriptwriting to refashion real-life stories is less of an imperative for the American made-for-TV movie.

IN PRAISE OF DISCONTINUITY

Television itself proves that there is nothing inherent in its technology that forces it to provide the experience of co-presence and the low level of narrative resolution that it characteristically employs. Television could well show movies or movie-type material made within the cinematic mode of historic narration. Entire channels do precisely that, and generally charge a premium subscription for doing so. They do so because they radically alter what is now the typical televisual experience – one of discontinuity.

Discontinuity is a social fact of television. It lies at the heart of the way television exists as a domestic medium. New television has integrated this social reality into the heart of its distinctive aesthetic. Almost all television programmes on almost all channels will be broken up by adverts and announcements, will be cut up into episodes, and so on. Even those rare channels that provide programmes with no breaks tend to make their own programmes according to this model (either for foreign markets or because the aesthetic is pervasive) or buy a considerable amount of material which was originally constructed to be so interrupted. This aesthetic of discontinuity results from the discontinuous attention which domestic viewers typically give to television.[8]

Television's process of working-through is crucially linked with the way that audiences use television. No one can watch everything that is on television nowadays, or even the entire content of one channel. Any completeness that television might offer will always escape any one viewer. Television is at once both continuous and incomplete. It exists as a facility which is used by its audiences according to the pattern of their domestic lives and to their desires for what they think television has to offer. Television constantly offers; viewers take up the offer only when they feel like it. Audience studies have shown both the low levels of attention given to television and the high degree to which individuals in particular circumstances find particular television material useful for the conduct of their daily lives.[9] This particular combination of disdain and involvement may seem disconcerting at first. It is important to emphasize that television nowadays is a highly intimate part of the domestic existence of almost everyone in the developed world. Television's special domestic status means that it is given a low level of attention much of the time; but it is the same low level of attention which is given to much else (and most other people) in the domestic space as well. Television is intimate, and therein lies its power. It underlies television's social status as a mechanism for working-through and exhausting society's preoccupations.

Most television has embraced this reality and has learnt to base its work on it. Television institutions around the world have intensified the medium's unique ability to source images of events happening almost in real time. News bulletins and entire news channels are able to bring these images and fragments of events into an initial interpretative structure that is inherently unstable, not least because the events shown in news bulletins are by turns radically inconclusive or catastrophic. Television then provides a wide range of forms which can, with varying degrees of co-presence with their audience, begin to work through the material that is brought in by the news, as well as bring in material of their own.

CONCLUSION

To return to Pierre Sorlin's (1998) initial insight, it is possible to define the degree to which the world beyond television has been processed by television by the pictorial qualities of the programmes in which they are worked through. Documentary images will have a more calculated sense of framing than does news footage; television fiction will be far more composed as a rule, except when it is consciously striving to imitate the roughness of news material. The degree of narrativization also contributes. But it is important to note that television is an inconclusive form. Its narratives use the historic mode tactically and carefully. Its more habitual forms are more open-ended. And the television process as a whole is managed neither intentionally nor unintentionally to move towards any specific conclusion or definitive interpretation of the world whose events it works through. Television refuses what Gellner called 'the advantages of certainty' in favour of the pleasure and pain of living in the uncertain present (Watkins 1995). Television, in this sense, acts as our forum for interpretations.

This forum has a definite shape, and hence definite limits and overall tendencies. Television tends to favour the psychological over the structural – or the personal over the political, to use an old distinction. Television is bound by rules which ban particular points of view. Television is pushed by the demand that it should entertain. It is pulled by the competition for audiences into any amount of trivia and sensationalism. Everywhere it is defined by the process of scheduling. But even these processes, while forming and limiting television's potential as a forum, also enable it to work through for its overwhelmingly domestic audience the enormity of a world full of information.

NOTES

1 'This "working through" of the resistances may in practice be an arduous task for the patient and a trial of patience for the analyst' (Sigmund Freud 1958).
2 As was vividly demonstrated by Klaus Bruhn Jensen's account of the UNESCO Newsday Project (Chapter 8).
3 See, for instance, Knut Helland's (1993) illuminating study of news as genre.
4 Sir Michael Bishop is now the Chairman of Channel 4 Television Ltd.
5 John Fiske (1987, 1989) advances such arguments. His position is elegantly undermined by Jostein Gripsrud (1995: 129 ff.).
6 The connection between narrative and certainty was further illuminated for me soon after delivering this paper, when I read an obituary of Ernest Gellner:

> I particularly remember a radio talk that he gave: *On Being Wrong*. Its theme was an asymmetry which, because of mankind's partiality for certainty and finality over uncertainty, always gives an unfair advantage to the bad side of the antithesis. It is rather poignant that in this talk he gave this example: life with its ever-present possibility of death is essentially precarious, but with death one retains a stable and absolutely unprecarious state. The word death is, in Gilbert Ryle's sense, an 'achievement word'. He cited a Gorki story about a peasant whose longing for finality incited him to multiple murder. Gellner suggested that the theological idea of the ever-present possibility of grace may be a cunning attempt to deprive the devil of his advantage by making the state of sin equally precarious.
>
> (John Watkins 1995)

This passage is illuminating not only because it makes explicit some of the problems inherent in our desire for narrative as an explanatory form, but also because it emphasizes the necessity of maintaining an openness even at moments of narrative closure.
7 Formalist theories of narrative in cinema demonstrate this very clearly. (See, for instance, Bordwell 1985).

8 Even on commercial television networks that do have advertising breaks, in Britain, these will tend to be less frequent than American ones. So even in Britain we have abrupt transitions both of mood and non-diegetic music because American series are very carefully paced and structured to use the fact that two scenes will be separated by an advertising break.

9 This point is made equally in empirical research such as that by P. Collett and R. Lamb (1986) and by those who are very critical of such approaches, like Ien Ang (1991).

REFERENCES

Ang, Ien (1991) *Desperately Seeking the Audience*, London: Routledge.

Bordwell, David (1985) *Narration in the Fiction Film*, London: Methuen.

Collett, P. and Lamb, R. (1986) *Watching People Watching Television*, London: Independent Broadcasting Authority.

Corner, John (1995) *Television and Public Address*, London: Edward Arnold.

Fiske, John (1987) *Television Culture*, London: Methuen.

—— (1989) *Understanding Popular Culture*, London: Unwin Hyman.

Freud, Sigmund (1958) 'Remembering, repeating and working through', *Standard Edition of the Complete Psychological Works*, trans. James Strachey, London: Hogarth.

Gripsrud, Jostein (1995) *The Dynasty Years*, London: Routledge.

Helland, Knut (1993) *Public Service and Comercial News: Contexts of Production, Genre Conventions and Textual Claims in Television*, Report no. 18, Department of Media Studies, University of Bergen.

Livingstone, Sonia and Lunt, Peter (1994) *Talk on Television*, London: Routledge.

Mehl, Dominique (1996) *Télévision de l'intime*, Paris: Seuil.

Nichols, Bill (1994) *Blurred Boundaries*, Bloomington and Indianapolis, IN: Indiana University Press.

Sorlin, Pierre (1998) 'Television and the close-up: interference or correspondence?', in Thomas Elsaesser and Kay Hoffman (eds) *Cinema Futures: Cain, Abel or Cable?*, Amsterdam: Amsterdam University Press.

Watkins, John (1995) 'Ernest Gellner: a tribute', *Guardian*, 8 November.

5

RHETORIC, PLAY, PERFORMANCE

Revisiting a study of the making of a BBC documentary

Roger Silverstone

INTRODUCTION

This chapter involves three moves. It involves an interrogation of a previous study of television documentary in the light of more recent work on television audiences and media consumption. It involves an interrogation of contemporary audience theory in the light of a concern with the nature of television's textuality. And it involves the beginnings of an attempt to rethink the nature of television's mediation in the light of the changing media environment, which is no longer dominated by, or dependent upon, broadcasting. All of these moves involve, of course, a consideration of the relationship between television and its audience. The chapter has, then, as its aim a modest sketch of an epistemology. Television documentary will be the focus of an effort to address the ways in which television itself is an address. The aim is to question how television grounds its appeal and how it can be seen to construct its own common ground.

THE NATURE OF A RETURN

In 1985 I published a study based on an ethnography of the production of a television science documentary (see also Silverstone 1983, 1984, 1987).[1] The study itself emerged from earlier work on television narrative, first of drama and then of documentary, which was set within a framework of the structural analysis of television texts. This argued that television was in an important sense a mythopoeic medium – and that this mythopoeic quality, and indeed mythopoeic function, was expressed through forms of narrativity. Television's narratives depended on, and expressed in various ways, classic folk forms of narration and the kinds of mythic logics that Lévi-Strauss (1969) had argued were at the heart of the relationship between myth and social practice in preliterate societies. It was the beginning of a stumbling attempt to understand television's mediation, to make some sense of how the medium and its various genres and forms found their way into the culture of our everyday lives.

The specific study of television science was designed to chart the production of a particular form of textuality – the science documentary. It was intended as a study of the ways in which television constructs its version of science, mediating between arcane forms of otherwise inaccessible knowledge and popular, everyday forms of understanding. Television produced its own narratives of science, occupying a space left vacant by the crumbling of Lyotard's (1984) grand narratives, but nevertheless arguably and perhaps forlornly articulating science in its utopian and dystopian modes to forms of storytelling that were still dependent on barely concealed traditional and persistent models and structures. The project as a whole sought to explore the dynamics of textual emergence, of television's creative process, and to try and understand how documentary science could possibly and recognizably emerge from the struggles of television production. Television's texts were seen, therefore, to be the product of creative work which had to be understood as institutionally mediated.

So to go back a few steps: what were the assumptions and arguments of the study and the book which, together with a number of earlier and one later paper, attempted to formulate a poetics of television documentary (Silverstone 1983, 1984, 1987; cf. Renov 1993)?

The first was based on a presumption of both a difference and an opposition between science and television as discourses, displaying in the dominant forms of their mediation (print v. image/sound) profoundly different forms of textuality, but a difference and an opposition which were also the product of different forms of work addressing different communities for different purposes and, above all, making different knowledge claims. This initial presumption was both obvious and in many respects wrong, and it was wrong principally because it was based on an inadequate view of science.[2] It was also based on a less than adequate view of the presence and meanings of science in popular discourse (especially after Hiroshima), as well as a less than correct presupposition about the nature of the interface that television science producers have with 'science'; that is, that it was based on their having to confront written products in journals and books rather than, as is mostly the case, with science in the form of scientists' own physical presence and forms of talk. The relationship between science and popular understanding was much more complex than one might expect. Nevertheless, it was hoped that science would provide a very strong test case of the work of 'popularization', or what the French call 'vulgarisation', and that it would throw some light on the way that art, politics and other forms of arcane knowledge would also be mediated by television.

Second, it was presumed that the work of television involves the construction of particular kinds of texts, which in so-called documentary involved, I argued, a mix of familiarity, novelty, accessibility, coherence and drama; the separable rhetorics of voice (finding a voice), image (the convertible image) and look (the camera's eye); the separable logics of argument and story, mimesis and myth, claiming authority and plausibility for the text's particular account of the world; and a perspective on the production process that suggested that the producer/director could be seen to be inventing the structures that were at the same time constraining him.[3]

Underlying many of these arguments, of course, was a particular model of narrative and of narrativity in culture. It was drawn – it was the 1970s, after all – from the formalists, structuralists and semioticians of the period, from Vladimir Propp (1968), Roman Jakobson (1960), Claude Lévi-Strauss (1968), A. J. Greimas (1966) and Claude Bremond (1970), most of whom were exploring, still quite unselfconsciously, the rule-governed preconditions for meaning and textuality in linguistics and in other expressions of culture, and searching – through the identification of these rules and structures, and with varying degrees of emphasis – universality and persistence in cultural forms. This approach to narrative was to a degree independent of the particular realization in film or television which, for example, both Christian Metz (1974) and David Bordwell (1985) would stress. It underplayed the specificity of the medium in the search for more generally identifiable and realizable narrative structures.

The 1970s structuralists are well known for having misconceived both the dynamics and indeterminacies in the texts they were analysing, and above all were challenged, and correctly so, with a failure to consider the capacity of readers to construct their own meanings alongside, in negotiation with, or in some sense and at some times against the forms and contents of what they were reading. This weakness was present in my own initial work with audiences, though I was keen to approach and understand audiences of various kinds for the transmitted programme, for example comparing scientists to lay audiences and seeking the views of those scientists who had been consulted during the making of the film once it had been transmitted. But I was also keen to contextualize reception by incorporating comments on the public texts, especially in reviews of the programme, and to assess audience response in relation to the producer's declared and perceived intentions. Most of this, and not just in hindsight, was unsatisfactory and inconclusive. It was undertaken without a convincing model of audiences as readers, and, as with much work with audiences, there was a sense of artificiality in the enquiry and therefore in the responses – especially with regard to something called science.

The limitations of the study are therefore easy now to identify. It was not sufficiently located in a political economy of the broadcasting industry, or the wider culture of the BBC. Despite the attention paid to the dynamics of the production process and to the text as an emergent product of that process, there is a sense in rereading the study of something quite static and rigid. The stress on structure, and the formal elements of story and argument which informed the analysis tended to overwhelm the particular characteristics of the content, although this was perhaps less the case in the ethnography itself, as compared with the earlier textual work. The model of the text and of the text's relationship with the producing institution makes it difficult to think about change. And, finally, as I have just indicated, there was an almost entirely inadequate model of the dynamics of reception.

DISCURSIVE SPACES

What I want to do in this paper is almost certainly foolhardy and certainly incomplete. I want to confront this early study in the light of the experience of more recent work on television and other media use – work that is in some respects in its turn quite insensitive to the textual specificities of the medium. And I want to open for discussion – nothing more – the relationship between text and audience, forcing myself to reconsider the importance of the text as a site for the analysis of television but trying to take a different approach to it.

What I am interested in here is the *discursive* spaces that contain both text and audience. The metaphor refers both to a literal space (the places and times of everyday life) and to a symbolic space (the place where meanings are negotiated and made). At issue are the conditions for the possibility of meaning in any given communicative interaction, an interaction in television which demands attention to the interrelationship of technology, text and audience. And I am interested in the nature of the activity that takes place in these spaces. This interest is in a strict sense a phenomenological interest, occupying its own discursive space between epistemology and ontology, and subject to increasingly sophisticated enquiry in the recent work of Tony Wilson (1996) and Paddy Scannell (1995).

I am therefore searching for a way of thinking about, and seeking the specificities and variations of, not just the *modes of address* within documentary science and other forms of television, but possible frameworks for understanding the *discursive spaces* within which those modes of address are presented and negotiated, the spaces in which viewers and listeners or readers participate in the construction of meaning – and the different ways in which they may do so. Given my starting point, my aim is to enquire into this construction not from the point of view of the viewer – the individual inside or outside an interpretative community – but from the point of view of the claimed authority of the text itself, rejecting the currently dominant epistemology of audience–text relationships.

This is a way, I hope, of going beyond David Morley's (1986) attempt to ground an understanding of viewers' relationships with the text in a mixture of context and primary sociological categories. It is also an attempt to go beyond the generalities of Scannell's approach to the phenomenology of television through the notion of 'the communicative ethos' of broadcasting, and also to move beyond those phenomenologies (including my own) which tend both to treat television as an undifferentiated medium and to treat as unproblematic its status as a broadcast medium. It will also attempt to offer a version of the relationship among text, technology and viewer/reader which does not prematurely foreclose the text's effectivity, seeking rather to address its constitutive agonistics: 'to speak is to fight, in the sense of playing' (Lyotard 1984: 10).

What I am going to propose is this: that we can identify different, non-discrete – I have already called them – *discursive spaces* from within which different relationships of text and reader are claimed and constructed. I shall describe three – minimally and inadequately – in order to argue that they provide a way of identifying distinct *textual claims*, inviting and legitimating different relationships both to knowledge and to reader response. Each articulates too – as a result, of course – a different textual politics.

I will call these discursive spaces the spaces of *rhetoric, play and performance*. I think it is possible to argue that any two of these can be seen to be subcategories of the third (that is, that play and performance can be considered versions of rhetoric; or rhetoric and play as versions of performance, and so on).[4] But I actually think it is worth trying to distinguish them for what they can reveal about the different textual strategies that television's texts can adopt, and, even more importantly, to see them as offering a different way of engaging an audience in a text-dependent discourse, exercising power through their inscription on the screen (cf. de Certeau 1984) and, of course, offering a legitimation of their own authority and truth claims, and in so doing laying claim to a particular kind of audience engagement. So, for example, I believe that it is possible to distinguish (though, as I have just indicated, by no unambiguous divide):

- *rhetoric* as the domain of cognitive truth and language to stimulate action;
- *play* as the domain of emotional truth and language conjoined with action;
- *performance* as the domain of experiential truth and language as action.

I am going to try and argue for an understanding of the relationship between text and audience as being dependent (in some degree) on the presence or absence of such discursive spaces. While each of these can be seen in literary manifestations, they have their origins in, and are sustained by, visual and oral (non-literary) culture. While each of these can be identified analytically as discrete, as one might expect in the empirical world, they are likely to overlap and sometimes compete or contradict each other within a given viewing experience. Likewise, it is possible to suggest that each of the three depends to different degrees on the dominance of text or technology, message or medium in the viewing experience.

While clearly not approximating to anything approaching interactivity with the specific sense of active participation in a common project by two or more participants, the sense of discursive space that I wish to convey can be profitably compared to Brenda Laurel's (1993) discussion of the creation of a 'common ground'. Her discussion of computer-mediated interaction stresses the need to go beyond a model of interaction as turn-taking 'conversation'. Following Clark and Brennan (1990), she argues that the common ground, both precondition and consequence of any interactive communication, is a jointly inhabited 'space' where meaning takes shape through the collaboration and successive approximations of the participants....The notion of common ground not only provides a superior representation of the conversational process but also supports the idea that an interface is not simply the means whereby a person and a computer represent themselves to one another; rather it is a shared context for action in which both are agents.

(Laurel 1993: 4)

This is not the place to engage in any discussion of 'conventional' television viewing as interactive, but it is nevertheless important to point out that there is a version of activity which is required in understanding audiences' relations to mediated texts – elsewhere I have called this 'engagement' (Silverstone 1994). And it is crucial to understand the importance of this 'common ground' as a mutual participation of (motivated) texts and readers, as well as a precondition of readers' participation in meaning-construction. It is also important to point out that the presence of common ground does not preclude failures of communication, surprise or other deviations from a supposed matching of intention and response. Indeed, it is my contention within this paper that we need to understand better than we appear now to do what elements make up the complex common ground, or indeed common grounds, which, in turn, make up the television experience.[5]

RHETORIC

The producer of the case study BBC *Horizon* documentary articulated his ambitions for the programme, a critique of post-Green revolutionary technology, in the following terms:

Minimally [to see] that...the relationship between technology and people's lives isn't understood....At least to question the assumption that the latest technology is necessarily better for people and to question the assumption that what works for us is bound to be right for them.

Maximally...to say that these guys mean well – the scientists. It is necessary for the stability of the world and for the well-being of the poor that they are supported in those things that they are doing, that they are right; and that they are no longer supported in those things that they are doing that are wrong for the poorest people. And it's even more important that those regimes which reinforce inequality and make the situation worse are not supported with aid, and that initiatives like the Proshika movement [a landless peasant movement in Bangladesh] should be supported.

(Martin Freeth, producer of *A New Green Revolution*;
quoted in Silverstone 1985: 181–2)

Documentary is perhaps, above all, the form of television that is most consistently persuasive, embodying, in a sense ideal-typically, the Lasswellian (1948) model of media communication. As Michael Renov suggests, 'The documentary "truth claim" (which says, at the very least, "Believe me, I'm of the world") is the baseline of persuasion for all non-fiction, from propaganda to rock doc' (Renov 1993: 30).

Rhetoric, in its Aristotelian or Ciceronian guise, is the science of persuasion. It involves both an aesthetic and a pragmatic agenda. We are encouraged to speak well and to some purpose.

Television, it could be argued, can be seen through the filter of rhetorical theory as a medium, and not just in documentary, of persuasion – persuading its viewers to believe or to suspend disbelief, to accept the claims for verisimilitude as well as the claims, literally, to be heard, understood and accepted. Different contemporary approaches to rhetoric stress its different functions: as persuasion (Burke 1962), as argument (Billig 1987) and as the structuring of knowledge (McKeon 1987).

Rhetoric has its divisions (invention, arrangement, expression, memory and delivery), its forms of argumentation (its figures and its tropes) and its mechanisms of engagement in its commonplaces (the short cuts in argumentation, the places of recognition). Rhetoric has been divined in the patterns, 'the perambulatory rhetorics', of everyday life (de Certeau 1984), in the homological narratives that link the literary and personal and structure time (Ricoeur 1980, 1983), and in the metaphors (Lakoff and Johnson 1980) of everyday life. Rhetoric involves appeals which are both cognitive and critical, intellectual and emotional – for attention, for assent; and, in the sharing of communication and understanding, for both common sense and community (see, especially, Billig 1987: 200ff.).[6]

A focus on the rhetoric of television and of its texts therefore involves the consideration not just of persuasion and appeal, but also of the mutual involvement by producer and consumer, addresser and addressee in the structuring of meaning and experience (Morley and Silverstone 1990). It also involves the rehabilitation of a notion of intention, as well as invention (*inventio*) and argument in the analysis of television's communication. We are required to see behind and within the text the agents and activities – individuals, groups acting both coherently and contradictorily – whose creative work in the construction of narratives and the mobilization of genre results in a series of textual calls and claims which on their own, or in the context of the wider (the widest) viewing experience, require response. To see this as a process of encoding and decoding is to see it too mechanically. What is missing from this formulation is a sense of the complex to-ing and fro-ing of meanings being defined in and through a common ground, a common ground of commonplaces (of received wisdoms, and the familiar metaphors and tropes of contemporary culture). And what is involved is simultaneously a process of cognition and recognition, as viewers engage with (or resist) television's rhetorical appeal. As Michael Billig notes:

> There has been [in recent research] a great emphasis upon examining the effects of different types of messages, especially those coming from

an organ of the mass media. The result has been a static rhetoric, in which the messages are seen to flow in a single direction from the broadcaster, advertiser or experimenter towards the audience. What is missing is a sense of the message being part of debate, in which arguments flow back and forth, and in which skills are needed to invent excuses and accusations. It is in the context of argumentation that we see not so much the propagandist seeking a science of presentation, but disputants exercising the arts of thinking.

(Billig 1987: 83)

My own framing of the *Framing Science* film (Silverstone 1985) was principally through a barely articulated model of rhetoric. And the construction of the audience study was similarly framed – that is, through an approach privileging intention, attention, cognition and meaning. Indeed, and once again this would be a site for critique, the text was configured in the analysis as *unproblematically* televisual. The fact that it was a text for and on television, for broadcasting, was left unexamined. Such a position ignores the significance of the common and contrary observation that television can 'only entertain', that, despite the intention of, for example, John Reith that it should inform, educate and entertain, it only really can be, and has been, able to do the latter. Of course rhetoric can entertain. Texts are rhetorical, in their structures, in both their form and their content, in their narrativity; but so are media. But it can also be suggested that television, as technology and medium, makes its own medium-specific rhetorical claims – claims for attention, assent, community. In making this observation, banal though it might appear, one is actually identifying both a complexity and a tension within television's mediation, and one which arguably affects documentary in an especially significant way. This is that documentary's rhetorics, both agonistic and irenic, are contextualized and compromised by, and may even depend upon, other textual claims, claims that find their source not only in the cognitive or in rational appeal or address, but in the claims of and for experience, and in the attempts to provide pleasure and to meet desire.

The rhetorical address, then, offers a distinct discursive space – both claiming and inviting – in which viewers of documentary, prototypically, as well as other television genres, negotiate their meanings: a space to think, a space to persuade and be persuaded, a space to affect and be affected. This discursive space is the one we in turn think of when we discuss effects on attitudes and influences on behaviour. It is the space in which things are learnt and where we may (or may not) be persuaded to change our minds. It is a space of attention, of primary viewing. But it is not the only discursive space released by television in general or documentary in particular.

PLAY

I want now to change focus slightly. I have already observed that textual claims are not simply the product of a text and that context too, in this case the context of the televisual, has to be understood as dynamic. The rhetorical appeal of a specific documentary, and the discursive space that it claims and enables, has therefore to be understood alongside or against another set of claims which derive as much from the medium as from the message. It is this other set of claims which I now want to consider. The claims concern play.

Play, it has been argued, is a central component of what is to be human. Jan Huizinga, in his seminal (but much criticized) essay on play in human society, defines it in the following way:

> [P]lay is a voluntary activity. Play to order is no longer play....A second characteristic is closely connected with this, namely, that play is not 'ordinary' or 'real' life. It is rather a stepping out of 'real' life into a temporary sphere of activity with a disposition all of its own....As regards its formal characteristics, all students lay stress on the *disinterestedness* of play. Not being 'ordinary' life it stands outside the immediate satisfaction of wants and appetites....Play is distinct from 'ordinary' life both as to locality and duration. This is the third main characteristic of play: its secludedness, its limitedness...[play] creates order, is order....All play has its rules. They determine what 'holds' in the temporary world circumscribed by play.
>
> (Huizinga 1970: 26–30)

For Huizinga, play involves, both literally and metaphorically, a bounded space. Play is the general category of which games are the specific embodiment, so the notion of play both exceeds and contains the game. Play is associated with ritual, and ritual with performance. Play involves the suspension of disbelief, not 'complete illusion' (*ibid.*: 41). Play lies outside morals. It is neither good nor bad. Huizinga's pursuit of play and games leads him, as other commentators have noted, into a less than satisfactory terrain of elitist and pessimistic judgements. His arguments also tend to misread the social significance of play and especially games, placing both play and games unreasonably outside the material world and excluding material interest. He also fails to develop any significant psychology of play, ignoring especially, as George Steiner (1970) points out, the contribution that psychoanalysis had already made at the time of his writing to an understanding of play.

I have argued elsewhere (Silverstone 1981) for a conceptualization of television which takes its relation to play seriously. In this conceptualization television's mediation is seen as being dependent on its capacity to engage an audience within spaces and times that are distinguished – marked off – from the otherwise relentless confusions of everyday life. This can be seen to be expressed in the physical presence of the television set and in the presence or co-presence of viewers within its range. It can also be found within the frame of the screen, and within the bounded security of the schedule and of narrative forms. It can be identified within the rules of behaviour and precedence that individuals and families insist upon, the more or less ritualized, taken-for-granted patterns of behaviour that mark the viewing experience (the control of the remote, the favourite chair, the rules of inclusion or exclusion; for example adults excluding children on the basis of judgements of suitability of programming, children excluding adults – especially in watching videos – for similar reasons). In each of these broad dimensions of television a distinct discursive space emerges, structured through textual claims and social practices quite different from those already identified as emerging from television's rhetoric.

Roger Caillois (1958) both develops and offers a critique of Huizinga. Play involves freedom within rule-governed limits. He, too, describes play as essentially free, circumscribed within limits of time and space, uncertain, unproductive, governed by rules under conventions that suspend ordinary laws, and involving make-believe. It is 'accompanied by a special awareness of a second reality or of a free unreality, as against real life' (ibid.: 10). Play is therefore simultaneously both inside and outside everyday life, contained within the holding structures of the ordinary, but released from and legitimated by that ordinary as distinct and, arguably, in their containment, as a consequence, relatively unthreatening.

Caillois goes on to distinguish four kinds of games or dimensions of play, each of which, it might be suggested, can be seen to have its manifestation in the ludic claims of distinct genres of television, as well as to offer an approach to the particular characteristics of the viewing experience claimed or released by television as a whole. These are *agon* (competitiveness), *alea* (chance),[7] mimicry (masquerade and identification – pleasure in passing for another)[8] and ilinx (vertigo, surrender, possession of a physical kind). He also distinguished between those kinds of games and play that emphasize spontaneity and improvisation (*paidia*), and those that are significantly rule-governed (*ludus*), a continuum leading from play to (civilizing) games. *Paidia*, as its name implies, is associated with childhood play and improvised games. *Ludus* betokens

> the specific element in play the impact and cultural creativity of which seems most impressive. It does not connote a psychological attitude as precise as that of *agon*, *alea*, mimicry or ilinx, but in disciplining the *paidia*, its general contribution is to give the fundamental categories of play their purity and excellence.
>
> (Caillois 1958: 33)[9]

Caillois's approach is at once sociological and normative. Within an emergent anthropology and history of play, he nevertheless expresses his own fear of the conjunction of mimicry and ilinx, detecting, perhaps unsurprisingly in the aftermath of world war and fascist excess, their dangers in public spaces (Callois 1958:

127) and their revival in modern society. Yet he notes, with approval, their constructive disjunction – in carnival, travelling fairs and the circus. What he would think of television is another matter entirely.

However, and without rushing to judgement, I want to follow Huizinga and Caillois in stressing the centrality of play to television, a centrality that can be explored both through the specificities of genre and programming and through the character of the viewing experience. Play involves, as does rhetoric, mutual participation; players and audiences, and audiences who become, even at one remove, players, together are involved in a specific discursive space that television claims and constructs. It is important to note here, as Caillois does particularly, the tensions identified in play and games between 'contained freedom', 'secure creativity', 'active passivity', 'voluntary dependence' – both of the TV experience as a whole (if such a thing exists), but mobilized and reinforced by particular kinds of texts, and by the continuities and consistencies of the textualities of the interruptible flow of television. There is a precariousness in television play, the product of this constant tension between the two sides of the oxymora of the medium. It is a precariousness recognized by the psychoanalyst D. W. Winnicott in his discussion of the relationship between playing and reality:

> Play is immensely exciting. It is exciting not because the instincts are involved, *be it understood!* The thing about playing is always the precarious-ness of the interplay of personal psychic reality and the experience of control of actual objects. This is the precariousness of magic itself, magic that arises in intimacy, in a relationship that is being found to be reliable.
> (Winnicott 1971: 55)

Winnicott places play at the centre of his psychology of childhood. He sees play as being at the heart of culture in a psychodynamic sense. His approach is based on the analysis of the pre-linguistic child and his or her object-relations, principally and initially with the mother, and then in a process of separation and individuation with transitional objects which become the site of fantasy, and the negotiation of illusion and disillusion. Here, too, play occupies a space, both liter-ally and metaphorically, in which the trusting child explores the world through the manipulation of objects and the construction of fantasy. Through play, and within an environment which offers trust and security, and in which play can be both stimulated and contained, a child pleasurably constructs for herself or himself a place in culture. Play occupies and depends on a transitional space, tran-sitional between the inner world and external reality in which, as it were, both can be tested against one another in a creative way. This is what the child does, argues Winnicott, in the manipulation of objects; playing is doing.[10] External reality is tested; internal reality is defined, gradually, through such testing and through the near-hallucination that play requires.

Here is a possible approach to the psychology of play which links closely with the broader culturalist theories so far discussed but which provides an element that neither of the earlier theories adequately provides. Together they find play to be a central component of culture, and in each case there is a tension between a view of play as both, or either, progressive and regressive. Despite the clinical approach in the psychoanalyst and the moral-political approach in the two cultural critics, play as such is not seen as essentially either negative or positive. What they share also is a sense of the specialness of play, its location in distinct spaces and times, protected and trusted spaces and times, and spaces and times in which all participants (all of whom might be considered as players) engage in a distinct if often extremely limited creative work.

Whereas it could be argued that it is the *commonplace* that provides the ground for a meeting of speaker and listener, a condition for the possibility of the participation of receivers in the discursive space created by *rhetoric* (a cognitive security), in *play* that role is taken by the trust of a shared or shareable set of rules and the consequent emotional security that this offers; and in *performance*, as I shall go on to argue, such participation is predicated on a shared or shareable *identification* – though, as I shall suggest, not in any singular or straightforward way.

I suggest that the textual claims of television involve both a rhetorical and a ludic appeal. In *Television and Everyday Life* (Silverstone 1994) I argued for an ontological security/transitional object model for television as a whole. This general and perhaps overly reductive approach requires some modification, confronted as it is now is with the complexity and specificity of the textual address, for example in the *Framing Science* case study (Silverstone 1985). The discursive spaces offered by television in and to which we as audiences contribute are clearly more complex than a singular model will allow. The claims that television makes are dependent on its status as a specific medium, until now an essentially broadcast medium, and one which is located and consumed principally in the home; but they also depend on the more specific textual claims. This is obvious and challenging, a challenge that is increased once it is recognized that such claims require a response and that they are indeed negotiated on the common ground that familiarity with the medium and with generic conventions both requires and constructs.

It follows, therefore, that we might wish to frame a documentary film like *A New Green Revolution* within a model that includes a sense of play as generated by the medium (as well as specific aspects of its programming, especially in its heroic narrative) and by its predominantly rhetorical mode of address.

PERFORMANCE

In a recent essay Bill Nichols (1994) draws attention to what he takes to be a new mode of documentary address, the 'performative documentary'. The performative documentary involves a suspension of the realist impulse which underpins, in one way or another, all documentary claims:

Performative documentary puts the referential aspect of the message in brackets, under suspension. Realism finds itself deferred, dispersed, interrupted and postponed. These films make the proposition that it is possible to know difference differently....Performative documentary clearly embodies a paradox: it generates a distinct tension between performance and document, between the personal and the typical, the embodied and disembodied, between, in short, history and science.

(Nichols 1994: 96–7)[11]

Performative documentary, in Nichols's view of it, involves a figurative aesthetic, claiming evocative rather than literal truth, iconic rather than indexical, and a dialectic between the particular and the general, the local and the global. Reality is embodied (the body is a social text). Priority is given to affect and to a politics of identity. Nichols suggests that performative documentary is the creation of its time, and in particular of the postmodern turning away from grand narratives and towards the fragmented, dispersed, diasporic cultures of the late twentieth century.[12]

I want to say both more and less than Nichols. Less, because I do not wish to construct specific documentaries as 'performative' necessarily, or even to argue a periodic classification of documentary form as he does. More, because I do want to identify the performative (and performance) as a distinct textual claim and the basis for describing an analytically distinct discursive space.

Performance is the thing done: memory, identity, desire, claimed or fixed, for the moment, in the act, the word, the image. In a sense, and from a certain point of view, the notion of performance is redundant, since the social in its entirety can be (must be) considered as performed in linguistic and symbolic as well as material work.[13] Yet the consideration of the social as performative dislocates action from any ontological grounding, from a security or fixity in time passing, or the mapping of social or physical space. Performance is of the moment, drawing on and in memory, both of performers and audiences, who become – and not even at one remove – performers too. Consideration of the social as performed, and of culture as performative, requires an acceptance that there is no prior reality on which the performance is based or on which it can call. Performance is based on an 'epistemology grounded not on the distinction between truthful models and fictional representations but on different ways of knowing and doing that are constitutionally heterogeneous, contingent and risky' (Diamond 1996: 1).[14] What is fixed, as Judith Butler (1990) argues, is only what is repeated.[15] Performance, then, is both pastiche and parody, yet in both the claims are for originality, for reinscription, redefinition, refiguration.

One thing that postmodernism insists on is the denial of the modernist separation between play and seriousness (Ehrmann 1968; cited in Benamou 1977). This, together with Raymond Williams's (1974) observation that we live in a society dramatized by television, offers a starting point for consideration of how television's mediation within and across its various genres can claim another kind of discursive space, both integrative and transcendent of those offered by rhetoric and play. On the one hand, we can identify the specificity of particular genres and modes of representation and address as Nichols (1994) does in his discussion of documentary. On the other hand, we can see in the fragmentation of television's new forms of textuality, as well as in the behaviour of audiences, in the displaced textuality that presupposes, and to a degree relies on, the mutual fragmentation of narratives and everyday life, the requirement to make and to perform choice and choices, as attention wanders, and as the culture of display becomes ever more insistent and, it might be said, ever more hysterical. At performativity's root is, perhaps, as Benamou (1977: 4) acknowledges an indeterminacy, a denial of the authority of the text, and the (re)assertion of the authority of reader and audience that present theory encourages us to accept. Intertextuality, citation, gossip and the traces of memory and experience are performed in collusion, but also against each other's grain, by texts and audiences together. The performative television text facilitates a discursive space in which its own authority is masked (but never entirely denied) by the liberating freedoms granted to audiences to be and to behave, singularly and collectively, as active participants both with and against the textual grain. Ludic boundaries are breached as games expand into everyday life, as they do perhaps most exceptionally in various manifestations of fan culture.[16] Fans, it could be suggested, are involved in television (and other) texts as, perhaps above all, performers.

As technologies invite more interactivity, as choices, which are perhaps not quite choices, are increasingly being required but at the same time constrained, the discursive spaces that television now creates are increasingly synthetic, both rhetorical and ludic, offering a common ground which is common only for the moment, and whose commonness is claimed as much by the reader as by the text. It is a claim that depends above all on the momentary (but profound) identification of situation and person, image and word, repeated, played back (both literally and metaphorically), structured and restructured in the incessant orality and the continuous interchange of performance.

Identification is a key component of audiences' relationship with what they see and hear on television, and the performative cannot lay claim exclusively to identification as the basis for the common ground which underpins the discursive space that audiences enter. Yet it could be argued that the performative privileges identification, offering experiential truth claims to audiences, truth claims that are grounded in the endlessly iterative figuration of character and situation. Of course, audiences participate in this discursive space, as in others, as social beings. There is no compulsion, no determination. Yet here, as elsewhere, there is a deal, a contract, implicitly made, not necessarily consciously made, among audiences, texts and media, a deal which involves both public and private identities, and public and private communications.

Indeed, within this performativity critics detect a new political space, for critique, for mobilization, and for the construction of both individual and communal identity. Such are the hopes. Yet this televisual performativity has to be understood not just in the relationships between texts and audiences, and in the discursive spaces that are constructed on the common ground between them, but in the compromising contexts of changing media environments. In this sense the naked promise of performance and performativity, as it is articulated in treatises on aesthetics and sexuality – that uniqueness and authenticity can be composed in the event and in its iteration – must be qualified. The new performativity, while distinct in its address from that of rhetoric and play, and inviting quite different modes of engagement, is a performativity mobilized by and on behalf of the same forces that have found in rhetoric and play a way of claiming attention and response. The differences are significant and, although one might be forgiven for supposing that the shift towards performativity is (as Vattimo (1992), for example, argues) symptomatic and even evolutionary, it is possible also to argue *both* that the baseline relationships of a political economy of media still hold *and* that the discursive spaces released by television are becoming more open, more variable and more contested.

CONCLUSION

A number of concluding observations can be made.

No single televisual text will create or intend to, or indeed can, create a unitary discursive space, any more than those who watch television operate within one. These spaces conjoin and confront each other, offering distinct, sometimes reinforcing, sometimes contradictory, frameworks for textual engagement or participation.

Scientists, and others, when complaining about the ways in which television treats their profession or their product, tend to base their complaints – principally that science is seen by the media as a singular and uniform activity, and that it is constructed through a very limited repertoire of frameworks – on two presuppositions: first, that television is itself a singular and uniform medium; and, second, that it is essentially passive. An approach which grounds our understanding of neither the medium as singular nor its audiences as passive needs to be based, I would argue, on a more thoroughgoing epistemology of the medium, one which is based on an understanding of what I have described here as the discursive spaces in which television creates and recreates itself each time it is switched on (and also in the secondary discourses and forms of talk that sustain it when it is not being watched – it is, of course, always on).

And in relation to the analysis of the case study film in *Framing Science* (Silverstone 1985), the flatness that I detect in retrospect in my textual analysis and its stability and resistance to change can be explained by a reluctance to identify the dynamic tensions in the discursive spaces released and created by the documentary, and, as a consequence, those spaces within which audiences (my audiences) would have to negotiate their own meanings and understandings.

This observation raises the question of the different terms under and within which viewers or receivers of communication are invited to participate in television's mediation. This is a question of the different epistemologies of viewing that draw together intentions and responses, in both of which agency is involved. Clearly, a sense of these non-discrete but identifiably distinct discursive spaces would force a re-evaluation of the encoding or decoding model of text–audience relationships. It would also challenge the equally reductive notion that audiences come to their viewing with class and gender positions fixed and determining. Finally, it would recover, and necessarily so in my view, a concern with both text and textuality (textuality that includes consideration of technology) as a precondition for any understanding of electronic mediation and for assessing the social and cultural production of knowledge in the late twentieth century.

NOTES

1 This may seem a mite self-indulgent. Indeed it is. But it arises as a request from Jostein Gripsrud to reflect on this early work in the light of more recent and differently focused research. I accepted the invitation with gratitude and hope that it is not just me who learns something from it.

2 Science is, of course, socially constructed (Knorr-Cetina 1981; Latour and Woolgar 1979); science is rhetorical (Gusfield 1976; Bazerman 1981); science is action (Latour 1987).

3 All these terms and their relevance to the study of science documentary are discussed by Silverstone (1983, 1984, 1985).

4 This characterization involves a deliberately fuzzy logic which I am not intending to resolve in this paper. To try to do so would involve a more extensive investigation of the conceptual relationship among rhetoric, play and performance than I can undertake here, and certainly a more sophisticated history and phenomenology than I am in a position to offer. The model is therefore merely an indication of some of the first steps necessary for thinking about audience reception and response within a framework that moves beyond the cognitive and takes seriously the different kinds and qualities of engagement (Silverstone 1994) of viewers and readers with their media texts.

5 One can characterize the relationship between common grounds and discursive spaces by suggesting that common grounds are both precondition and product of the work that takes place in the various discursive spaces within which audiences participate.

6 'We must bear in mind that the *sensus communes* can be both the good common-sense envisaged by Cicero, as well as the evil prejudices feared by Plato. The present point is a much simpler one: whether the common-sense of a community appears to us as *le bon* or *le mauvais sens*, it nevertheless will exert its control over the individual orator, *who seeks to make an audience of that community*' (Billig 1987: 202; last emphasis mine).

7 *Agon* and *alea* imply opposite and somewhat complementary attitudes, but they both obey the same law – the creation for the players of conditions of pure equality denied them in real life. For nothing in life is clear...Play, whether *agon* or *alea*, is thus an attempt to substitute perfect situations for the normal confusion of contemporary life.

(Caillois 1958: 19)

8   With one exception, mimicry exhibits all the characteristics of play: liberty, convention, suspension of reality, and delimitation of space and time. However, the continuous submission to imperative and precise rules cannot be observed – rules for the dissimulation of reality and the substitution of a second reality. Mimicry is incessant invention. The rule of the game is unique: it consists in the actor's fascinating the spectator, while avoiding an error that might lead the spectator to break the spell. The spectator must lend himself to the illusion without first challenging the décor, mask, or artifice which for a given time he is asked to believe in as more real than reality itself.

(Caillois 1958: 23)

9   In a general way, ludus relates to the primitive desire to find diversion and amusement in arbitrary, perpetually recurrent obstacles. Thousands of occasions and devices are invented to satisfy simultaneously the desire for relaxation and the need, of which man cannot be rid, to utilise purposefully the knowledge, experience, and intelligence at his [sic] disposal, while disregarding self-control and his capacity for resistance to suffering, fatigue, panic or intoxication.

(Caillois 1958: 32–3)

10   To get to the idea of playing it is helpful to think of the preoccupation that characterises the playing of a young child. The content does not matter. What matters is the near-withdrawal state, akin to the concentration of older children and adults. The playing child inhabits an area that cannot be easily left, nor can it easily admit intrusions....This area of playing is not inner psychic reality. It is outside the individual, but it is not the external world.

(Winnicott 1971: 60)

11   I am grateful to John Corner for drawing my attention to Nichols's (1994) essay.

12   Performative documentary takes up those strategic locations called for by the shifting terms of identity politics and a post-modern disposition for cyborg affinities. By relying on a dispersed, associative, contextualising, but also social and dialectical mode of evocation, performative documentary is a particularly apt choice in a time when master narratives, like master plans, are in dispute....By restoring a sense of the local, specific, and embodied as a vital locus for social subjectivity, performative documentary gives figuration to and evokes dimensions of the political unconscious that remain suspended between an immediate here and now and a utopian alternative.

(Nichols 1994: 105–6)

13   There is a strong tradition in sociology and anthropology which grounds the study of the social in a notion of performance, for example in the work of Goffman (1959), Garfinkel (1967) and Turner (1974). This needs to be both remembered and understood as we enter the current debates within postmodernism, especially in the study of gender and sexuality, which is in danger both of reinventing the wheel and of mistaking the significance and originality of its own insights.

14 Cf. Austin (1975):

> In real life, as opposed to the simple situations envisaged in logical theory, one cannot always answer in a simple manner whether it is true or false....The truth or falsity of a statement depends not merely on the meanings of words but on what act you were performing in what circumstances.
>
> (Austin 1975: 143–5)

15   The subject is not *determined* by the rules through which it is generated because signification is *not a founding act, but rather a regulated process of repetition* that both conceals itself and enforces its rules precisely through the production of substantializing effects. In a sense all signification takes place within the orbit of the compulsion to repeat; 'agency', then, is to be located within the possibility of a variation on that repetition.

> (Butler 1990: 145)

16 I am indebted to Matthew Hills, who has encouraged me to confront fan culture in all its complex psychodynamic manifestations.

REFERENCES

Austin, J. L. (1962/1975) *How To Do Things With Words*, Oxford: Oxford University Press.

Bazerman, Charles (1981) 'What written knowledge does: three examples of academic discourse', *Philosophy of the Social Sciences* 11: 361–87.

Benamou, Michael (1977) 'Presence and play', in Michael Benamou and Charles Caramello (eds) *Performance in Modern Culture*, Madison, WI: Coda Press.

Billig, Michael (1987) *Arguing and Thinking: A Rhetorical Approach to Social Psychology*, Cambridge: Cambridge University Press.

Bordwell, David (1985) *Narration in the Fiction Film*, Madison, WI: University of Wisconsin.

Brémond, Claude (1970) *Logique du récit*, Paris: Éditions du Seuil.

Burke, Kenneth (1962) *A Rhetoric of Motives*, New York: George Brazillier.

Butler, Judith (1990) *Gender Trouble: Feminism and the Subversion of Identity*, London: Routledge.

Caillois, Roger (1958) *Man, Play, and Games*, New York: Free Press.

Clark, Herbert H. and Brennan, Susan E. (1990) 'Grounding in communication', in L. B. Resnick, J. Levine and S. D. Behrend (eds) *Socially Shared Cognition*, American Psychological Association.

de Certeau, Michel (1984) *The Practice of Every Day Life*, Berkeley, CA: University of California Press.

Diamond, Elin (ed.) (1996) *Performance and Cultural Politics*, London: Routledge.

Ehrmann, Jacques (ed.) (1968) *Game, Play, Literature*, Boston, MA: Beacon Press.

Garfinkel, Harold (1967) *Studies in Ethnomethodology*, Englewood Cliffs, NJ: Prentice-Hall.

Goffman, Erving (1959) *The Presentation of Self in Everyday Life*, Harmondsworth: Penguin.

Greimas, A. J. (1966) *Sémantique structurale*, Paris: Larousse.

Gusfield, Joseph (1976) 'The literary rhetoric of science: comedy and pathos in drinking driver research', *American Sociological Review* 41: 16–34.

Huizinga, Jan ([1949] 1970) *Homo Ludens*, London: Maurice Temple Smith.

Jakobson, Roman (1960) 'Closing statement: linguistics and poetics', in Thomas A. Sebeok (ed.) *Style in Language*, New York: MIT Press and John Wiley.

Knorr-Cetina, Karin D. (1981) *The Manufacture of Knowledge: An Essay on the Constructivist and Contextual Nature of Science*, Oxford: Pergamon Press.

Lakoff, George and Johnson, Mark (1980) *Metaphors We Live By*, Chicago, IL: Chicago University Press.

Lasswell, Harold (1948) 'The structure and function of communication in society', in L. Bryson (ed.) *The Communication of Ideas: A Series of Addresses*, New York: Harper & Brothers.

Latour, Bruno (1987) *Science in Action*, Milton Keynes: Open University Press.

Latour, Bruno and Woolgar, Steve (1979) *Laboratory Life: The Social Construction of Scientific Facts*, Beverley Hills, CA: Sage Publications.

Laurel, Brenda (1991/1993) *Computers as Theatre*, Reading, MA: Addison-Wesley.

Lévi-Strauss, Claude (1968) *Structural Anthropology*, Harmondsworth: Penguin Books.

—— (1969) *The Raw and the Cooked: Introduction to a Science of Mythology*, London: Jonathan Cape.

Lyotard, Jean-François (1984) *The Postmodern Condition: A Report on Knowledge*, Manchester: Manchester University Press.

McKeon, Richard (1987) *Rhetoric: Essays in Invention and Discovery*, Woodbridge: Ox Bow Press.

Metz, Christian (1974) *Language and Cinema*, The Hague: Mouton.

Morley, David (1986) *Family Television: Cultural Power and Domestic Leisure*, London: Comedia.

Morley, David and Silverstone, Roger (1990) 'Domestic communication: technologies and meanings', *Media, Culture and Society* 12(1): 31–56.

Nichols, Bill (1994) *Blurred Boundaries: Questions of Meaning in Contemporary Culture*, Bloomington, IN: Indiana University Press.

Propp, Vladimir (1968) *The Morphology of the Folktale*, Austin, TX: University of Texas Press.

Renov, Michael (1993) 'Towards a poetics of documentary', in M. Renov (ed.) *Theorizing Documentary*, New York: Routledge.

Ricoeur, Paul (1980) 'Narrative time', *Critical Inquiry* 7(1): 169–90.

—— (1983) *Time and Narrative*, vol. 1, Chicago, IL: University of Chicago Press.

Scannell, Paddy (1995) 'For a phenomenology of radio and television', *Journal of Communication* 45(3): 4–19.

Silverstone, Roger (1981) *The Message of Television: Myth and Narrative in Contemporary Culture*, London: Heinemann Educational Books.

—— (1983) 'The right to speak: on a poetic for television documentary', *Media, Culture and Society* 5(2): 137–54.

—— (1984) 'Narrative strategies in television science: a case study', *Media, Culture and Society* 6(4): 377–410.

—— (1985) *Framing Science: The Making of a BBC Documentary*, London: British Film Institute.

—— (1987) 'The agonistic narratives of television science', in J. Corner (ed.) *Documentary and the Mass Media*, London: Edward Arnold.

—— (1994) *Television and Everyday Life*, London: Routledge.

Steiner, George (1970) 'Introduction', in Jan Huizinga ([1949] 1970) *Homo Ludens*, London: Maurice Temple Smith.

Stephenson, William (1988) *The Play Theory of Mass Communication*, New Brunswick: Transaction Books.

Turner, Victor (1974) *Dramas, Fields and Metaphors: Action in Human Society*, Ithaca, NY: Cornell University Press.

Vattimo, Gianni (1992) *The Transparent Society*, Cambridge: Polity Press.

Williams, Raymond (1974) *Television: Technology and Cultural Form*, London: Fontana.

Wilson, Tony (1996) 'Television's everyday life: towards a phenomenology of the "televisual subject" ', *Journal of Communication Inquiry* 20(1): 49–66.

Winnicott, D. W. (1971) *Playing and Reality*, Harmondsworth: Penguin.

6

MEDIATED KNOWLEDGE

Recognition of the familiar, discovery of the new

Sonia Livingstone

MEDIATED KNOWLEDGE AND ACTIVE AUDIENCES

The modern mass media possess a hitherto unheard-of power to encode, preserve, manipulate, reproduce and circulate symbolic representations of knowledge. In this paper I shall address the relationship between audiences and mediated knowledge, using the opportunity to consider some broader problems currently facing audience reception research. How shall we think about the relationship between audiences and mediated knowledge, why are audiences not overwhelmed by the constructive power of the media, and in what ways, if any, are audiences the beneficiaries of mediated knowledge? Much depends on how we conceptualize the audience. Thus we may regard audiences as citizens who need knowledge for informed participation and public opinion (the public right to know, public service ethic, etc.; Corner 1991). We may see them as consumers who place some market value on having their social surveillance or informational needs met by the media (Rubin 1984). Or we may see them as workers in need of diverting entertainment whose uncritical stance makes them vulnerable to varieties of misinformation (including significant silences and overrepresented mainstream images of society; Gerbner and Gross 1976; McCombs and Shaw 1972; Noelle-Neumann 1974).[1]

My analysis is partly based on broadening out an argument developed during an empirical text–reader analysis of 'audience discussion' or audience participation programmes (Livingstone and Lunt 1994). In this new genre it is more than usually unclear whether the audience is best conceived of as the public/citizen-viewer, the consumer, or the mindless and voyeuristic masses (as I shall argue later, this generic ambiguity may be part of the appeal). Programmes such as the American *Donahue* and *Oprah Winfrey* and the British *Kilroy* and *The Time, The Place* centre on the studio audience, thus involving potential participation, access and interpretative activity from the audience both at home and in the studio (Bierig and Dimmick 1979; Rose 1985). Topical social, moral and political issues are debated by a mixed studio audience of experts and lay people, and the discussion varies in approach and seriousness depending on topic, host and target audience. Unlike many other media forums, the genre specifically focuses on publicizing the experiences of ordinary people, often members of marginalized social groups. Viewers and participants, as well as critics, are ambivalent about these programmes; are studio debates a new form of public space or forum, part of a media public sphere, or are they a travesty of political debate with no 'real' consequences?

The project relates to audiences and mediated knowledge in two ways. First, *what* can viewers come to know through this genre – a question of lay knowledge and its relationship to media. Second, *how* may viewers come to know about the world (including their place in it) from media representations – a question of lay epistemology and its relationship to media. Our analysis suggested that the question of lay knowledge depends significantly on the question of lay epistemology.[2] Thus it may be more productive to regard the interaction between text and viewer not as a potential clash of knowledge (what the text 'tells us' versus what the viewer knows from elsewhere) but as a negotiation on the appropriate ways of knowing, for epistemological assumptions frame both images in the text and the relevance of viewers' daily experiences to the process of viewing. A central means by which this genre, and by extension other genres, manages the construction of particular kinds of knowledge is by managing the various discursive positions available to the participants (expert and lay), and thus establishing what it is legitimate for each to say and in what manner utterances should be regarded by the studio and home audiences. While mediated knowledge depends on the genre or 'interpretative contract' between text and reader (Livingstone 1998a), the audience discussion programme specifically problematizes this contract by mixing generic formats in its version of 'infotainment' in a manner suggestive of future trends in evolving media genres and modes of address.

Textual analysis of discussion programmes reveals a multiple, often confused, mode of address in which, for example, experts are requested to inform the public and then ridiculed for their jargon; similarly, the host stimulates opposition to accepted views and then claims to be on the side of the majority (typically constructed as the 'underdog'). Some studio participants take part because it seems like fun or they find the media glamorous; others claim a public service motive, wanting to exercise a perceived right to have their say, contribute to public debate and inform people of their experience. Viewers are divided in their response to the genre. For some, experts are trained professionals who should inform and convince us, and accordingly deserve respect and time to develop their arguments; for others, the label of expert depends on who makes the best contribution and is as likely to be applicable to a member of the public as to a professional. For the former group of viewers, the logic of an argument is a key criterion in assessing a debate; for others, logic may be a means of exclusion, and the breadth of a debate, particularly insofar as it includes ordinary people we do not usually hear on television, offers a better criterion of assessment.

How audiences relate to a specific genre, what they consider to be of value and how they position themselves in relation to it all frame what they may gain from it, in terms of 'what knowledge' is at stake. If experts are considered to be lacking in personal experience while ordinary people are seen as authentic, the value of what each says will be regarded differently than it will be by those who consider that experts are more credible and more knowledgeable than ordinary people. Those who most value the contributions of ordinary people are most likely to feel that they gain something from watching and that their own perspective is represented among the opinions expressed (Livingstone, Wober and Lunt 1994). How viewers respond to the implicit invitation of this genre to identify home with studio audiences is a matter not only of interpretation, but also of identity – involving the positioning of oneself in relation to perceived others, including those on television. This is particularly pertinent to genres which are presented as primarily concerning ordinary people 'just like you' (in contrast to the elite world of early television or the middle-class world of 1950s television, these offer the dialects, the dialogue and the diversity of 'everyday life'). Do viewers accept this representation of 'ordinary people', or do they consider the studio audience to be 'idiots' or people acting a part? Are the experts 'expert' or patronizing time-wasters? Are the single parents in the studio debate relevant to viewers' own lives as single parents or is the divorce under discussion like their divorce? Not only are the debates in the studio often heated, so too are the debates in front of the set, for the negotiation of the genre is also a negotiation of oneself and one's relations with others. In this sense the personal is political, and the social dramas enacted among the studio participants are significant insofar as they serve to reproduce the identities and perceived legitimacy of the various participants.

TOWARDS A RESEARCH AGENDA FOR MEDIATED KNOWLEDGE

Questions of what knowledge the media may offer and of how audiences do or might come to know it form part of a broad research agenda which we can derive by characterizing the significance of the modern media in terms of 'the institutionalized production and diffusion of symbolic goods; the instituted break between production and reception; the extension of availability in time and space; and the public circulation of symbolic forms' (Thompson 1990: 219), as follows:

- *Who knows?*: questions of the transmission of knowledge and of differential access to ideas and knowledge (e.g. inequality, marginality and knowledge gaps), the extent to which audiences are becoming homogenous or fragmented, what knowledge resources audiences may draw upon in engaging with media, who is considered expert (whose knowledge counts, is considered worthy of transmission and, as a consequence, who has the power to produce rather than consume mediated knowledge).
- *How do we know?*: questions of changing modes of communication from face-to-face to mediated communication (how is knowledge mediated, how is it

constructed in the presence or absence of recipient feedback or reciprocity, what is the significance of para-social interaction, are new forms of interactivity becoming available).

- *What do we know?*: questions of the implications and consequences of extended space–time availability (what can be known, what is the relationship between global and local contexts of use, how is knowledge contextually dislocated and re-embedded, how is knowledge transformed in the process of this dislocation and re-embedding).
- *Whose knowledge is being (re)produced?*: what are the implications of different kinds of mediated knowledge for the boundary between public and private, for the public sphere, for the regulation of knowledge, and for the political voice of elite and marginalized groups.

The dimension of time is crucial to this agenda, for the kinds of mediated relationships available are undergoing continuous change and diversification. Forms of media, and the rapid changes which these are undergoing, raise new questions about communicative relations between media and audiences (and among audiences, insofar as these are mediated).[3] This changes, and locates historically, our understanding of what knowledge, whose knowledge, how it is mediated and to whom. The emerging mixed 'infotainment' genres and new multimedia formats render problematic key terms hitherto standard in discussions of mediatized knowledge – expert, information, recipient, discursive rules, ignorance, personal experience. Thus in access or viewer-made programmes (e.g., in Britain, *Video Diaries*, *Video Nation*) ordinary people may be producers as well as the recipients of programmes, the lay public may seek to inform as well as be informed by the supposed experts in a field, and personal experience may be validated as worthy knowledge, while expert facts may be rejected as irrelevant or ungrounded. Indeed, the problems raised may be seen as the point of the genre, for what gives audiences pleasure is not only learning about how others live, or seeing their own lives in the context of others, but also debating the value of hearing from ordinary people, what the outcome of a discussion was, how it related to one's own experience, whether the experts had a valuable contribution to make, and so forth. The talking heads, expert commentary and careful sequencing of argumentation of the documentary genre, for instance, may be implicitly questioned by these other formats.[4]

The four questions of mediated knowledge outlined above may be mapped on to the standard tripartite organization of the field of media and communication. The study of texts, production and audience raises issues concerning media and knowledge. The most obvious focus for such issues is questions of representation: what do we know and what kinds of knowledge do the media represent or convey or construct? A second focus locates these questions in relation to media institutions: whose knowledge, by what organizational means and purposes, and in whose interests is such mediated knowledge constructed? And, third, what of the audience: who knows, or what role does mediated knowledge play in their lives and how does mediated knowledge relate to other forms of everyday knowledge and experience? The significance of the audience, once a separate topic or even a legitimate omission from media theorizing, has recently come to be taken for granted,[5] notwithstanding concerns about whether the media are being used primarily for communication among elites rather than from elites to the laity (Schlesinger and Tumber 1994; see also the debate on the role of the media in the public sphere in Curran 1991; Garnham 1990). The addition to the above agenda of the question of how we know focuses attention once more on the form or channel of communication (Lasswell 1947; McLuhan and Fiore 1967), more recently discussed by Meyrowitz (1985).

THEORIZING KNOWLEDGEABLE AUDIENCES

Despite paying relatively little attention to the forms or channels of communication (see later), a central achievement of Hall's (1980) encoding–decoding model was to emphasize the dynamic interrelations among the three elements of text, production and audience, moving us away from the limitations of hitherto dominant models which arranged them in a broadly linear and unidirectional path from sender via message to receiver. Questions of media and knowledge, under this latter model, had become questions of how elites use the media to inform, educate, persuade or control the laity, with their success depending in part on the efficiency of the communication channel and the receptivity of the audience. The theoretical and methodological difficulties encountered by media-effects research have led many to consider other ways of asking about the relationshp between mediated representations and audiences (Livingstone 1996), although various specific models of how mediated knowledge may inform audiences continue to enjoy some success (e.g. agenda-setting, cultivation theory, knowledge gaps; Fejes 1984).

Carey (1975) has been particularly critical of the imperialist presumptions behind this 'transmission' model of communication. As a consequence of these and similar critiques, the very notion of knowledge has become problematic for media scholars, for to ask about knowledge may appear to suggest the return of supposedly doomed lines of inquiry concerned with administrative control, media effects or media imperialism – models which are taken vastly to underestimate the institutional/epistemological basis of media production, the polysemic/multilayered complexities of message meanings and the interpretative and contextualized activities of the (plural) audiences. Even Hall's encoding–decoding model has been criticized for a similar tendency to revert to the transmission model through the concept of the 'preferred reading', the means by which Hall retained some determining power for the text over its readers (Grossberg 1994; see also interview with Stuart Hall in Cruz and Lewis 1994).

Yet it is not so evident from Carey's work that he meant to halt research on the transmission of information; rather, he intended to supplement it with questions of meaning, performance, tradition and interpretative community through a 'ritual' model of communication. This model focuses on the ways in which knowledge is socially generated from the activities and relations of an interpretative community (Schroeder 1994) rather than imposed from on high for the supposed benefit of an ignorant and needy mass. The media are conceived of as a resource by which, almost irrespective of their institutional purposes, meanings are circulated and reproduced according to the contextualized interests of the public. Knowledge becomes, not the pedagogy or propaganda of the transmission model, but the *habitus*, the shared representations, the lived understandings of the community.[6]

Undoubtedly, many analyses of texts and audiences have been productively fuelled by this ritual model of communication. For example, Taylor (1989) insightfully analyses the popularity of family and workplace-based situation comedies as providing an expression of culturally and socially generated anxieties about changes in family and work arrangements, particularly during the 1970s. Work on soap opera suggests that, whatever its possibly hegemonic message about the limitations of women's lives, the genre is used by audiences to celebrate the strengths of women and local communities (Hobson 1982; Seiter *et al.* 1987). Similarly, the topics of talk shows are suggestive of the range of contemporary cultural anxieties, while some hosts (Squire 1994) and viewers regard the genre as an opportunity to express, even celebrate, ordinary experience (especially that of women).

RECOGNITION OF THE FAMILIAR, DISCOVERY OF THE NEW

Such culturally informed work has seemed more successful recently than that conducted under the transmission view, where studies of how media have changed knowledge or attitudes or brought about different behaviours or values have been fraught with methodological and theoretical problems, not least as regards the assumptions about the kinds of knowledge supposedly conveyed by the media[7] and about the kinds of prior knowledge supposedly held by audiences.[8] However, the kinds of research studied under the ritual communication model are not accidental; they deal primarily with media portrayals of everyday life, portrayals of a world about which we have prior knowledge and which we can match up to our own lives so as to appropriate or recontextualize media images with relative ease. Such immediacy, such familiarity of reference points (albeit a constructed familiarity, a cultural achievement), facilitates questions about circulation of familiar images, about the appropriation of meanings into different personal and domestic contexts, and about how different backgrounds support different kinds of readings. Clearly, many media images concern the representation of that for which we have personal, located experiences; their significance may thus be understood through processes of recognition, validation and reinforcement. Modleski's (1982) analysis of the parallels between the textual rhythms in the soap opera and the domestic rhythms of women's daily lives (repetitive, cyclic, constrained in their opportunities, etc.), and the immediacy with which Schlesinger et al.'s (1992) female audiences related to images of violence against women provide good examples. The knowledge at stake concerns processes of re-knowing, and of coming to value and find pleasure in, what is already familiar.

Yet when we stand back and think about media and knowledge these are not necessarily the first kinds of knowledge which come to mind. Surely the amazing thing about the modern mass media is that we gain all kinds of knowledge about the world that we precisely did not have before – about other countries, past periods in history, other lifestyles, inaccessible institutions (the Houses of Parliament, law courts) or rarely encountered places (hospitals or prisons), even inside our own bodies via medical science programmes. We meet unique people (the president), unusual people (the oldest person on earth), people unlike ourselves (the aristocracy) – and so forth and so forth. Mediated knowledge is not just about recognition of the familiar or legitimation of the known, but also about the discovery of the new, about becoming familiar with the unknown, about legit-imating the hitherto marginalized. The media have 'created what we could call a "mediated worldliness": our sense of the world which lies beyond the sphere of our personal experience, and our sense of our place within this world, are increas-ingly shaped by mediated symbolic forms' (Thompson 1994: 34) – we know about places and times we have not personally visited, and when we do visit them it is from within that knowledge context.[9]

To understand the significance of such ready access to diverse images we need both models of communication; new ideas and knowledge are indeed transmitted to audiences by those who have direct access to such specialist sources and places (and the imperialist connotations of this process are often appropriate), but we also need a ritual model to understand such knowledge in terms of local mean-ings and shared assumptions, not simply in terms of the supposed accumulation of information. Information is significant only insofar as it becomes known, is appropriated and made useable by being incorporated into and interpreted within the set of assumptions and understandings of everyday life. Otherwise it washes over us, as do most television images, as an excess of 'information' with which we do nothing and so which does not become knowledge. To distinguish between recognition and discovery as processes of mediated knowledge is to cut across Corner's (1991) distinction between public information and popular culture. Instead, the distinction depends on the audience's prior state of knowledge (for familiarity and novelty depend on what audiences are or are not already familiar with) and on the epistemological framing of the mediated knowledge (e.g. a genre concerned with education for citizenship, such as the documentary, or with the reproduction of the normative, such as a sitcom), although many genres mix the two. It allows both discovery and recognition to be sources of pleasure; more-over, the former is not necessarily 'better' – we may associate it with learning but also with the voyeurism of the talk show or the imperialism of Carey's (1975) transmission model, as in certain traditional forms of the documentary. Moreover, while recognition is usually understood as the relationship between a particular viewer-in-context and a particularly resonant television scene or event, knowledge is usually understood as making some claim on the general, usually with some normative or mainstreaming connotations (Gerbner et al. 1982). Here again, the epistemological claims of a genre and the audience's critical response to these are important for understanding its potential for mediating knowledge.

The media also make an epistemological claim that is potentially transformative of our relations with our everyday context, for they imply that everything is potentially transmittable, that no knowledge, no place or time or aspect of life can escape being included within the vast scope of media representations (even if for practical or commercial reasons it happens not to be so included); everything may be the subject of a documentary or a studio debate. Thus the portrayal of the familiar and the everyday, in addition to any mainstreaming effect it may have through repetition, salience and typicality, gains a normativity precisely through not portraying the unfamiliar. The sitcom family is familiar because it resembles our own (and so may reinforce certain assumptions about family life and offer the pleasures of recognition), but it is also safe, comforting, because it does not challenge us with other images of family life that we now know about, say through a documentary about family life at other times or in other places. The nostalgia with which sitcoms and soaps are imbued derives in part from our intertextual and extratextual knowledge of other ways of living, knowledge which is routinely excluded from these genres as if we were still living in a time when such knowledge was not available. Yet the same viewers, after the sitcom or soap, may watch (indeed, may actively seek out) a documentary, a current affairs discussion or even a talk show in which different and unfamiliar portrayals are now, but once were not, commonplace.

KNOWLEDGE, SPACE AND TIME

Writers in the phenomenological tradition have long stressed the importance of analysing the spatio-temporal context of social situations and relationships (Goffman 1974; Meyrowitz 1985; see Drotner 1994 on the legacy of Schutz's work; most recently, Giddens 1984 discusses 'time–space distanciation'). As Drotner notes, 'mass communication is of course precisely defined (among other aspects) by its dislocation of such time–space relations' (Drotner 1994: 351). Goffman's argument that different social settings arrange time and space differently (Jary 1991) is useful for analysing the significance of the media in portraying images of life beyond, as well as within, the viewer's immediate locale. We may then draw out the ways in which different media forms provide the technical underpinning for new kinds of social settings which position audiences in new relations to absent others, transforming the kinds of knowledge which may be (re)produced in these settings as a consequence.[10] In a similar vein, Thompson develops Horton and Wohl's (1956) concept of para-social interaction in his discussion of 'mediated quasi-interaction', which, despite being monological and non-reciprocal, is still interaction in the sense that 'it creates a certain kind of social situation in which individuals are linked together in a process of communication and symbolic exchange' (Thompson 1994: 36); as a consequence, the media may be said to have altered 'the interaction mix' of social life (ibid.: 37). This more phenomenological analysis may productively develop the somewhat ill-defined terms of 'context' or 'embedding' which are current in audience ethnography and which are central to cultural studies (Grossberg 1994).

Once symbolic forms gain extended availability across time and space the traditional boundary between public and private may be transformed; hence 'the private domestic setting – has become a principal site of mediated publicness' (Thompson 1994: 243). As Urry points out, this increased availability to audiences of certain kinds of information or knowledge may be directly counter to the desires of specific social groups, for television in particular has 'made all backstages public property and hence served to undermine such a demarcation' (Urry 1991: 171). Thus, in direct opposition to the emergence during modernity of specialized systems of knowledge, the media open up the possibility of the 'de-sequestration of experience' (Thompson 1994: 227), revealing portrayals of experience to which people would not otherwise have access in their day-to-day lives: 'the media produce a continuous intermingling of different forms of experience, an intermingling that makes the day-to-day lives of most individuals today quite different from the lives of previous generations' (ibid.: 227). Problematically for the concept of space–time distanciation, this sequestration to which the media provides a counterforce may occur close to home (e.g. the prison, Westminster, etc. may be within one's locale but entirely inaccessible to the laity).[11] Thus the media offer an alternative, delocalized agenda of issues and values, and they open up the possibility of what Thompson calls a despatialized commonality, an imagined community based on shared knowledge without a shared locale.[12] Even more than everyday experience, mediated experience or knowledge requires precisely the active process of re-embedding in local contexts that audience researchers have been exploring in recent years, but it is also a process which may transform viewers' experience and understanding of the local.

In analysing the social consequences of time–space distanciation, Giddens (1984) suggests that despite, or even because of, the increased availability of information individuals are faced with increased risk, coming under pressure to make decisions in situations of uncertainty rather than in the context of adequate knowledge. This creates the burden of endlessly seeking further knowledge, creating an informational dependency which the media are only too happy to address, some might say exploit. Particularly in the domain of identity politics, it also opens up the possibility of greater experimentation or vulnerability. The process of re-embedding or recontextualizing knowledge about absent or other kinds of experience may be a creative – or, more pessimistically, a manipulable –

one, allowing both opportunities and dangers for the individual not hitherto possible or legitimate. Thompson sees this positively as 'a major new arena [which] has been created for the process of self-fashioning' (Thompson 1994: 43). Reception theory, more neutrally, has long been aware of this; Iser notes that 'as the reader passes through the various perspectives offered by the text, and relates the different views and patterns to one another, he sets the work in motion, *and so sets himself in motion too*' (Iser 1980: 106; emphasis mine). Baudrillard (1988) and Habermas (1987), among others, are far more pessimistic about the possibilities for the self/lifeworld escaping from the system world.

MEDIATED AND NON-MEDIATED KNOWLEDGE

The question of self-fashioning, or the active appropriation of mediated meanings, brings us back to the issue of the active or knowing audience, which, as I suggested at the outset, has sometimes appeared to displace the question of mediated knowledge. While the popularity of the active audience concept has multiple justifications (Livingstone 1993), it has tended to set up an opposition between text and reader in which the relationship is one of struggle rather than mutual interaction over time. In the present context it is particularly relevant to note that audience-reception theory appears to assume that viewers' interpretative resources (i.e. knowledge and ways of knowing) are constructed entirely independently of the media and, moreover, also used by people for understanding their non-mediated everyday experience. This opposition between mediated and non-mediated knowledge lies implicit beneath discussions of the possible interpretations and effects of media representations, especially in arguments about the role of prior experience and the extent to which prior knowledge or interest may reconstrue media representations and so undermine media effects (Philo 1993).[13] Rather, as Thompson has noted, we must 'put aside the intuitively plausible idea that communication media serve to transmit information and symbolic content to individuals whose relations to others remain fundamentally unchanged' (Thompson 1990: 4). To take another example, while expressing concerns that audience research is subordinating media questions to questions of everyday discourses, Schroeder agrees that 'individuals have no identity as simple receivers of such [media] products' (Schroeder 1994: 340), for 'individuals/subjects precede the media products they consume: they and their cultural repertoires have been formed by multiple discourse (interpretive communities?) throughout their lives' (ibid.: 340). Yet individuals are surely born into media cultures just as they are born into a particular linguistic environment (and a separation between culture and media is hard to sustain). Media cultures provide not only interpretative frameworks, but also sources of pleasure and resources for identity-formation which ensure that individuals certainly have a complex identity of which part includes their participatory relations with particular media forms. The strength of arguments about the transformative potential of time–space distanciation (as brought about in part by the mass media) is that it allows us to avoid the assumption of a confrontation or opposition between lay knowledge and media knowledge by suggesting that we conceptualize people as primarily located in particular time–space relations but with access via the media (and other means) to others. Furthermore, this access to non-physically present experiences and relations may transform the construction of those experiences and relations which are directly available in one's locale. The focus on interaction and process prevents us posing chicken-and-egg questions about which comes first.[14]

As was suggested earlier, ways of knowing made salient by the media may be as significant as – if not more so than – the nature of the knowledge promoted or reinforced by the media. This demands an analysis of how different media genres, forms or channels establish different communicative relations, or different mediated social settings, between text and reader. Again, reception does not just involve a negotiation between media contents and prior interpretative frameworks. Rather, part of becoming a knowledgeable and experienced viewer involves learning media-specific and genre-specific interpretative skills – frameworks of interpretation, modes of involvement, expectations of events, narrative structures (Livingstone 1998a). Allen (1985) argued that soap opera fans make more 'paradigmatic' readings of the genre which focus on the play of possibilities among characters involved in specific events, while non-fans, often including media critics, make 'syntagmatic' readings which focus on the generally repetitive sequencing of events and the absence of conclusions. Similarly, audience discussion fans construe the genre differently from non-fans, valuing the conjunction of contributions from diverse lay publics, seeing these debates as of social value, and relishing the confrontation of elite experts and ordinary people, while non-fans are more concerned about whether the debates are emotional, ill expressed, include non-normative views or 'fail' to reach a consensual conclusion (Livingstone and Lunt 1994). New forms of interaction, mediated or not, require the emergence of new forms of interactional competences; mediated interaction is a skilled achievement on the part of the viewer as well as the text. Moreover, such cultural and media 'literacy' may provide a resource of greater applicability than just to the media, since our interpretative resources do not stay in neat compartments.[15]

IMPLICATIONS FOR AUDIENCE-RECEPTION RESEARCH

I have argued that a focus on time–space relations in late modernity provides a useful framework for refocusing some of the ways in which audience researchers have considered the problem of mediated knowledge and contextual embedding. In so doing, I have suggested that we abandon certain dichotomies which have structured the field – transmission v. ritual models of communication, public information v. popular culture approaches to study, learning v. pleasure, and mediated knowledge v. personal knowledge. The advantage for audience-reception research is that time–space distanciation offers an audience-centred framework and so fits the now widespread recognition that audiences crucially mediate media knowledge processes (or that encoding and decoding are both necessary parts of the whole, or that apparently micro-processes of reception are necessary to macro-processes in the circulation of knowledge; Livingstone 1993). Specifically, both time and space (and the power to access otherwise sequestered domains) are measured in terms of distance from the audience, the knowing subject, and, consequently, the familiar and the unfamiliar are defined according to the prior knowledge of the audience.[16] The analysis of different mediated knowledge processes then follows from this distance from the audience. For the familiar, media research has argued that the key processes are those of recognition, validation and mainstreaming; for the novel, media research has argued that the key processes are those of discovery, learning and surveillance. Finally, for both physically absent and physically present events, the dimension of time–space distanciation foregrounds the means of coming to know (whether through face-to-face or mediated interactions) rather than the possession (or presumed absence) of knowledge. The case of the audience discussion programme, used as an example of emerging media genres which transform or challenge traditional formats for mediating knowledge, has been valuable in illustrating these points, for it is a genre which places the audience, and the audiences' knowledge and ways of knowing, centre stage, and it combines the recognition of the familiar with the discovery of the new. Most importantly, it problematizes the epistemology of media representations, showing how increasingly critical viewers may negotiate, and gain pleasure from negotiating, the 'rules' by which knowledge is mediated.

This interactional view of audience reception refocuses reception analysis on the ways in which people stand in relationship to each other, rather than as a thing (the audience, which stands in a certain relation to that other thing, the media) of which people may or may not be a member and whose peculiar ways we need to discover (cf. critiques of audience reception research by Ang (1990) and Allor (1988), among others). Our analysis of audience discussion programmes set out to discover what kind of relationships were established among people as an audience for different television genres – were viewers acting as citizens or as consumers, in what ways were they engaged, critical, mindless or responsive to the diverse modes of address in this genre? Most particularly, we wanted to consider the notion of the relationship between text and viewer as one concerned with 'publicness', with acting as a public or with communicating as part of a public. The current debate on Habermas's (1969) theory of the public sphere framed our concerns well (Curran 1991; Garnham 1990), since the question for Habermas was not what the public is, what it thinks, how it acts and what influences it, but, rather, in what ways people in their everyday activities constitute a public, what forms of communication are appropriate for a public sphere and what discursive or institutional threats it faces. More generally, I suggest that audience research should chart the possibilities and problems for communication or relations among people, insofar as these are undermined or facilitated, managed or reconstituted by the media, rather than ask about the various reifications of the audience, the public or the market. Our understanding of mediated knowledge surely depends on our understanding of the communicative relationships established among people, and these include those supported or managed by the media.

NOTES

1 Questions of mediated knowledge have received less attention in recent research than questions of audience knowledge or social positioning (i.e. 'How do knowing audiences approach texts?' rather than 'What knowledge do texts convey to audiences?'), and questions of the pleasures and the practices associated with media consumption (Livingstone 1998a; Silverstone 1994).

2 By epistemology, I mean to refer broadly to a set of questions concerning what can be known, ways of knowing, criteria and rules for establishing and legitimating relations between evidence and conclusions, frameworks to guide the construction and application of knowledge, and so forth.

3 We should be careful, however, when asking how changes in media forms raise new questions about communication and knowledge not to fall into a technological determinism which assumes simply that social change follows technological change; instead, we should also ask what is it about certain social and cultural formations that some technologies develop and are used in certain ways and not others.

4 Certainly, our research suggested that this epistemological negotiation has implications for the reception of other genres; for example, while some viewers complained that a documentary develops its arguments more carefully, uses representative examples and gives experts more time to express their expertise, others considered that the few examples in a documentary are of more dubious representativeness than the multiple voices of the studio audience, that the experts often fail to say anything of significance and that a documentary is more easily biased than a discussion programme (Livingstone and Lunt 1994).

5 The agenda for audience research has, over the past fifteen years or so, successfully moved research on from problematic assumptions about fixed and given textual meanings, passive and vulnerable audiences, and the homogenous mass 'audience'. In so doing, its most significant achievement has been to make visible an audience which was hitherto devalued, marginalized and presumed about (Livingstone 1998b).

6 The role of media institutions is unclear on this view and may be too easily reduced to a kind of functionalist analysis whereby knowledge circulates through the media in order to provide for the ritual needs of the community of receivers; can there, for instance, be dysfunctional, voyeuristic or harmful rituals?

7 An example would be the question from cultivation research of whether the statistical patterning of 'television reality' (e.g. overrepresentations of the police force as an adult occupation) affects knowledge of such statistical patterning in real life (overestimation of the number of police officers) or whether it conveys a second-order symbolic message (society values law and order). While the second hypothesis has generally been regarded as both more plausible and more interesting (as in the many content analyses of television's 'symbolic annihilation' of women, where the supposed message is not that there are more men in the world but that men are more important), it has proved easier to support the former empirically than the latter (Hawkins and Pingree 1983).

8   In order to contrast audience knowledge or experience with mediated knowledge, researchers tend to posit an implausible opposition between the two. For example, Philo (1993) argues that personal experience of the miners' strike – presumably entirely unmediated – acts as a counterforce against the influence of media representations of the strike, without either a processual view of the construction of social reality from multiple sources or a means of analysing interpretations when personal experience accords with the media representation. Morgenstern (1992) notes with some irony that audience researchers assert the power of audiences to undermine media representations when audiences express counternormative positions, while asserting the power of the media when audiences express normative positions; as she says, the test is one not of the strength of mediated knowledge but of whether the audience espouses an implicit left-wing theory.

9   Of course, books have traditionally provided a source of knowledge of that which is distant from us in space or time, but such knowledge differs from mass-mediated knowledge in key ways, being circulated among a smaller audience in a relatively ad hoc rather than common manner, and being subject to relatively little institutional management. Audiences for mediated knowledge may generally assume that theirs is a shared experience, and this facilitates interpersonal relations among audiences as well as relations between audiences and media.

10 See Giddens's (1984) emphasis on the transformative potential resulting from the 'stretching' of social relations over time and space, so that face-to-face interaction with others in a shared locale is increasingly supplemented by interaction with others who are physically absent.

11 For example, the issue of televising the activities of the Houses of Parliament in Britain involved questions both of what the public should know and of whether the desequestration of parliamentary debate would itself be transformative of that debate. Such desequestration results in conjunctions which have hitherto been segregated by the media; for example, in the audience discussion programme a homeless woman may have an argument with, and even get the better of, a government minister for housing and this may alter the public regard in which both parties are held.

12 By watching an audience discussion programme or a drama documentary the teenager suffering from anorexia, the mother of a drink-driving victim, the gay man who cannot tell his parents may all discover that they are not alone, that others exist in their position who share their experiences.

13 Empirical research tends in any case to confuse neat theoretical distinctions. For example, in their recent study of women viewing violence Schlesinger et al. (1992) show substantial differences in the viewing of violent images between women with and without personal experience of violence. But what knowledge was at stake? Largely irrespective of prior experience, most of the viewers were reasonably cynical about the police and the workings of law-and-order agencies; most were fairly familiar with the nature of the violent episodes portrayed (in the sense that they claimed not to have learnt much, although they were committed to the idea that others would learn about violence by seeing such images and so believed an educational value for others was at stake). The differences lay more in the consequences of being reminded of their common knowledge – those with prior experience viewed the scenes with greater emotion, with greater empathy, with a clearer ability to predict narrative developments, with a greater sense of fear for themselves and with a greater cynicism about men as perpetrators of violence. There are differences, then, in the process of relating to the world and the positioning of oneself within it, but not necessarily in information about that world, for a realm of shared representations is already available to women concerning the continued threat to themselves of violence from men and this forms part of the context within which they themselves encounter their personal experiences.

14 The theory of media-systems dependency (Ball-Rokeach and DeFleur 1976) raises an interesting exception, namely the question of how audiences respond when they become dependent on the media for knowledge which is critically unavailable or inaccessible within their immediate locale, as in times of crisis.

15 Watkins (1988) suggests that, while 'light' viewers tend to use interpretative frameworks from everyday life to retell a television narrative, 'heavy' viewers tend to reverse this, being more likely to use mediated frameworks to retell events from everyday life.

16 As the media themselves are part of the immediate locale of the audience, past media experiences become part of the familiar (although they are experienced via mediated rather than face-to-face interaction). 'Prior knowledge' (frequently shown to make a difference to media reception (Livingstone 1998a; Philo 1993; Schlesinger et al. 1992) may thus be either mediated or directly experienced by viewers and cannot be simply contrasted with new mediated representations – the president of the United States is not available to us directly, but, like J. R. Ewing, he is no longer unfamiliar to us (indeed, viewers often are unclear about the source of their information; Lewis 1991).

REFERENCES

Allen, R. C. (1985) *Speaking of Soap Operas*, Chapel Hill, NC: University of North Carolina Press.

Allor, M. (1988) 'Relocating the site of the audience', *Critical Studies in Mass Communication* 5: 217–33.

Ang, I. (1990) *Desperately Seeking the Audience*, London: Routledge.

Ball-Rokeach, S. J. and DeFleur, M. L. (1976) 'A dependency model of mass-media effects', *Communication Research* 3: 3–21.

Baudrillard, J. (1988) 'The masses: the implosion of the social in the media', in M. Poster (ed.) *Jean Baudrillard: Selected Writings*, Cambridge: Polity Press.

Bierig, J. and Dimmick, J. (1979) 'The late night radio talk show as interpersonal communication', *Journalism Quarterly* 56: 92–6.

Carey, J. W. (1975) 'Communication and culture', *Communication Research* 2: 173–91.

Corner, J. (1991) 'Meaning, genre and context: the problematics of "public knowledge" in the new audience studies', in J. Curran and M. Gurevitch (eds) *Mass Media and Society*, London: Methuen.

Cruz, J. and Lewis, J. (eds) (1994) *Viewing, Reading, Listening: Audiences and Cultural Reception*, Boulder, CO: Westview Press.

Curran, J. (1991) 'Rethinking the media as a public sphere', in P. Dahlgren and C. Sparks (eds) *Communication and Citizenship: Journalism and the Public Sphere in the New Media Age*, London: Routledge.

Drotner, K. (1994) 'Ethnographic enigmas: "the everyday" in recent media studies', *Cultural Studies* 8: 341–57.

Fejes, F. (1984) 'Critical mass communications research and media effects: the problem of the disappearing audience', *Media, Culture and Society* 6(3): 219–32.

Garnham, N. (1990) 'The media and the public sphere', in *Capitalism and Communication: Global Culture and the Economics of Information*, London: Sage Publications.

Gerbner, G. and Gross, L. (1976) 'Living with television: the violence profile', *Journal of Communication* 26(2): 173–99.

Gerbner, G., Gross, L., Morgan, M. and Signorielli, N. (1982) 'Charting the mainstream: television's contributions to political orientations', *Journal of Communication* 32(2): 100–27.

Giddens, A. (1984) *The Constitution of Society: Outline of the Theory of Structuration*, Cambridge: Polity Press.

Goffman, E. (1974) *Frame Analysis*, Harmondsworth: Penguin.

Grossberg, L. (1994) 'Can cultural studies find true happiness in communication?', in M. R. Levy and M. Gurevitch (eds) *Defining Media Studies: Reflections on the Future of the Field*, New York: Oxford University Press.

Habermas, J. ([1969] 1989) 'The structural transformation of the public sphere: an inquiry into a category of bourgeois society', Cambridge, MA: MIT Press.

—— (1987) *The Philosophical Discourse of Modernity: Twelve Lectures*, Cambridge: Polity Press.

Hall, S. (1980) 'Encoding/decoding', in S. Hall, D. Hobson, A. Lowe and P. Willis (eds) *Culture, Media, Language*, London: Hutchinson.

Hawkins, R. P. and Pingree, S. (1983) 'Television's influence on social reality', in E. Wartella and D. C. Whitney (eds) *Mass Communication Review Yearbook*, London: Sage Publications.

Hobson, D. (1982) *Crossroads: The Drama of a Soap Opera*, London: Methuen.

Horton, D. and Wohl, R. R. (1956) 'Mass communication and para-social interaction', *Psychiatry* 19: 215–29.

Iser, W. (1980) 'Interaction between text and reader', in S. R. Suleiman and I. Crosman (eds) *The Reader in the Text: Essays on Audience and Interpretation*, Princeton: Princeton University Press.

Jary, D. (1991) 'Society as time-traveller: Giddens on historical change, historical materialism and the nation-state in world society', in C. G. A. Bryant and D. Jary (eds) *Giddens' Theory of Structuration: A Critical Appreciation*, London: Routledge.

Lasswell, H. D. (1947) *The Analysis of Political Behaviour: An Empirical Approach*, London: Kegan Paul.

Lewis, J. (1991) *The Ideological Octopus: An Exploration of Television and Its Audience*, London: Routledge.

Livingstone, S. M. (1993) 'The rise and fall of audience research: an old story with a new ending', *Journal of Communication*, special issue, *The Future of the Field* 43(4): 5–12.

—— (1996) 'On the continuing problem of media effects research', in J. Curran and M. Gurevitch (eds) *Mass Media and Society*, London: Edward Arnold.

—— (1998a) *Making Sense of Television: The Psychology of Audience Interpretation*, second edition, London: Butterworth-Heinemann.

—— (1998b) 'Relationships between media and audiences: prospects for audience reception studies', in T. Liebes and J. Curran (eds) *Media, Ritual and Identity: Essays in Honor of Elihu Katz*, London: Routledge.

Livingstone, S. M. and Lunt, P. K. (1994) *Talk on Television: The Critical Reception of Audience Discussion Programmes*, London: Routledge.

Livingstone, S. M., Wober, J. M. and Lunt, P. K. (1994) 'Involvement and participation in audience discussion programmes: an analysis of viewers' preferences', *European Journal of Communication* 9: 355–79.

McCombs, M. E. and Shaw, D. (1972) 'The agenda-setting function of the mass media', *Public Opinion Quarterly* 36: 176–87.

McLuhan, M. and Fiore, Q. (1967) *The Medium is the Message*, Harmondsworth: Penguin.

Meyrowitz, J. (1985) *No Sense of Place: The Impact of Electronic Media on Social Behavior*, New York: Oxford University Press.

Modleski, T. (1982) *Loving With a Vengeance: Mass-produced Fantasies for Women*, New York: Methuen.

Morgenstern, S. (1992) 'The epistemic autonomy of mass media audiences', *Critical Studies in Mass Communication* 9: 293–310.

Noelle-Neumann, E. (1974) 'The spiral of silence: a theory of public opinion', *Journal of Communication* 24(2): 43–52.

Philo, G. (1993) 'Getting the message: audience research in the Glasgow University Media Group', in J. Eldridge (ed.) *Getting the Message: News, Truth and Power*, London: Routledge.

Rose, B. G. (1985) 'The talk show', in B. G. Rose (ed.) *TV Genres: A Handbook and Reference Guide*, Westport, CT: Greenwood Press.

Rubin, A. M. (1984) 'Ritualized and instrumental television viewing', *Journal of Communication* 34(3): 67–77.

Schlesinger, P. and Tumber, H. (1994) *Reporting Crime: The Media Politics of Criminal Justice*, Oxford: Oxford University Press.

Schlesinger, P., Dobash, R. E., Dobash, R. P. and Weaver, C. K. (1992) *Women Viewing Violence*, London: British Film Institute.

Schroeder, K. C. (1994) 'Audience semiotics, interpretive communities and the "ethnographic turn" in media research', *Media, Culture and Society* 16: 337–47.

Seiter, E., Krentzer, G., Worth, E. M. and Borchers, H. (1987) 'Don't treat us like we're so stupid and naive: towards an ethnography of soap opera viewers', *Remote Control*.

Silverstone, R. (1994) *Television and Everyday Life*, London: Routledge.

Squire, C. (1994) 'Empowering women? The Oprah Winfrey Show', *Feminism and Psychology* 4(1): 63–79.

Taylor, E. (1989) *Prime-time Families: Television Culture in Postwar America*, Berkeley, CA: University of California Press.

Thompson, J. B. (1990) *Ideology and Modern Culture: Critical Social Theory in the Era of Mass Communication*, Cambridge: Polity Press.

—— (1994) 'Social theory and the media', in D. Crowley and D. Mitchell (eds) *Communication Theory Today*, Cambridge: Polity Press.

Urry, J. (1991) 'Time and space in Giddens' social theory', in C. G. A. Bryant and D. Jary (eds) *Giddens' Theory of Structuration: A Critical Appreciation*, London: Routledge.

Watkins, B. (1988) 'Children's representations of television and real-life stories', *Communication Research* 15(2): 159–84.

7

IMAGINARY SPACES

Television, technology and everyday consciousness

Peter Larsen

YOU PRESS THE BUTTON, WE DO THE REST

The first people who saw Gutenberg's printing machine in action were duly struck with wonder. But at least they had a fair chance of understanding how this ingenious, revolutionizing invention of his worked. It was, after all, a relatively simple mechanism, based on well-known physical principles, not radically different from the tools most of his contemporaries used in their everyday life. Anyone who watched him at work in the shop could instantly *see* what he and his machine were doing.

It was far more difficult to understand what was going on when Niepce and Daguerre made the first photographs in the early nineteenth century. And things did not get any easier as time went by. While professional photographers and ardent amateurs learnt to master the mysterious physical and chemical processes involved, ordinary people learnt to rely on specialists – and George Eastman made a fortune with his small, cheap Kodak camera and the famous slogan 'You press the button, we do the rest'. This is still the way it is with photography. We all press the buttons; the 'rest' – developing and copying the pictures – is done somewhere else by someone else.

Moving images are just as mysterious. Sitting in the cinema we enjoy the moving images on the big screen, but we have only a rather vague notion of how they are produced and we have all forgotten what the teachers once told us about the strange physiological defect in our eyes, which deceives us to such a degree that we believe that these flickering images are really 'moving'. On the other hand, we know at least that they are stored on large rolls of film, that they arrive at the cinema in tin cans, and that they are projected on to the screen through a hole in the wall by a machine that sometimes can be heard humming faintly in the background.

When it comes to television our ignorance is much greater. Most of us only know that the images on the small screen are 'electronic' in some mysterious way, that they are 'recorded' somewhere else and that they are 'transmitted' from far away. We have not the faintest idea of how this is done; we just press the button and – miraculously! – images appear on the screen. The chosen few who actually have some understanding of the basic technological principles involved are not much better off. As soon as they turn on their TV set, they forget what they know; they are quite unable to relate their theoretical knowledge to the concrete, everyday experience of watching moving images on a small screen in the living room.

From Gutenberg onwards it has been like this; media history is the story of a constantly widening gap between theoretical knowledge and practical experience. And it is true to say that the same story could be told about most everyday technologies. There was a time when people knew how to build their own radio sets and repair their own cars. Those days are over. We buy our computers and CD players at the local electronics market, and when we come home we simply take them out of their boxes and plug them in. Nobody would dream of fetching a screwdriver when the hairdryer breaks down. A look inside the video recorder will not tell you why it suddenly died.

We are surrounded by incomprehensible gadgets. Our knowledge about them is fragmented. But, although we do not understand them intellectually, we use them, they are a vital part of our daily life, and we deal with them in reasonable, practical ways. We press the button and something inside the black box does 'the rest'. We do not know exactly what 'the rest' is, but at least we usually press the right button, and we know very well what would happen if we pressed another one.

So we do know something after all. But what is it, more precisely, that we know, and how is this everyday knowledge structured? What do we think we are doing? What mental strategies enable us to deal with these complex, incomprehensible technologies? I will use these questions as guidelines in the following chapter, in which I discuss the ways we deal with television in a multi-channel environment.

The stories we tell each other about the simple, general, everyday experience of 'watching TV' are a good point of departure – and probably the only one we can choose for an initial discussion of this type. Therefore my material will be the formulas of everyday language, the stock phrases we use when we talk about TV, about switching from one channel to another etc. The quotations I discuss have not been collected in any systematic way. Most of them are merely sentences, phrases, metaphors and so on that constantly turn up in conversations with family members, friends, colleagues or in television reviews. In a few cases I quote from interviews made during a study of Norwegian viewing habits.[1]

BEARINGS

'What did you do last night?' somebody asks in the lunchroom. 'I watched TV,' says one; another answers: 'I went to the cinema.' The first is talking about a 'passive' state (that of 'receiving' something); a *situation* is tacitly implied: he or she was sitting in front of a TV set, watching. The other person is talking about an activity, about going somewhere, about a small *journey*. Of course, people will usually specify what they did at the cinema, but they mention the journey all the same, and they usually do so before they even begin describing the film they saw: 'I went to the cinema and saw the new Batman movie.' Simply saying 'I saw the Batman movie last night' will, under normal circumstances, mean that the movie was seen on TV.

This simple structure, this opposition between situation and journey, turns up again and again when we compare descriptions of everyday life: 'I read the news-paper', 'listened to the radio', 'heard a record', etc., but 'I went to the theatre', 'to the opera', 'to the Albert Hall'. The reason is obvious: Most experiences (and most descriptions) of everyday activities are 'oriented', structured according to a simple spatial opposition. Everyday activities take place in a centred world: There is a base, a 'home', and what is not 'at home' is 'outside', 'elsewhere'.

Psychologists tell us that the development of an individual's space conception has three major phases (see Piaget and Inhelder 1948). As infants we live in a *topological* space in which the prime perceptual categories are closeness, contiguity and continuity; then comes the *projective* stage, in which all activities and objects are experienced in relation to a single, subjective point of view; finally, by the age of 6 or 7 we have the *Euclidean* space, with its geometrical proportions and coordinates, a space in which the perceiving subject has become 'decentred' and knows how to imagine itself as one object among many within an all-embracing grid of relations.

The centred space of everyday life bears some resemblance to the space perception characteristic of the second stage. But, while the projective space is liquid, movable, always related to the position of the spectator-subject, the everyday space is a stable one; the point of view is locked on to one and the same locality. 'Home' is the mental point of reference, a position from which everything else is measured regardless of where the subject may be at present. Activities taking place 'somewhere else' are 'outside', 'beyond', 'at a distance'; they are deviations from the centre of the universe, and in descriptions of everyday life this deviation is always marked linguistically ('I went to work, to town, to the supermarket'), while 'home' activities are described with unmarked terms ('I did the dishes').

PLACES AND SPACES, MAPS AND TOURS

Before we discuss such descriptions in more detail, it might be useful to introduce two basic distinctions from Michel de Certeau's analysis of the spatiality of everyday life (de Certeau 1988: 115 ff.). The first one is the distinction between *place* and *space*. De Certeau writes:

A place (lieu) is the order (of whatever kind) in accord with which elements are distributed in relationships of coexistence. It thus excludes the possibility of two things being in the same location (place). The law of the 'proper' rules in the place: the elements taken into consideration are *beside* one another, each situated in its own 'proper' and distinct location, a location it defines. A place is thus an instantaneous configuration of positions. It implies an indication of stability.

(ibid.: 117)

The counterpart of the ordered, stable 'place' is 'space' – which in de Certeau's sense of the word is defined by vectors of direction, velocities and time variables:

Thus space is composed of intersections of mobile elements. It is in a sense actuated by the ensemble of movements deployed within it. Space occurs as the effect produced by the operations that orient it, situate it, temporalize it, and make it function in a polyvalent unity of conflictual programs or contractual proximities. On this view, in relation to place, space is like the word when it is spoken, that is, when it is caught in the ambiguity of an actualization, transformed into a term dependent upon many different conventions, situated as the act of a present (or of a time), and modified by the transformations caused by successive contexts. In contradistinction to the place, it has thus none of the univocity or stability of a 'proper'.

(ibid.: 117)

The place is turned into a space by means of actions. Or, as de Certeau puts it, '*space is a practised place*' (ibid.: 117). His example is the way people walk through a modern city: 'the street geometrically defined by urban planning is transformed into a space by walkers' (ibid.: 117).

The second distinction is one which is directly derived from the stories of everyday life, from 'oral descriptions of places, narrations concerning the home, stories about the streets' (ibid.: 118), etc. In this case de Certeau refers to the work of the American socio-linguists Charlotte Linde and William Labov (1975). They once analysed the descriptions a group of New York residents gave of their apartments and found that these descriptions could be divided into two distinct groups. The first one included sentences like 'the girls' room is next to the kitchen'; in the second there were sentences like 'you turn right and come into the living room'.

The first type presents a kind of verbal *map*; the second describes a *tour*. In the New York corpus only 3 per cent of the descriptions were of the 'map' type; the rest were 'tours': 'You come in through a low door' etc. The tours were for the most part descriptions of 'operations' one must perform in order 'to enter' the rooms in an apartment, but they also included (or were based on) maps; they presented a minimal series of paths by which one might go into each room, and these 'paths' could be analysed further into series of units that had the form of either 'static' vectors ('to the right', 'in front of you', etc.) or 'mobile' vectors ('if you turn to the left' etc.).

111

De Certeau summarizes these findings by saying that spatial description oscillates between the terms of an alternative: either seeing (the knowledge of an order of places) or going (spatializing actions). Either it presents a tableau ('there are...') or it organizes movements ('you enter...', 'you go across...', 'you turn ...'). Of these two hypotheses, the choices made by the New York narrators overwhelmingly favoured the second (de Certeau 1988: 119).

In other words, the place–space dichotomy has a discursive counterpart in descriptions like these. The verbal map is obviously a description of a 'place', a description with, we might add, 'projective' or perhaps even 'Euclidean' features, the place *as seen* from a subjective, elevated point of view ('to the left there is...'). The discursive tour describes a 'space', the way a place is being *practised* ('you turn to the left...'). Or, to use the example of the city, the map description is the genre preferred by city planners; the tour belongs to 'walkers', to the people using the city at street level.

De Certeau is primarily concerned with the various relationships between these two types of description, between *acting* and *seeing*, between itinerary ('a discursive series of operations') and map ('a plane projection totalizing observations'). It is, he says, as if two symbolic and anthropological languages of space are being spoken in these descriptions, indicating two poles of experience. And he goes on to show how these languages interact, how maps constantly intervene in tours and vice versa. Although tour descriptions predominate, 'an element of mapping' is usually 'the presupposition of a certain itinerary' (*ibid*.: 120). In fact, most descriptions of everyday spatiality have 'the structure of the travel story: stories of journeys and actions are marked out by the "citation" of the places that result from them or authorize them' (*ibid*.: 120).

AN INSTITUTIONAL STORY

What kind of stories do we tell each other about television, about our journeys across the imaginary borderline in the living-room, about the many places and spaces we see behind the screen? What kind of stories does television itself (its presenters, anchorpeople, cable operators) tell us? Which 'symbolic and anthropological languages of space' do we use, do they use?

Let us start by listening to an institutional story which is a bit different from all the others, the story told by a large Norwegian cable system to its new customers. First-time subscribers to the BSS system receive a leaflet which greets them with the following words:

> Welcome to BSS Cable Television. Congratulations! You are now attached to BSS Cable Television through the cable television network. This means that you have the possibility of choosing among a multitude of different television channels. BSS transmits approximately 20 channels through the cable television network at the moment.

The rest of the text is a simple manual telling new subscribers what to do with their TV sets in order to receive the signals from this 'multitude of different television channels'. When the set is tuned correctly it is possible to choose the right signal simply by operating the remote control. The reader is told that a number is assigned to each individual channel, and that this number will light up on the TV display whenever the signal from this particular channel is received by the set. On the last page there is a brief summary in the form of a simple list describing which numbers are assigned to which channels.

The manual is pedagogical, easy to understand, but it is clearly written by someone (the cable operator) for whom television is basically a question of transmitting and receiving electronic signals. Of course, we all talk like this from time to time – precisely when we are referring to reception conditions ('Do you get SkyNews?', 'How does Deutsche Welle look on your screen?'), but normally when all things technical are in order we forget about cables and electronics and use another language, indicating another kind of experience.

First-time subscribers are quick learners. As soon as they start using their new toy they forget all the sensible things the manual told them. They press the buttons on the remote control; they watch the numbers change on the TV display whenever images from a new channel appear on the screen – and they immediately understand that these numbers refer to locations within a landscape. Each location is a kind of 'site' on which a certain channel is 'placed'. In short, they construct an imaginary map based on how their actions with the remote control affect what is shown on the screen. And later, consulting the list of channels in the leaflet, they use it like a driver uses a road map – as a helpful tool providing an overview, showing the most efficient way to move from one place to another.

TRAVEL STORIES

The new cable subscribers 'translate' the channel list into something else; they read it as if it were an externalization of their own mental map, as if the sequence of numbers indicated a sequence of locations. They read it as if it were an indication of possible itineraries. They are ready to travel.

'I switched to Sweden,' says a respondent when interviewed about yesterday's viewing. She is obviously referring to what she did with the remote control ('I switched'), but she actually describes a movement in space: by her action she moved to another location ('to Sweden'). The solemn cable operator would probably say that by operating the remote control the viewer made something move inside the TV set. The viewer describes it as if she moved herself from one location to another. She was apparently on a tour.

This is the way it is. Talking about television, we constantly refer to tours: 'Stop here,' we say to the irritating, restless zapper. 'Stay here,' we say when the teenager declares that he wants to 'move to MTV'. 'Go back to CNN,' we yell when he does not obey our orders.

Our phrases refer to tours. Many times we actually use the very word itself. When we do not feel like watching a particular channel or programme we say, 'Let's take a tour.' One viewer tells us that she 'took a tour and landed on Sweden' – apparently she was flying. Danish zappers talk jokingly about going on a 'kanal-rundfart', a pun referring to sightseeing excursions on the canals of Copenhagen – they 'sail' through the channels/canals.

We walk, drive, fly, sail; we *travel*. And when you travel through an unfamiliar landscape you need a map in order to make the right movements, the right decisions. Of course, it is possible to grope one's way, but it is far more efficient to ask the locals: 'How is it? Is BBC after or before TV Cinq?' After a while we all get our bearings. We do not need to read the leaflet or consult the locals. The map has been internalized; it is a part of our mental equipment, and we generously share our knowledge: 'No, no, Super is just before CNN', 'Screensport comes after Lifestyle, Eurosport lies at the other end', etc.

Once again, the cable operator knows better. He knows that all the signals from all the various channels are received on one and the same screen. The only thing his leaflet actually told us was how to change the reception conditions inside the TV set. In terms of technology, the screen is nothing but a 'place', in de Certeau's sense of the word; as we know, 'the law of the "proper" rules in the place' (de Certeau 1988: 117), signals from two different channels cannot be received at the same time. But in practice we experience the screen as an opening through which we get access to another place, a place in which channels lie 'beside' each other. And as we move through this opening we 'practise' this imaginary, other place, transforming it into a space, our own 'television space'.

TOUR GUIDES

There are probably as many mental maps and as many imaginary places as there are viewers. But the design of the remote control seems to have a certain unifying effect.

Some controls allow you to zap continuously through the channels, and when there are no more possibilities the next press on the button will bring you back again to channel number one. Viewers with this type of remote control tend to imagine they are touring in a 'topological' space defined neither by distances nor by relational projectivity, but by proximities. In this kind of space the channels lie side by side, each one connected by contiguity to the previous and the next one, like pearls on a string. The viewers move like nomads through the landscape, they find their way to the preferred oasis by going from one significant landmark to the next. These topological spaces are seldom mapped; they are merely told, they remain in the mind as memories, as stories of previous tours, as fixed sequences of operations which one has to perform in order to get from one channel to the other. If they actually do settle into mental overviews the image of the topological space is usually organized as a circle; the rudimentary map maintains the structure of the string of pearls.

On other remote controls the numbers from 1 to 9 are laid out in a regular pattern similar to that on the pocket calculator or the cellular phone. In these cases the viewers tend to think of the channel universe as a rectangular space, and their mental maps are more like real maps. The channels seem to be arranged within a stable grid of coordinates, in stable relational positions. Some are close to each other; others lie at a distance. The space is ordered, organized, a pattern easily grasped. It is possible to jump from one end of the space to another; one can make shortcuts, detours, etc. This space is obviously a kind of 'Euclidean' space, but not quite, for while Euclidean spaces are 'abstract' structures, independent of the position of the subject, all 'television spaces' are very 'concrete' ones, which usually, regardless of all other, individual variations, have a basic 'orientation'.

In some cases the orientation is 'build into' the TV set. Every time it is turned on it shows the signal from channel number one. In other cases the viewers may decide where they want to start, but even in these cases there is a kind of fixed point within the imaginary universe, a channel functioning as a base from which you start and to which you usually return after the trip. In short, the viewers' maps and tours are structured according to the home–elsewhere dichotomy.

In Scandinavian countries it is usually the national public-service channel which is the centre of the universe. 'Let's go home again,' Norwegians say when they are heading for the NRK, the old public-service channel. At least, this is the case with older viewers. The younger ones do not have the same kind of loyalty towards the fallen monopolies; they establish bases of their own in the channel universe. When the teenager of the house has been watching television the MTV logo inevitably appears on the screen the next time the set is turned on. The youngest member of the family leaves his or her imaginary space via Children's Channel.

IN THE FLOW

When we go to the movies we leave our base and go on tour. On arrival we enter an institutional place, the cinema, and we practise this place by looking passively into an imaginary space in which imaginary persons are actively moving around. Obviously, the TV viewers' 'place' resembles the cinema; here, too, the core activity is that of looking across the borderline into an imaginary space. There is another similarity as well. Although 'watching television' means staying at home, the TV viewers cannot begin to practise their 'television place' before they, too, have been on a tour. In order to watch what goes on in the imaginary space of, say, a sitcom they have to leave 'home' in search of the 'right' place. But in this case the tour takes place across the borderline, as it were; it is as if the viewers were touring 'behind' the TV screen, inside the imaginary space.

'I switched to Sweden to see if there was a good movie there. But this was not the case, so after a few minutes I went back again,' a respondent says to the media researcher. A channel is placed on a specific site but is apparently also a site in itself, a site on which programmes are 'placed' ('Let's see what's on FilmNet') or on which programmes are shown ('What are they showing on TV3?'). If we are lucky we will find a 'good movie' on the Sweden site, but we cannot be sure; something else may be showing, some boring documentary for instance. If we do not like what we find we will simply 'move on' to another, more interesting site.

In his seminal work on television as cultural form, Raymond Williams (1975) used the term *flow* to describe the sequence of programmes transmitted by a given channel. The term suggests a movement in time, but also in *space*. The metaphor refers to a fixed position from which an object is seen as it moves by. It is actually a quite adequate metaphor, since, as seen from the position of the viewer, programmes do actually 'move by', they succeed each other on the screen, and many programmes are, furthermore, organized as sequences of minor units (in news programmes reports give way to interviews, commentaries, etc.).

However, behind the screen, inside the imaginary subspace, people use a quite different spatial language when they talk about what is happening on a particular channel. According to television's own discourse, it is not the programmes that 'move by', but the viewers who 'move in' or 'move on'. Even in this kind of story, one hears the anthropological language of the tour description. And, once again, the home–elsewhere dichotomy is at work.

At the level of the programmes, the announcer functions as a tour guide monitoring our movements back and forth between home and elsewhere: 'Now we are going to visit the Ewing family in Dallas', 'Now we are going home again'. At the micro-level, within the individual programmes, a similar strategy is adopted: 'Now we are going to the Persian Gulf,' says the news anchorperson; 'Back to the studio,' says the reporter. 'Before we continue with more international stories, let's have a look at the weather at home.'

SCREEN: OPENING, WINDOW PANE, BORDERLINE

When we are moving through the first imaginary space, that in which the channels are located, we constantly meet people who urge us to continue the tour; they beg us not to move on to another channel site, but to stay where we are, to explore this particular site – there are other tour possibilities here; we can move into new, secondary spaces from where we are right now.

The screen opens up to the channel space, but on each channel site there seems to be another screen, a new opening through which we may enter other spaces. In many cases the channel turns out to be a nest of Chinese boxes. Inside the channel space there is the news room; the news room opens up to the journalist's space in a faraway country; within this space there may be features which open up new spaces, etc. At each stage of the journey we may stop and watch what goes on behind a new screen, in a new space.

In the TV viewers' own stories the character of the space is constantly changing; the topological space of the itinerary is transformed into the projective space of the overview and vice versa. Their stories often refer to this oscillation between tour and map, to the double experience of travelling and watching. But even in such cases the stories are 'oriented'. They usually end up being stories about watching, which is not so strange: the reason the viewers embarked on the tour in the first place was that they wanted to 'see something'.

In these cases they often use the window pane as a metaphor for the TV screen. Explaining how he reacts to television news, one respondent says:

> You may sit inside a room where you can't see a thing, and then some-body says: It's raining outside. Oh yeah! Is it raining? You don't know that, for you can't see it. But if somebody says it's raining outside, and you go to the window and look out, then you are at least convinced that it's raining outside.

This viewer uses the story of the rain to illustrate the difference between reading a newspaper and watching the news on TV. The images on the screen are more 'convincing' than the written text, he argues; they have a special 'reality effect'. But implicitly he also describes a familiar experience. At some point there are no more imaginary spaces; you cannot go any further, you just have to stand there watching, with your face pressed to the pane. It is raining on the other side. You cannot feel the rain, you do not know if it is real rain, but you think it is, for you can see it raining, and seeing is believing, as they say.

We move around, and we watch. The screen is constantly changing. Now it is an opening, now a window pane. In the last instance it becomes what it was in the first place, a borderline. The movement cannot go on forever; there comes a time when we must stop in front of the final screen, the final pane, and look into the final space – before we resume the journey and move backwards through all the imaginary spaces, from the rain to the studio, from the studio to the channel, through the channel space 'home' to our 'own' channel site and, finally 'home' to the living-room.

MAPPING

Let us sum up. The way viewers talk about watching TV, about how they choose channels, how they think of individual programmes, and so on, indicates that all of these activities are experienced as movements in and out of imaginary spaces. And, as we have seen, these stories bear a striking resemblance to the way real locations are described in everyday language. The viewers' television spaces are oriented, 'centred'; their stories are structured according to the tour–map dichotomy; the experiences seem to have a series of features in common with 'real', topological or projective, spatial experiences.

Given the fact that experiences of modern media technology are described in the language normally used in descriptions of real spatial experiences, one might ask what is the link between these two realities? Why is it that a spontaneous media experience *can* be translated in this way? Why is it that it *can* result in stories about imaginary spaces?

It is easy to get lost if one poses questions such as these. By doing so, one has in a way already indicated that there is some kind of direct connection, that the viewers' spatial models should be understood as semiotic *representations* of the television experience, as something which 'stands for something else…in some respect or capacity', to quote C. S. Peirce's old definition of the sign (Peirce 1931; quoted in Eco 1979: 15). But it is not as simple as that. Maybe the function of these imaginary spaces can best be illustrated by reference to the art of memory as it was taught in the old rhetorical treatises.[2]

Rhetors facing the task of memorizing long, complex speeches were advised to start by dividing the text into a series of small units. Then they should imagine that they were walking through a familiar space, the interior of the local church, for example. On their imaginary tour they should stop at various points – at the altar, at the pulpit – and 'lay down' a textual unit at each location. When, finally, it was time to deliver the speech in front of an audience they would have only to embark on the imaginary journey once more, this time stopping to 'pick up' the units in exactly the same order as they originally had been 'placed' there.

It is fairly obvious that this mnemonic activity was not a representation in the ordinary sense of the word. The relation between a rhetor's discourse and his imaginary space was not semiotic. The space did not 'symbolize' the content of the speech and, although the units of speech would in many cases be represented iconically by 'images' which were placed within the space, the space itself was not related to the speech by means of 'iconical' likeness or 'indexical' causality. The imaginary space merely served as a practical, mental tool; it was an external grid which was pressed on to the discourse, a formal division which could be used to articulate any discourse regardless of content.

We all follow in the old rhetors' footsteps from time to time. Faced with difficult problems, we use the same kind of mental tools, the same kind of mental strategies; we construct imaginary, spatial models. Sometimes we do it consciously, as the rhetors did, but most of the time we do it automatically, without really thinking about it. We 'translate' complex situations into mental spaces; we divide troublesome phenomena into units; we 'place' these units on various 'locations' within a space. Some units seem to be 'beside' or 'close to' each other; others lie 'opposite' each other, and so on.

In their book *Metaphors We Live By* (1980), George Lakoff and Mark Johnson argued that metaphor is one of the most effective mental tools we have at our disposal. In a later book Lakoff uses the term *mapping* when describing the function of the metaphor (Lakoff and Turner 1989). In traditional rhetoric, metaphor is a linguistic trope based on some kind of similarity between two experiential fields, but when Lakoff uses the term 'mapping' it is not this kind of direct mirroring he has in mind. Obviously, the map and the mapped area may have a series of common denominators which may strengthen and 'naturalize' the metaphorical articulation, but this is not an absolute necessity. In Lakoff's understanding it is precisely the process of *articulation* which is the essential feature. A metaphor works by transferring the structure of a (familiar) field of experience to another (unfamiliar) one, regardless of whether there are common denominators between the two fields or not. And, as Lakoff and Johnson pointed out, spatial or 'orientational' metaphors are the most common of all, something which presumably has to do with the fact that mental mapping is 'grounded' in fundamental bodily experiences. Spatial metaphors arise, as they put it, 'from the fact that we have bodies of the sort we have and that they function as they do in our physical environment' (Lakoff and Johnson 1980: 14).

So we map our world, our experiences. Sometimes we construct mental maps of actual locations, and in these cases we make representations in the traditional sense of the word – a map represents a geographical area on the basis of an iconical likeness (the map was Peirce's prime example of iconical signs). But in most other cases we spontaneously and unconsciously use the spatial models as metaphors, as abstract systems or grids which are mapped on to fields of experience which have no spatial structure of their own. In many cases we simply use our experience of handling physical objects in space to articulate a complex, troublesome phenomenon. As Lakoff and Johnson put it: 'Once we can identify our experiences as entities or substances, we can refer to them, categorize them, group them, and quantify them – and, by this means, reason about them' (Lakoff and Johnson 1980: 25).

As far as our television experiences are concerned, one might argue that the mapping is meant to articulate and organize a phenomenon which actually has some spatial features of its own. Sitting in front of the screen we get the spontaneous experience of looking into a space, and in short sequences it is possible to maintain an elementary topological, spatial experience even though the images and the depicted spaces constantly and abruptly change. However, if one listens to the viewers' stories it is quite obvious that this is not the kind of spatial experience they are trying to map.

The screen is a 'place' in de Certeau's sense of the word, we said; two things cannot be in the same place *at the same time*. The problem the viewers talk about and which the construction of the imaginary space is meant to solve is precisely this: the problem of time, the flow of time. Images, programmes, features, etc. do actually and necessarily follow after each other on the screen during the actual experience of watching TV, since the TV set cannot receive more than one signal at a time. But, as the cable operator told us, we have 'the possibility of choosing among a multitude of different television channels'. We know that at any given time there is an abundance of programmes 'out there', programmes that could be there on the screen instead of the one we are watching at the moment. By translating this experience into a spatial model and by mapping this imaginary space on to the place of the screen, we make the experience of simultaneity *visible* in the 'mind's eye'. Time becomes a 'physical' object we can handle. Simultaneity becomes as a series of site-objects which can be watched from an elevated point of view; the flow of time becomes a sequence of operations one may 'leaf through'.

Regarded as semiotic representations, the viewers' maps are, like most other mental maps, 'misleading', 'wrong', for they are not analytical models based on exact, theoretical knowledge; they are simple summaries of how situations and phenomena are experienced in the everyday mind. Nevertheless, or perhaps therefore, they function very well. They enable us to grasp and to remember complicated, confusing phenomena, to perform the routines of everyday life in a practical, sensible way. They enable us to live with and handle the television set, to comprehend an incomprehensible technology.

ACKNOWLEDGEMENT

This chapter is a revised version of a paper presented to the IAMCR conference in São Paolo, Brazil, in August 1992. The question of 'imaginary spaces' in relation to contemporary science fiction films is discussed in another paper (Larsen 1995).

NOTES

1 The interviews were done by Ingunn Hagen as part of her PhD thesis on the reception of television news in Norway (Hagen 1992).
2 The old treatises all rely on the 'memoria' section in *Ad Herennium* (86–82 BC), the only surviving Latin presentation of the classical 'art of memory' (see Yates 1966).

REFERENCES

de Certeau, Michel (1988) 'Spatial stories', *The Practice of Everyday Life*, Berkeley, CA, London and Los Angeles, CA: University of California Press.

Eco, Umberto (1979) *A Theory of Semiotics*, Bloomington, IN: Indiana University Press.

Hagen, Ingunn (1992) *News Viewing Ideals and Everyday Practices*, Bergen: Department of Mass Communication, University of Bergen.

Lakoff, George and Johnson, Mark (1980) *Metaphors We Live By*, Chicago, IL: University of Chicago Press.

Lakoff, George and Turner, Mark (1989) *More Than Cool Reason: A Field Guide to Poetic Metaphor*, Chicago, IL: University of Chicago Press.

Larsen, Peter (1995) 'The cities of the future, the future of the cities', paper presented to the conference on Movies and Metropolis, Centre for Urbanity and Aesthetics, University of Copenhagen, December.

Linde, Charlotte and Labov, William (1975) 'Spatial networks as a site for the study of language and thought', *Language* 51: 924–34.

Peirce, C. S. (1931) *Collected Papers*, Cambridge, MA: Harvard University Press, section 2.228.

Piaget, Jean and Inhelder, Bärbel (1948) *La Réprésentation de l'espace chez l'enfant*, Paris: Presses universitaires de France.

Williams, Raymond (1975) *Television: Technology and Cultural Form*, London: Fontana/Collins.

Yates, Frances (1966) *The Art of Memory*, London: Routledge & Kegan Paul, 1966.

Part III

GENRES

8

KNOWLEDGE AS RECEIVED

A project on audience uses of television news in
world cultures

Klaus Bruhn Jensen

INTRODUCTION

In 1992 a tiny majority of the Danish population voted against full membership
of the new European Union (EU). This happened in spite of the fact that almost
the entire Danish political establishment and practically all Danish news media
supported the EU. A year later, in a second referendum, a somewhat larger, but still
quite small majority of the Danish electorate voted for the EU, provoking, among
other responses, unprecedented riots in the streets of Copenhagen.

During the early 1990s the wider European public witnessed, through the
news media, several other developments that might be difficult to account for. In
Eastern Europe and the former Soviet Union the political, economic and military
unions of the past dissolved. This happened in spite of the fact that a number of
powerful interests, both within the countries and in international political-
economic cooperation, both inside and outside the media, presumably would
have preferred a stable framework supporting production and the rest of social
life, at least during an interim period. Concurrently, cultural, ethnic and religious
sentiments reappeared on the surface of society, having been 'forgotten' for ages,
at least in many political circles and media.

All of these developments can be interpreted as evidence that a significant
aspect of the phenomenon which news media and politicians commonly refer to
as the formation of 'public opinion' goes unnoticed in the media. In certain cases
the undercurrents of communication and interaction in society apparently accu-
mulate to produce momentous change. The project entitled News of the World
examines the everyday frames of understanding and communicative processes that
audiences bring to bear on political mass communication within different cultural
contexts. The research question may be summed up thus: what happens to the
flow of information in the world once it is received and used by the audience-
public?

This chapter outlines the background, aims and methods of the project. The study takes advantage of recent developments in basic research, applying the models and analytical tools of qualitative reception analysis to issues in international communication with major policy implications. The first section surveys previous research about, on the one hand, the flow of news in the world and, on the other hand, the audiences for television news. Second, the chapter presents the design of the project, which is the first specifically cross-cultural study of television news viewers in international reception studies. The research questions focus on the potential uses of television news by viewers as a resource for citizenship – locally, regionally, nationally and, in principle, transnationally. In conclusion, the chapter discusses the explanatory value of the study as an intervention in the ongoing research debate about the active, localized audience versus the entrenched, global structures of media institutions. Comparative cross-cultural studies may have particular relevance, not only for theory development, but also for assessing the relative determination of audience decodings and uses of media by texts and social contexts. The challenge for communication studies remains one of explaining not only what media do to audiences, or what audiences do with media, but also how media and audiences interact as agents of what one of the founding fathers of semiotics, Ferdinand de Saussure, called 'the life of signs in society' (de Saussure 1959: 16).

THE FLOW OF INTERNATIONAL NEWS

Issues and debates

Since the 1970s public debate on the flow of information in the world, particularly news, has been intensifying (for summary position statements, see MacBride 1980). A major complaint has been that the international news media significantly misrepresent local political and cultural realities around the world, perhaps unwittingly for institutional or organizational reasons, but with potentially damaging consequences both for such local communities and for international communication in the true sense of the word. The debate is, in part, a legacy of colonialism, addressing decolonization in the areas of culture and communication; it also is restating the question – particularly following the break-up of communist political systems in Eastern Europe after 1989 – of the degree to which a free market may ensure a balanced flow of information.

While much of the debate has centred on the role of the international news agencies as gatekeepers in international communication (for an overview, see Boyd-Barrett and Thussu 1992), the debate has further implications for the structure of modern societies, in technological as well as institutional terms, and for the public's access to the means of communication in these societies. If a society may be looked upon as a system of communication, both the available technologies of communication and their specific institutional form represent enabling conditions of the entire social structure, its reproduction and reformation. In

Giddens's (1984) terms, the media exercise an agency that is constitutive of the social structure. One of the historical characteristics of modern society is the use of communication technologies for the reorganization of time, space and social relations on an unprecedented scale (Thompson 1990). One measure of democracy in modern societies is the extent to which communication technologies are organized so as to enable public access, not just to media as such, but to the contexts of social action that media inform and facilitate. At stake is the right not just to speak, but also to be heard in relevant contexts, whether community politics or international cooperation.

These implications of the news-flow debate, together with its historical links with questions of colonialism and cultural identity, help to explain its vehemence and persistence in international media politics. The issues have also been high on the agenda of international communication research since the 1970s.

Contents and organizations

Two bodies of research, in particular, have examined news flow. On the one hand, content analyses have been carried out to document the distribution of different categories of news, their coverage of different regions of the world, their origin in the news organizations of different nations and their retransmission to different cultural contexts. The question posed, in sum, is whether the international news media discriminate against particular geographical regions or cultural traditions when representing them to themselves and others, either by neglecting them through non-selection or selection only in the incriminating case, or by reconstructing them within a foreign frame of understanding with negative connotations and marginalizing implications.

An early example of such a content analysis – which was not, however, conceived to address the world information order – was Wilbur Schramm's (1959) study of one day of information reported in newspapers from around the world in 1956, at the time of the Hungarian and Suez crises. This study assessed the newspapers as a basis for action by national leaderships, and found that 'quality' papers offered more non-local and serious news to this end, even if they still contained an average of about 60 per cent news about their own country. With Galtung and Ruge's (1965) analysis of news criteria, the agenda was set for a broader examination of how the news media represent the world to world audiences, and with what implications (but see the incisive critique of this classic by Hjarvard 1992).

Since then a variety of studies have examined international news flow, especially television news, many of them in the context of the UNESCO discussions of the New World Information and Communication Order (NWICO), which became the political arena of the flow debate (see, for example, Varis and Jokelin 1976; for an overview, see Wallis and Baran 1990). Even though studies have documented what are arguably specific imbalances of content, the further conclusion that international television news flow is characterized by the same imbalance between North and South, and between West and East, as is found in the exchange of other television programming (Varis 1985) would need more empirical substantiation. Moreover, the charge of imbalance raises several theoretical problems, one of them arising from the fundamental difficulty of defining a standard of balance in the reporting of events from economically, politically and militarily powerful, as opposed to not so powerful, nations. And behind this massive research effort lurks the danger that it may, in the end, provide ammunition for shooting the messenger who both identifies and is symptomatic of certain, more profound imbalances in the distribution of material and symbolic resources.

On the other hand, studies of the production of television news have consistently found that the routines of news work take precedence over both personal and ideological factors that might shape the news. Following early studies which conceived of journalists and editors as gatekeepers on the avenue leading from sources to audiences (White 1950), the 1970s, in particular, witnessed major studies which highlighted the financial and bureaucratic constraints of journalism, as well as the routinized interaction of journalists with officials and other sources (see, especially, Gans 1979; Golding and Elliott 1979; Tuchman 1978). Later studies have specified, for example, the role of visuals in the selection and formatting of television news stories (Cohen et al., 1996). In relation to the flow debate, the production studies suggest that news media essentially work like other modern bureaucracies, being dependent on specific resources and competences which may only be modified marginally, incrementally and in the long term.

News as received

Whereas the potential 'effects' of media are undoubtedly the most widely researched aspect of mass communication – and, indeed, the main social justification of the field – earlier research addressing issues of flow focused on the structures of news content and on the routines and organizations of journalism. This may have been due, first, to the importance of establishing a concrete standard of reference for policy discussions: An inventory of news items – in terms of their availability as information from particular sources to particular national or international news organizations, as well as in terms of their selection for presentation to a specific local or national audience – is a necessary condition for any informed debate on balance, or lack thereof. Second, knowledge of the standards and procedures which may explain how journalistic organizations come to select and present particular items of information as news is indispensable, not just for explaining the anatomy of contemporary news media, but also for attempting any reform of news media, whether at the level of individual journalists, organizational practices or institutional frameworks.

Third, although the 'effects' issue can be detected at the heart of the flow debate – including its concern about 'cultural imperialism' since, for example,

Schiller's (1969) classic statement – the familiar problems of how to establish the direction of causality, or even of how to establish a determining factor in a complex social and cultural context, are multiplied in a cross-cultural study of how audiences respond to transnational news. The standard survey and experimental methodologies of audience research, which parallel the quantitative content analyses predominating in earlier flow studies, have important limitations for the task at hand.

So far, no specifically comparative, cross-cultural studies of audience interpretation, experience and uses of (television) news have been available. Such studies, while highlighting similarities and differences between nations and cultures, would also be able to address the question of how audiences participate in the production and circulation of meaning in society, with implications for both political participation and the engagement of different cultures with global issues. By analogy to other forms of production, meaning production has its bottlenecks, a strategic one being the audience; unless audiences comprehend the basic information and perceive it as relevant to their perspective on the world, the news media must be said to face a crisis of legitimacy as fourth-estate institutions (Habermas 1989).

Since the late 1970s theories, models and methods for addressing the question of audience participation have been developed within several traditions of qualitative reception analysis. Reviews of the literature (Jensen 1991a; Morley and Silverstone 1991) suggest that recent research recovers and re-articulates an historical undercurrent of both social-scientific and humanistic communication research while beginning to integrate the two research traditions. The common denominator has been the development of qualitative methodologies relying on interviews, observation and records to probe the categories and criteria that audiences apply to media as they incorporate mass communication into the rest of their everyday practices.

NEWS OF THE WORLD: PROJECT OUTLINE

Sponsored by UNESCO and the International Association for Mass Communication Research (Jensen 1991b), the News of the World project has applied several methodologies to questions of news flow and reception in seven different countries (Germany took part in several early stages of the project):

- Belarus;
- Denmark;
- India;
- Israel;
- Italy;
- Mexico;
- the USA.

From the outset we had to choose between two possible strategies for this type of comparative project: we would either have to translate all the materials into a common working language, thus losing important linguistic and conceptual distinctions; or we would have to conduct the collection and analysis of data in the 'local' languages according to common detailed guidelines, to be supplemented with translated excerpts which could be discussed in theoretical and methodological terms at meetings of the project group. Whereas practical and financial considerations suggest the latter strategy, it is also recommended by theoretical deliberations. It is crucial that the analysis stays close the 'language', concepts, or signs that respondents employ (Pike's (1967) 'emic' categories), before constructing more general, 'etic' categories to articulate distinctions and relationships in the material across the participating countries. This theoretical point is supported by preliminary empirical findings.

The project comprises three main elements. First, during the week of 5–11 May 1993, dubbed 'Newsweek', the main newscasts from all national channels in all the countries were recorded. Local, regional and transnational (e.g. CNN) newscasts were not recorded, but they enter into the studies to the extent that they were brought into discussions by the respondents. The purpose of the recordings was partly to prepare for a comparative content analysis of newscasts, partly to document a significant element of the news coverage – including, importantly, the visuals – which could be expected to inform the interviews with viewers about 'important events in the news'.

Second, individual interviews were conducted with all the members of the households that participated in the project, preferably in the household, otherwise by telephone, in advance of the subsequent household interview. The individual interviews addressed 'the most important events currently in the news'; sources of information about these events; and the respondents' background data. The purpose was, on the one hand, to allow each respondent to consider the issue of important news events before interacting with the others in the household interview. On the other hand, it would be possible to compare the general principled statements concerning news value that are implied in such individual interviews with the more concrete statements occurring in the household interviews with reference to a specific programme that had been watched jointly by the household and interviewer.

Third, on 11 May 1993, dubbed 'Newsday', all the participating countries conducted group interviews with selected households after the members of each household had watched a news programme of their own choice. During viewing and during the interviewer's two visits in the household a brief observation was conducted, including preparation of a diagram of the room where the viewing took place.

The household interviews constitute the pivot of the study in each country. Furthermore, within the household interview the respondents' retelling of 'the most important stories', both national and international, in their own words was of special importance, since the retelling bears witness to the conceptual categories and frames of understanding with which viewers encounter the news. On the basis of close analyses of the interview discourses, special attention was given to four aspects of news reception:

- viewer assessments of TV as compared to other news media;
- the place of TV news in the immediate context of viewing and its everyday routines;
- uses and relevance of news in other social contexts;
- and 'super-themes', defined as the thematic constructs by which viewers are able to establish a link between the world of news and the world of everyday life.

Our epistemological premise has been that different scientific methodologies serve different ends; 'how' depends on 'what' and 'why' (Kvale 1987). While drawing on the available evidence about the ratings and demographics of news audiences, the project addresses questions which shorter, standardized interviews with larger samples of respondents could hardly address in a valid manner. A relatively small number of household interviews (10–15 in each country), in addition to the equivalent number of observations and individual interviews, have been conducted, producing large data sets of interview discourses and observation notes, and a documentation of the news content. Media discourses and audience discourses are the analytical points of access to the process of reception, being discursive and cognitive interfaces between medium and viewer. Preliminary findings from Denmark about the super-themes suggest the types of answer which the project may produce.

PRELIMINARY FINDINGS

One element of the findings can be summed up in the form of the model in Figure 8.1. Despite many specifications and variations, the model may be thought of as a matrix of the respondents' conception of the world, as mediated in part through the news. As discussed below, the axes can serve as an analytical point of departure for comparisons between societies and cultures, whereas the specific super-themes referred to in Figure 8.1 derive from the Danish data.

The *horizontal* axis indicates the space in which the viewers find themselves, together with the events in the news. It should be stressed that this is both a mental and a social space, bounded not by absolute geographical distance, but by experienced distance from the event. In the respondents' own concepts, events can be placed on an axis from 'our little corner of the world', which is almost too close to home, to 'the war', which is far afield in a no-man's land of social madness.

The *vertical* axis refers to the ranking of 'those who take the rap' under 'those who are in charge'. Even if the interviews document differences in terms of how respondents place themselves on this axis in relation to different events, it is clear

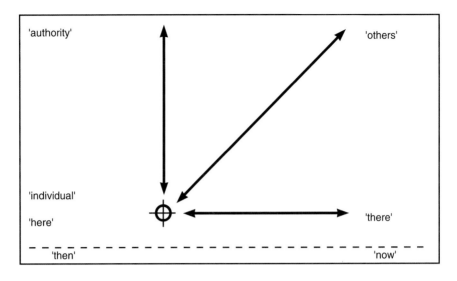

Figure 8.1 A model of news reception

that the relations of power between social institutions and the individual viewer are the key to the interpretation of specific news items.

The *diagonal* axis establishes the relationship between the viewer, the symbol in the bottom left-hand corner, and his or her significant others (Mead 1934). The point is that we derive our identity – socially, culturally, ethnically – from our interaction with others and their perspective on us. 'The others' may be the family, an interest group, a religious formation, and so forth. The respondents refer to the axis, for example, when they compare themselves to people in developing countries or in the former Yugoslavia, and when they place themselves in a group that 'takes the rap'. In other words, the respondents assign meaning and relevance to the horizontal and vertical axes according to the categories and values that are generated from the diagonal axis. We become 'ourselves' only in relation to 'others' in the rest of the social structure and the world.

An *historical* axis, finally, is introduced by the respondents as a means of orientation in relation to current events. One example of an historical event orienting present interpretations is the Second World War, specifically the German occupation of Denmark in 1940–5, which appears in the Danish interviews both as a parallel to the events in the former Yugoslavia and as a background to the debate on the EU, including the role of Germany in the Europe of the future.

The main implication for further comparative analysis is the possibility of accommodating two different perspectives on the news experience within the model. According to Kenneth Pike (1967), an analytical distinction should be made in studies of communicative and other social action between what he calls 'emic' and 'etic' perspectives. Pike extrapolated his categories from the study of linguistic sounds, which distinguishes between a phonetic approach assuming a universal set of sounds and a phonemic approach focusing on the distinctive set of sounds constituting a particular language (*ibid.*: ch. 2). The emic–etic distinction is matched by a further set of conceptual pairs, including internal–external, specific–cross-cultural, and relational–absolute units of analysis. In anthropology and other social sciences the distinction has emphasized the importance of a dual approach to meaning, exploring both the categories of understanding from the perspective of the participants in the culture and the possibility of developing a conceptual common denominator that enables a comparative analysis of several cultural perspectives.

In the present context the super-themes in the Danish material represent the emic perspective. These are categories of understanding that may enable viewers to make sense of the news from the perspective of their particular social and cultural setting. It is for further analysis to determine whether the four thematic headings indicated here constitute the emic perspective as such, or whether they make up a medium level of analysis between certain overarching super-themes of reception, such as 'power corrupts', and the abstract, analytical axes. The analytical axes, then, represent the etic perspective, incorporating common categories of social structure, including time, space and institutional as well as interpersonal relations. The explanatory value of comparable mental schemata is suggested by current cognitive approaches to culture and meaning (for example Johnson 1987), and the peculiar flexibility of the super-themes, which are interpretative constructs that are simultaneously abstract–general and concrete–complex, may be accounted for by recent network models of meaning as developed within both semiotics and cognitive science (see Jensen 1995: ch. 10). The next step in the project will be to assess the extent to which the current model may serve to specify and explain similarities and differences between the data sets of the participating countries.

IMPLICATIONS FOR THEORY AND POLICY

Both this project and other reception analyses have found that media audiences are able to identify, interpret and appreciate other, hidden, realities behind the surface discourse of text and image. It is this ability, in part, that has led studies to characterize audiences as sophisticated and critical users of mass communication. However, the ability of these Danish respondents to account for such hidden realities and their reliance on the super-themes are of at least two different kinds. Moreover, two modes of reception appear to be related to the respondents' social background, implying two social as well as interpretative formations. It should be underlined that the study does not speculate on quantitative measures such as what percentage of Danish viewers belong to one or the other formation, or what percentage rely on particular themes in their reception and uses of news. The qualitative methodology, instead, documents the existence of two types of reception, which are distinguished by their specific articulation and configuration of themes, as well as by the social background of the actual respondents articulating them.

133

The first group refers to a double reality in terms of 'conspiracies'. Such arrangements may be seen to underlie both news events and the fact that certain events are covered in the news (even though reference to manipulation in the news is not a major criticism here). Examples include coverage of the taxation of vans which clearly shows vehicles of a particular make, perhaps by agreement between the journalist and the automobile salesman, and developments in the meat industry that might be accounted for as a conspiracy between the industry and the supermarkets marketing their products, and against the best interests of both workers and consumers. This group of respondents, however, finds it difficult to go beyond the super-themes to specify agendas, issues, decisions and implications regarding a particular news item. From their perspective, at least some news may be grasped through super-themes only. In socio-demographic terms, the respondents articulating this reception have a relatively shorter education, up to between two and four years of studies following ten years' basic schooling.

The other group represents an educational elite, primarily with a longer professional or university education. Whereas references to the same super-themes are found among these respondents – and while they appear to reproduce the same mental matrix of axes in the interview discourses – they are able to move beyond the super-themes, for example discussing both the details of the issues in the meat-industry conflict and its social implications concerning a gap between the top and the bottom of the union movement. Regarding the double realities, these respondents indicate the importance in society of 'structures', rather than individuals or particular organizations, as factors determining the impersonal 'decisions' and 'developments' that affect the ordinary viewer.

In conclusion, the model begins to suggest an interpretative framework which, in different articulations, may structure the reception and social uses of television news. These findings supplement the respondents' assessment of different news media, for example according to criteria that might make them both comprehensible and relevant in the everyday context. The findings also suggest the difficulties of developing an institution of political communication, in both organizational and discursive terms, that would fulfil the promise that news can be a resource for political and other social action. The super-themes make up a two-edged sword, facilitating sense-making, but discriminating against those who may not be able to act on their meaning.

ACKNOWLEDGEMENT

This paper, given at the symposium on Media and Knowledge: The Role of Television at the University of Bergen, in Norway, from 30 September to 1 October 1995, is a revised version of working papers from the News of the World project presented to conferences of the International Association for Mass Communication Research, Seoul, Korea, in 1994, and of the International Communication Association, Albuquerque, New Mexico, USA, in 1995.

REFERENCES

Boyd-Barrett, O. and Thussu, D. (1992) *Contra-Flow in Global News*, London: John Libbey.

Cohen, A., Levy, M., Roeh, I. and Gurevitch, M. (1996) *The Eurovision News Exchange: Global Newsrooms, Local Audiences*, London: John Libbey.

de Saussure, F. (1959) *Course in General Linguistics*, London: Peter Owen; originally published 1916.

Galtung, J. and Ruge, M. (1965) *The Structure of Foreign News*, in J. Tunstall (ed.) (1970) *Media Sociology: A Reader*, London: Constable.

Gans, H. (1979) *Deciding What's News*, New York: Pantheon.

Giddens, A. (1984) *The Constitution of Society*, Berkeley, CA: University of California Press.

Golding, P. and Elliott, P. (1979) *Making the News*, London: Longman.

Habermas, J. (1989) *The Structural Transformation of the Public Sphere*, Cambridge, MA: MIT Press; originally published 1962.

Hjarvard, S. (1992) 'Reconsidering a paradigm: Galtung and Ruge. An empirical, methodological, and theoretical examination of "The structure of foreign news" and the "Structural theory of imperialism"', paper presented to the 18th Conference of the International Association for Mass Communication Research, São Paulo, Brazil, 16–21 August.

Jensen, Klaus Bruhn (1991a) 'Reception analysis: mass communication as the social production of meaning', in K. B. Jensen and N. W. Jankowski (eds) *A Handbook of Qualitative Methodologies for Mass Communication Research*, London: Routledge.

—— (1991b) *News of the World: The Reception and Social Uses of Television News Around the World. A Project Outline*, Paris: UNESCO.

—— (1995) *The Social Semiotics of Mass Communication*, London: Sage Publications.

Johnson, M. (1987) *The Body in the Mind*, Chicago, IL: University of Chicago Press.

Kvale, S. (1987) 'Validity in the qualitative research interview', *Methods* 1: 37–72.

MacBride, Sean (1980) *Many Voices, One World*, Paris: UNESCO.

Mead, George Herbert (1934) *Mind, Self, and Society*, Chicago, IL: University of Chicago Press.

Morley, D. and Silverstone, R. (1991) 'Communication and context: ethnographic perspectives on the media audience', in K. B. Jensen and N. W. Jankowski (eds) *A Handbook of Qualitative Methodologies for Mass Communication Research*, London: Routledge.

Pike, K. (1967) *Language in Relation to a Unified Theory of the Structure of Human Behavior*, 2nd edn, The Hague: Mouton.

Schiller, H. (1969) *Mass Communications and American Empire*, New York: Kelley.

Schramm, W. (1959) *One Day in the World's Press*, Stanford, CA: Stanford University Press.

Thompson, J. (1990) *Ideology and Modern Culture*, Cambridge: Polity Press.

Tuchman, G. (1978) *Making News*, New York: Free Press.

Varis, T. (1985) *International Flow of Television Programs*, Paris: UNESCO.

Varis, T. and Jokelin, R. (1976) *Television News in Europe: A Survey of the News-film Flow in Europe*, Tampere, Finland: Institute of Journalism and Mass Communication.

Wallis, R. and Baran, S. (1990) *The Known World of Broadcast News*, London: Routledge.

White, D. (1950) 'The "gate keeper": a case study in the selection of news', *Journalism Quarterly* 27: 383–90.

9

FINDING OUT ABOUT THE WORLD FROM TELEVISION NEWS

Some difficulties

David Morley

INTRODUCTION

> Trying to find out what's going on in the world by watching the television news is like trying to find out what time it is by watching the second hand on the clock.
>
> Walter Lippman

Autobiographically speaking, the above quote certainly informs my own media consumption patterns. I watch very little television news, except when reports in another medium have alerted me to some possibly interesting visual dimension to a news event, in which case I may decide to watch it on television, specifically to see what the event *looks* like. The advantages of print seem obvious to me, so far as news goes. I can choose a newspaper designed to address my interests, in a way that I cannot on television. I can then use the printed medium more efficiently, imposing my own schedule and sequence of selections on it, starting with the back or middle pages, if I choose, scanning or skipping through the bits I am bored by, or going directly to what interests me (cf. Hagen 1992 for similar findings among middle-class viewers in Norway). With a newspaper I do not have to sit through the imposed chronology of television time (or, the postmodern equivalent, have to scroll through the interminable pages of junk on my computer screen before I finally get what I am after).

However, I notice that often the thing I do first with my morning newspaper is turn to the television pages – to see if there's 'anything on' that I may want to watch on television that evening. Thus the first thing I use my newspaper for is to give me 'news' about television, in relation to the one obvious form of action that I can take in response to items in the paper – i.e. my decisions concerning what, if anything, to watch on television. So, one of the few areas in which the newspaper gives me 'news' on which I can act is in relation to what's available to me as a consumer of other media.

What is at stake in all this? Perhaps some very old questions remain on our agenda. I have noted elsewhere (Morley 1992: ch. 12) the continuing relevance, in my own view, of Merton's and Lazarsfeld's (1948) anxieties about what they called the 'narcoticizing dysfunctions' of contemporary news media. They were concerned that exposure to a flood of media information might 'narcoticize' audiences rather than motivate people to action. Thus, in their image of the (necessarily masculine?) media consumer, they suggest that

> He is concerned. He is informed. He has all sorts of ideas about what should be done. But, after he has gotten through his dinner and listened to his favorite radio programmes and read his second newspaper, it really is time for bed.
>
> (Merton and Lazarsfeld 1948; quoted in Morley 1992: 252)

In a similar way, Brian Groombridge, writing in the early 1970s, pointed to the fact that, for most people, most of the time, 'the news' has little real significance for them, in so far as for most people, most of the time, it is not clear what, if anything, can be done with most of the information received from the news. Hence it is very badly assimilated, if at all. The audience's sense of powerlessness over the world reported on the news frames their fundamental attitude towards any specific news story/report (see Groombridge 1972). It is this issue – the sense of alienation from the 'world of news' – that concerns me here.

In England, both Graham Martin (1973) and Raymond Williams (1974) have analysed the role of popular newspapers in addressing that large majority of politically disenfranchised readers for whom news and political events are simply not news about a world in which they feel they can meaningfully act. For such people, these media can only offer a 'surrogate' sense of connection to this 'wider world' by means of the reported activities of 'stars' and 'personalities', who function in a kind of analogy to actual known or observed persons (cf. Hello magazine for a contemporary example of this type of journalism, now being busily reinvented in televisual terms by Channel 5 in the UK; see also Gripsrud 1992 on the role of the popular press in supplying melodramatic stories – sensationalized and personalized – for otherwise alienated readers).

Groombridge (1972) argues that it is the gap between the availability of lots of information via the news media and the lack of opportunity to act, in practice, on any of that information (except, perhaps, the local traffic news) that accounts for what he calls the paradoxical (or perhaps wilful?) 'ignorance' of the public at large in this information/media-rich environment. It is exactly this same sense of powerlessness, I believe, which informs the following account, by a working-class British woman (who I interviewed in an earlier project; see Morley 1986) as to why she rarely watches national television news (cf. Hagen 1992 on the 'more local orientation' of working-class viewers in Norway). Her strong preference is for local news, which pertains to a universe to which she has an intensely practical relationship, and her reasons for this preference are, to my mind, perfectly cogent:

> Sometimes I like to watch the news, if it's something that's gone on – like where that little boy's gone [an abduction] and what's happened to him. Otherwise I don't, not unless it's local, only when there's something that's happened that's local....National news gets on my nerves....I can't stand *World in Action* and *Panorama* [prime-time British current affairs programmes] and all that. It's wars all the time. You know, it gets on your nerves....What I read in the papers and listen to on the news is bad enough for me. I don't want to know about the Chancellor Somebody in Germany and all that. When I've seen it once I don't want to see it again. I hate seeing it again – because it's on at breakfast time, dinner time, and tea time, you know, the same news all day long. It bores me. What's going on in the world? I don't understand it, so I don't like to listen to that. I watch – like those little kids [the abduction] – that gets to me. I want to know about it. Or if there's actually a crime in [my local area], like rapes and the rest of it, I want to read up on that; see if they've been caught and locked away. As for like when the guys says 'The pound's gone up' and 'the pound's gone down' I don't want to know all about that, 'cause I don't understand it. It's complete ignorance really. If I was to understand it all, I would probably get interested in it.
>
> (Morley 1986: 169)

The same finding emerges from a more recent newspaper survey of the British public's level of information about 'current affairs' as reported in the media. In a report by Helen Fielding (1995) a large number of people were interviewed about events 'in the news' at that time, and the majority of those interviewed displayed a strikingly low level of knowledge and understanding of these events. One of Fielding's interviewees, a 31-year-old community development officer, who had mistaken Israel for Alaska when shown a map of the world, and who was unable to name the leader of the British parliamentary opposition party, cheerfully explained to the journalist that the simple reason for her 'ignorance', in these respects, was that:

> These things have nothing to do with me. I'm a single mother, black, working with homelessness and young people on the streets. I'm not interested in people at the top. They don't help us. The people who help are local people. I could name you 30 friends of mine that don't vote. I like soaps, I know about jazz and soul and fashion.
>
> (quoted in Fielding 1995)

Clearly, knowledge and expertise come in a large number of different forms and genres (cf. Bourdieu 1984), and one person's 'ignorance', is another person's irrelevance. 'Knowledge' is always a matter of class, race and gender positioning, among other things.

This story developed a further twist when, late in 1995, the BBC decided to introduce a 'test' of knowledgeability about popular culture for its prospective trainee producers as part of a strategy to ensure that they did not 'lose touch' with their audience. Helen Fielding herself then further complicated matters when, in her fictional persona Bridget Jones ('The Diary of Bridget Jones' was a weekly column in the *Independent* newspaper, and since then has been published in book form), she boasted about her own confidence in passing such a 'popular culture' test (Bridget was a researcher in a small independent TV production company). Bridget's confidence was founded on the fact that she had no problem, for instance, in giving the full names of various pop stars' children and politicians' mistresses. Unfortunately, this expertise availed her little; on the day of her test, it transpired that, unfortunately for her, her own company had plans to go 'up market', into business news. Thus Bridget's particular form of highly developed (popular) 'cultural capital' gave her little advantage in the face of questions concerning the exact workings of European monetary union. She was, it seemed, after all, just an 'ignorant girl' who possessed the wrong sort of (in her case gendered) 'knowledge', and she was penalized accordingly. If the mode of address of traditional public-service news and current affairs programming can be characterized as 'serious, official and impersonal...aimed at producing understanding and belief' (Fiske 1992; quoted in Branston 1993: 5), then it is clear that the 'believing subject' which it aims to interpellate is by no means always available for conscription. In this connection Gripsrud quotes Sparks's (1988) comments to the effect that many working-class people are 'much more interested in sport and entertainment and sexual scandal than in knowing about the world of politics' simply because 'political and economic power in a stable bourgeois democracy is so far removed from the real lives of the mass of the population that they have no interest, in either sense, in monitoring its disposal' (Gripsrud 1992: 93). As Gripsrud observes, in such a situation it may be quite rational for working-class people to respond along such lines as 'society is run by others, or runs its own course. It does not seem to be my business. Why should I care? Why not concentrate on the apolitical, which normally has greater entertainment value' (*ibid.*: 93).

One fundamental question here concerns the relative importance of 'fact' and 'fiction' on television. The simple fact (sic) is that most people watch fiction on television most of the time. Notwithstanding this, media studies, in many places, has long continued to grant special emphasis and importance to the study of 'serious' factual programming. However, in societies like many of those in the West – with rapidly declining indices of overall public participation in political affairs (as measured by voting etc.) and increasing numbers of people excluded or alienated, for one reason or another, from the process of formal politics on which 'serious television' focuses – this may well be an inadvisable strategy. To transpose a famous saying of Brecht's, it seems as if, the viewers having failed ('serious') television, some in media studies think that it may be necessary to dissolve the audience and 'elect' another. Of course, the other alternative would be to pay attention to whatever it is that the audience does seem to think is 'real', 'important' and/or 'serious', rather than to berate (or ignore) them when their choices are at odds with our presumptions.

DECODING THE TELEVISION NEWS

Given my own research background and interests in matters of media consumption, I will now attempt to focus on some of these issues more sharply by addressing a number of difficulties that have arisen in debates concerning the decoding of television news in recent years. For my own part, I continue to believe that Hall's encoding–decoding model remains our best starting point, but it clearly needs amending in various ways (Hall 1980). In particular, there is a need to differentiate the moment of comprehension more clearly from the moment of interpretation/evaluation of 'messages' (cf. Corner 1980). Hall's model tends to focus primarily on the second of these issues. In particular, it tends to be concerned with mapping the limits of dominant readings and the extent of 'negotiated' or 'oppositional' readings as indexical of the limits of ideological power. It can also be argued that the model is based on what could be called an 'integration-fearing' conceptual framework (where the 'danger' is the integration of subordinate groups into some dominant ideology) and it will always (correspondingly) tend to celebrate moments of 'resistance'. However, there is another sociological tradition (cf. the work of Mann 1973; Abercrombie *et al.* 1984) which argues that we should not be so worried about the 'dangers' of the political integration of the working class into some dominant ideology (or so thrilled when we find evidence of their 'escape' from it). For these theorists, the main political 'danger' is not, in fact, one of ideological integration or incorporation, but of 'incoherence' – in particular, a kind of disempowering, cynical, alienated, uncommitted incoherence experienced especially by many working-class people, as well as other marginalized groups.

From this perspective, we might also want to re-emphasize the comprehension–incomprehension dimension of decoding rather than the acceptance–rejection of ideology model. What we might perhaps then focus on is not so much moments of 'resistance' to ideology, but moments of disaffection, incomprehension and resignation, where many people may fail to make 'dominant' readings of the news, for example, but where this failure is not necessarily anything to celebrate. These people may simply lack the particular forms of literacy and other cultural resources necessary to read this material at all. Alternatively, they may have strong cultural reasons for deciding not to bother with it but, at the same time, lack the resources to develop any coherent alternative perspective on the events reported in the news media, so that, by default, if and when their attention is turned to these events, they are still reliant on what the news media tell them.

In *The Ideological Octopus* (1991) Justin Lewis points to an important issue concerning the formal structure of television news. As he notes, television news lacks the narrative structure (or suspense-development dynamic) which, in other genres, serves to capture viewer interest and thus motivate viewing. Lewis posits this as one of the key reasons why (1) television news often fails to interest people and (2) why, when they do watch it, people often cannot understand it. Lewis argues that one fundamental problem with watching television news is that its narrative structure means that the viewer is offered the punchline before the joke – because the main point (the headline) comes right at the beginning, after which the programme, by definition, deals with less and less important things. Thus, in television news our interest is not awakened by an enigma which is then gradually solved, to provide a gratifying resolution – as often happens in fictional narratives. In Lewis's terms, in television news there is no hermeneutic enigma, the solution of which will motivate the viewing process. As he baldly states, 'If we decided to try to design a television programme with a structure that would completely fail to capture an audience's interest, we might well (finally) come up with the format of the average television news show' (Lewis 1991: 131).

What Lewis also does is offer an interesting contrast, in this respect, between the high-status phenomenon of television news and the low-status genre of soap opera. The latter, he observes, offers the most highly developed use of effective hermeneutic/narrative codes. To that extent soap opera, with its multiple narratives, could then be seen, in formal terms, as the most effective type of television for the cultivation of viewer interest, and certainly as a far more effective form than that of television news for this purpose. Clearly, some of Lewis's speculation here is problematic. There are counter-examples of his arguments (e.g. instances of programmes such as sports news which share the problematic formal features he points to but which are nonetheless popular – at least among certain types of viewers). Moreover, he may perhaps overstress the importance of formal features as against content relevance in providing the basis for programme appeal. Nonetheless, I would suggest that his argument, in this respect, is of considerable interest.

THE WORLD AND THE TELEVISION WORLD

Lewis argues not only that soap opera is more narratively interesting than television news, in formal terms, but, moreover, that the world of television fiction in general is much closer to most people's lives than that presented in the news. This, he claims, is because the world of television fiction often *feels* to people like their own lives. They can, for example, identify readily with the moral issues and personal dilemmas faced by the characters in a favourite soap opera. Conversely, the world of television news is much more remote in all senses; it is a socially distant world populated by another race of special or 'elite' persons, the world of 'them' not 'us'. This is also why 'most people feel more able to evaluate TV fiction than television news…because it seems closer to their own lives and to the world they live in…[whereas] the world of television news…might almost be beamed in from another planet' (Lewis 1991: 152). It is as if the distant world of 'the news' is so disconnected from popular experience that it is beyond critical judgement for many viewers. Hence, however alienated they feel from it, they nonetheless lack any alternative perspective on the events it portrays.

One consequence of this, Lewis argues, is that, precisely because of this distance, people who feel this kind of alienation from the 'world of news' nonetheless use frameworks to understand news items which come from within the news itself. This, he argues, is because in the absence of any other source of information or perspective they are forced back on using the media's own framework. Many viewers are simply unable to place the media's portrayal of events in any other critical framework (where would they get it from?). To this extent, Lewis argues, Gerbner and his colleagues (see Gerbner et al. 1986; Signorielli and Morgan 1990) may perhaps be right in thinking that the dominant perspectives and 'associative logics' offered by the media may often simply be soaked up by audiences by sheer dint of their repetition. This is not to suggest that such viewers necessarily believe, or explicitly accept these perspectives, but simply to note that they may have no other place to start from, however cynical they may be, at a general level, about 'not believing what you see on television', and they may thus tend, in the end, to fall back on 'what it said on TV'. In one sense this could be said to the converse of Hall's 'negotiated' code (1980), as taken over from Parkin (1973). Parkin had argued that many working-class people display a 'split consciousness', whereby they accept propositions from the 'dominant ideology' at an abstract level, but then 'negotiate' or 'discount' the application of these ideological propositions to the particular circumstances of their own situation. Here, by contrast, we confront a situation where people often express cynicism in general (so that 'not believing what you see in the media' is no more than common sense), but then in any particular case they often find themselves pushed back into reliance on the mainstream media's account of anything beyond the realm of their direct personal experience, simply for lack of any alternative perspective.

An important point arises here – that television news may be watched, by many viewers, in a frame of mind somewhat resembling the 'suspension of disbelief' traditionally associated with the mode of consumption of drama and fiction. This is to suggest that many viewers watch television news with the premise that it is describing some distant, other world (decisively not where they live) – a world disconnected from their familiar everyday logic: a 'television world' or environment with its own 'facts of life', its own personnel (the Pope, Madonna, the President, Yasser Arafat), who we will never meet. It is a separate world (a parallel universe?) with its own forms of dramatic hazard (volcanoes, earthquakes, floods), which most of us will never experience direct, and its own distinctive types of problems (unemployment, inflation, interest-rate changes), which most people cannot make sense of, but which the people on television seem to know about. As Lewis puts it, 'events like "inflation" [are] entities whose significance is located not in our world but in the alien world of news' (Lewis 1991: 155). Thus to win elections, for example, politicians do not, in fact, 'seem to need to offer solutions to people's everyday problems. The world they need to govern well is another, rather different world – the world of television news' (ibid.: 156). This is also, perhaps, the world of what Baudrillard (1995) has called 'virtual media events', where television, rather than providing information about (or access to) the real, produces 'informational events' which 'stand in for the real and which "inform" public opinion, which in turn affects the course of subsequent events, both real and informational' (Patton 1995: 10).

EVALUATING THINGS YOU DO NOT KNOW ABOUT

The point here is that once people watch television news in an alienated mode (and for good reason – i.e. the absence of the cultural competences necessary to do otherwise – it is arguable that this is how most people do watch it), then, in a curious way, they are likely to be particularly gullible, in relation to its specific propositions, regardless of how cynical they claim to be in general. More particularly, one likely consequence is that viewers will absorb quite contradictory ideas (cf. Morgan 1989) without being aware of them as contradictions. Lewis (1991) argues from this position that, by way of an example, as long as the presidential candidate seems like a 'stand-up' kind of guy viewers will vote for him, even if all his particular policy suggestions can be demonstrated to be impractical or self-contradictory, in relation to the 'real' (non-television world). Similarly, Meyrowitz notes that, during the televised nomination hearings for Supreme Court Justice Clarence Thomas in the USA:

> Observers who had compared what Justice Thomas had written and said before to what he was saying during the hearings questioned the honesty of his oral testimony. A number of those who focused on a review of his resumé questioned whether he had sufficient experience to sit on the highest court in the land. Yet, because the hearings were televised, the focus, in most journalistic accounts, was on Thomas' personal being: his self-assured presentation, his easy laugh, his deep voice, the displayed bond with his wife. Indeed, on television, the senators who kept trying to return to the 'record' often appeared to be needlessly badgering Judge Thomas.
>
> (Meyrowitz 1992: 460)

The point here, according to Meyrowitz, is the extent to which television's increasing resort to the 'personalization' of issues, as a way of involving the viewers and overcoming their potential alienation, has the price of fostering the use of what he calls 'dating criteria' ('What is he like as a guy?') over 'resumé criteria', ('What is his record in office?') as the audience's principal mode of response and critical judgement in relation to public figures as represented in the media. As he puts it, 'we seem to be evaluating potential presidents today by drawing...on the type of criteria people use in choosing bowling partners' (Meyrowitz 1992: 459), i.e. whether they 'personally like' a candidate, even if they disagree with them on 'the issues'. This may sound like irrational behaviour, but what alternative do viewers have? Meyrowitz notes, to take one example, that about one-third of President Reagan's votes in the 1980 American presidential election came from just such supporters. In this sense, as he says, it seems that it has become more important for a politician on television to impress, rather than to convince, the viewers. Or, insofar as television news, with its fragmented narrative and highly segmented form, offers the viewer only a series of disparate images, 'as long as these associations appear to float above the ebb and flow of historical reality, they are immune from the contradictions it may expose' (Lewis 1991: 156). If you cannot grasp the 'policy' issues (and who can, in any full sense?), then what else can you do but decide who to vote for on the basis of their 'personality'?

MEDIA DEPENDENCY THEORY: REAL CONFUSIONS

The further point here concerns the problematic relationship between the television world and the real world. One does not have to buy into a Baudrillardian (1988) model of the 'end of the real' in order to accept that many people really do spend much of their time living in the represented world of television. Thus the norms of that 'television world' – chronically overpopulated as it is by professionally successful, physically fit, white, sexually attractive middle and upper class people – naturally come to define, for many people, the basic contours of how it *really* is, out there in the big wide world, beyond their immediate personal experience. As Hall (1972) argued many years ago, in a world with a complex division of labour, where groups lead highly segregated lives (cf. Davis 1990 on the socio-geographical extension of this process, in the creation of literally closed, 'gated communities' in many parts of the USA), we necessarily become increasingly dependent on the media for our knowledge of anything, anyone or anywhere beyond the horizons of our immediate environment. It is this that the novelist Don De Lillo captures in his remark that 'for most people there are only two places in the world – where they live and their television set' (De Lillo 1985: 66).

This does produce a potentially schizophrenic situation for viewers. If their immediate (necessarily limited and often literally segregated) sphere of personal experience gives them no point of reference from which to evaluate what the media say about a given topic, they are thus rendered the more vulnerable and gullible towards (or at least bemused by) media representations (cf. Sibley 1996 for an account of how social consciousness is systematically structured by a 'geography of exclusions'). Thus in Lewis's study of decodings of The Cosby Show (1991) one of his white American respondents explained his belief that the programme's representation of the (statistically improbable) black Huxtable family's elevated economic status was perfectly realistic, by reference, ultimately, to his own lack of *personal* experience of racism. For him, the question of whether racism still existed in the USA to an extent that made the Huxtable's economic success unlikely in reality, for most black families, was settled by reference to the court of appeal of his immediate personal experience. As he puts it: 'I've never seen anybody ask a black to sit on the back of the bus because they are black…I've never seen it' (Lewis 1991: 182). Although Lewis's respondent went on to acknowledge that he knew 'theoretically' that racism still exists, the absence of any personal experience of it makes this 'knowledge' seem, precisely, 'theoretical' (and, to that extent, unconvincing) to him. In this respect, Lewis's study serves only to confirm, from another angle, the early work of Hartmann and Husband (1972) in the UK, who found that among the white children they interviewed, racist attitudes were most pronounced among those who lived in areas where they had little direct contact with black people, and who were thus the more heavily dependent on the media for information and images of race. In Lewis's case, the point is that if the American media represent a world in which racism is no bar to upward social mobility for (fictional) blacks, and if white viewers themselves have little or no social contact with actual blacks (as is evidenced by the residential segregation patterns of the USA; cf. Davis 1990 and Sibley 1996), then white viewers have little or no basis on which to disbelieve what the media say about blacks.

Moreover, there may well be an increasing tendency in the USA towards what the journalist John Carlin (1995) has called a form of 'TV apartheid', by which black and white people not only live in physically segregated areas, but also tend to watch quite different programmes on TV. Indeed, such viewers are often disturbed when these physical or symbolic boundaries are transgressed (cf. Bodroghkozy 1992 on the outraged response of the white viewers of Julia, pleased with their success in keeping blacks out of their physical neighbourhood, who were thus all the more outraged by the programme's role in (symbolically) bringing (images of) black people 'into the living-room'). Thus Carlin reported that, 'none of the top ten programmes watched by white audiences are on the list of the black top ten' (Carlin 1995). Carlin went on ironically to contrast this form of 'TV apartheid' with his own previous experience in South Africa, where, he reported, even in the days of apartheid The Cosby Show itself had been as popular among whites as among blacks. In this case, though, as Carlin notes, a different set of confusions applied concerning media representations of race and their relation to the real world. Carlin quotes the case of the teenage Afrikaner girl who said that she 'loved the Cosby Show', but just wished there weren't so many Kaffirs in it' (ibid.). A case, perhaps, to misquote Jhally and Lewis (1992), of 'unenlightened racism', but a case which nonetheless opens up some important issues and questions for us.

Jhally and Lewis's (1992) analysis of the success of The Cosby Show in the USA is exemplary for the way in which they trace the endless shifting of perceptions of the Huxtables' 'normality' (or otherwise) among different groups – the point is that the family can be perceived as perfectly 'normal' in terms of the rules of the 'television world', which, in the USA, seems to have a growing proportion of successful black middle class people in it. Thus Gates (1996) notes that *The Cosby Show*'s success led to a succession of TV sitcoms in the USA featuring successful black middle-class characters. It is, of course, true that the fictional Huxtables have attained a level of affluence actually shared by only a very small minority of black people in the USA. Indeed, the same period that produced *The Cosby Show* saw an overall deterioration in the economic status of most black people in the USA. To that extent, as Gates (*ibid.*) notes, there is little connection between the position of fictional blacks on American television and their actual position in American society. However, if the Huxtables' class position would be exceptional in the real world of America, it is, of course, perfectly normal for most fictional characters on television to be affluent, attractive professionals. Moreover, these days a growing number of the black characters on American television are precisely affluent, attractive professionals. Given that most white middle-class Americans live in more or less exclusively white neighbourhoods, the only black people that many of them ever 'meet' are the fictional ones on their TV screens. One of Lewis's white respondents observes that nowadays 'We have black millionaires all over the place' (Lewis 1991: 199) – as an explanation of his belief that, in reality, the USA is not a racist society. While this would contradict the actual experience of black people (as Lewis's own black respondents testified), the observation would seem quite justified in relation to the world of American television drama.

Herman Gray (1995) argues that that 'Cosby moment', as he calls it, was in fact a key transitional point in the development of television representations of blacks – or, in his terms, in 'the struggle for Blackness'. As far as Gray is concerned, the show 'repositioned and re-coded blackness and black (middle-class) subjectivity within television's own discursive and intellectual practices' (*ibid.*: 83), opening up a 'vast and previously unexplored territory of diversity within blackness – that is, upper middle-class life' (*ibid.*: 81), in contrast to American TV's historically persistent portrayal of blacks as poor, downtrodden victims, villains or figures of fun. *The Cosby Show*, as Gray notes (quoting Dyson 1989), was perhaps most radical insofar as it simply 'presented a black universe as the norm' (Gray 1995: 82), while strategically using the Huxtables' upper-middle-class status to invite audience identifications across race, gender and class lines. If the Huxtable family was widely 'appealing...because it is a middle class family that happens to be black', it is also, and crucially, 'impossible simply to laugh at these characters and make their blackness an object of derision...blackness co-existed in the show on the same discursive plane as their upper-class success' (*ibid.*: 80–1). They and their success were thus normalized.

As Lewis observes, 'we may realise that normality in the television world is rather different from the normality of the world beyond it: but since we spend so much time watching television, we are liable to lose our grip on distinctions between the two' (Lewis 1991: 186). The problem here, as Meyrowitz notes, is that:

> Not only does reality become drama on television, but drama becomes reality. When a programme such as *Roots* or *The Day After* appears on television, for example, everyone realises that it is fictional. But the widespread knowledge of the programme – and all the discussions of it on news and talk shows, in schools, and at work – makes it into a real event and gives it a social reality. Such programmes are massive, shared experiences that everyone perceives as massive, shared experiences. Through such conscious sharing, they come to seem as real as – sometimes more real than – the varied and less shared experiences of our individual lives.
>
> (Meyrowitz 1992: 466)

THE SITCOM AND THE VICE-PRESIDENT: PARADOXES OF THE REAL

Once we recognize that shared media experience has the kind of social function that Meyrowitz (1992) outlines, we must also recognize that the lines between reality and fiction become even more blurred. One interesting case of this kind concerns the furore in the USA some years ago over the fictional character Murphy Brown becoming an unmarried single parent. This fictional disruption of traditional social norms sparked off an enormous political row about 'family values', with the then vice-president, Dan Quayle, leading the chorus of outrage. In a speech two days after the riots in Los Angeles in 1992, Quayle argued that this televisual instance of Hollywood's 'glamorization of illegitimacy', as he described it, had played a crucial role in encouraging the 'poverty of values' which then gave rise to the 'lawless social anarchy' of the riots (cf. Walkowitz 1997).

John Fiske's (1996) *Media Matters* offers a sophisticated analysis of the conjunctional significance of three 'media events' in the USA: the coverage of the Anita Hill/Clarence Thomas hearings, the LA riots and the *Murphy Brown*/Dan Quayle farrago. Fiske's interest in these events is, on the one hand as, in Baudrillard's (1988) terms, 'hyper-real'. However, he is further concerned with their significance as conjunctional markers in the cultural struggle over the dominant 'structure of feeling' of North America. In his view, these three events mark the 'right wing extremity of the electoral pendulum' (Fiske 1996: 15); the (cultural) 'end of Bush–Reaganism' (*ibid*.: 24); the point where the white Republican Christian fundamentalist coalition that had kept the Republican party in government throughout the 1980s finally broke down. For Fiske, these events 'were sites where Americans struggled to come to terms with, and exert some influence on...social changes...as the US transforms itself from a society organised around a relatively homogenous, Eurocentric consensus to a more diverse, multi cultural social order' (ibid.: 13). Fiske's argument is that, in the cultural struggles around these media events, we can trace the rise and fall of emergent and residual cultures (cf. Williams 1977) struggling over the story that the USA tells itself concerning its identity, through the media. Fiske's point is not at all to attribute magical powers to the media in all of this. Indeed, he identifies that mistaken approach as crucial to the Republicans' failure, arguing that Dan Quayle's attack on Murphy Brown followed an established Republican tradition of misunderstanding the role of the media by blaming Republican electoral setbacks on the liberalism of the 'Hollywood elite' (of whom Murphy Brown was obviously a leading member). Fiske's argument is that, rather than being the causes of the breakdown of traditional/family values bemoaned by conservatives, the media function as 'relay stations', through which emergent structures of feeling reflecting the actual changes in society are articulated (such as those, for example, which are decentring the position of the white nuclear family in the USA). In the case of the Murphy Brown incident, Quayle rapidly had to back down in his criticisms of the TV show, in the face of public hostility to his pronouncements. Indeed, his climbdown was so rapid that he ended up announcing to the media that he had sent toys to Murphy Brown's (fictional) baby as a gesture of conciliation (cf. Fiske 1996: 26). However, in this connection Fiske rightly argues that, if, in this instance, television was more powerful than the White House and Murphy Brown more influential than Dan Quayle, 'we must not understand this in terms of a 'cause-and-effect' model of television, or as a sign of television's powerfulness…Murphy Brown "won" because she was more closely aligned with the emerging (cultural) currents than was Dan Quayle' (ibid.: 24).

The complex formal and institutional modalities through which the Brown–Quayle battle was fought out repay close analysis. In the first instance, the vice-president of the USA criticized a fictional character in a television sitcom for choosing to be a single mother. This fictional choice, he argued, would constitute one more undesirable televisual influence on the breakdown of 'family values', and this, he claimed, was crucial because it was the breakdown of such values and the consequent failure of socialization in single-parent families that had (somehow) caused the LA riots. The public, as Fiske (1996) notes, tended, in the event, to back Murphy Brown rather than Dan Quayle. Quayle had to backtrack, and when, later that year, the actress Candice Bergen won an Emmy Award for her portrayal of Murphy Brown she thanked Quayle for inadvertently helping her to win it.

In the autumn of the same year, on the opening night of the TV show's new season, the fictional character Murphy Brown 'replied' to her real vice-presidential critic. As Fiske reports it:

> the episode replayed CBS News' sound-bite of the Vice President's speech attacking Murphy, and allowed its heroine to reply on air to his accusations. Murphy Brown is a television journalist who works on a current affairs show called FYI. She delivered her reply, in character, to FYI's

fictional and unseen audience but, as she spoke, all signs of her fiction-
ality were erased from our screens and she appeared to be speaking
directly to us, the real, not fictional, audience, answering a real, not
fictional, Dan Quayle.

(Fiske 1996: 24–5)

On the night of this broadcast, in a bid to demonstrate that he was not personally antagonistic to single mothers, Quayle had himself filmed by the media
watching Murphy Brown's fictional riposte in the company of a group of single
mothers at a hostel, and this film was itself then shown on the late evening news,
after the Murphy Brown broadcast. One does have to concentrate hard to keep a grip
on all this but, as Fiske puts it, the essential sequence of events was as follows:

The fictional Murphy Brown watches the news report [incorporated into
her sitcom] of the 'real' Dan Quayle criticising her single motherhood.
One hour later, TV news shows Dan Quayle, in the company of single
mothers, watching Murphy Brown watching him. The report ends with
the information that he has sent her fictional baby a real toy.

(Fiske 1996: 61)

As Walkowitz (1997) describes it, in her analysis of the same events, in the
programme's riposte to Quayle

Murphy Brown made fiction look like fact; her persona as sitcom TV
anchorwoman took on all the cues of broadcast journalism....Brown, in
her news anchor clothes...sits behind a news desk, poised for a
programme on 'the American family and family values' to answer
Quayle's attack on single motherhood. Murphy Brown looks straight at
the TV audience and the camera tightens to a familiar head and shoulders
shot. She has become the authority, and she is telling the truth....Is
Murphy Brown a real news anchor or does she just function as
one?...'Fact or fiction?', asked Boston's local news anchor, Liz Walker,
that night on the 11 o'clock broadcast. 'Hard to tell', her co-anchor
responded.

(Walkowitz 1997: 334)

As Fiske notes, the distinction seemed to be beyond Dan Quayle's staff as well in
the end. When asked why the vice-president had sent a real toy to a fictional baby
Quayle's spokesman replied: 'You tell me where fiction begins and reality ends in
this whole business' (Fiske 1996: 26).

Walkowitz's own approach to this question is to further analyse Quayle's 'geography' of the 'real America' (Walkowitz 1997: 331) and his claim that Hollywood
'ought to come out with me to where the real America is' (ibid.: 325). It transpires
that, although Quayle proposes an empirical (or even epistemological) contrast

between Hollywood 'illusions' and mainstream 'realities', the issue is in fact a more complex one. As Walkowitz notes, 'Real journalism and "real America" are not just about what's true, but what's true to whom' (ibid.: 331). It turns out that, for Quayle, 'real' functioned as a synonym for 'authentic' or 'legitimate' (rather than a description of an empirical reality); 'family values' are those that the 'real America' already possesses, and Quayle's claim to knowledge of these matters was, it turned out, ultimately based on a mystical belief. As Walkowitz notes, Quayle's claim (to the Southern Baptist Convention in Indianapolis) to know 'what was in the heart of America' depended, in the end, on nothing more substantial than the rhetorical force of his own claim to 'know', through the strength of his own emotional convictions, 'where the real America is' (ibid.: 333). Clearly, for Quayle the one place it was not was on the nation's TV screens – at least not while *Murphy Brown* was showing.

In such a promiscuous flux of postmodern simulacra, and with the seeming collapse of any hierarchical distinctions between the discourses of truth, actuality and fiction, one might be forgiven for despairing of any form of certainty here. However, as Fiske (1996) notes, notwithstanding these complications, we do not actually live in a postmodern world, but, rather, in a world where the modern and the postmodern coexist uneasily. Indeed, Fiske goes further (rightly, in my view), claiming that our sense of the differences 'between different modes of representation...is not killed off as easily as post-modernism assumes' (ibid.: 63). As Fiske points out, while the discursive complexities here are manifold, the realities of ownership, for example, remain pretty straightforward. He notes that:

> On September 21 1992, *Time* put Murphy Brown/Candice Bergen on its cover and gave her a prominent lapel button that read 'Murphy Brown for President'. *Time* is a news magazine [and] the lapel button is a fiction that did not occur even in the fictional TV series....This post-modern fluidity, however, overlaps a modern certainty: Warner Bros owns both *Time* and Murphy Brown, this issue preceded Murphy's reply to Dan Quayle by a week, it carried teasers from the script, and, in a hoped-for self-fulfilling prophecy, called the episode a 'sure-fire ratings block-buster'.
>
> (Fiske 1996: 63)

In an article on recent developments in American television the *Independent on Sunday* (Carlin 1997) reported a possibly even more convoluted case – the media frenzy generated by the news that the lead character (played by Ellen DeGeneres) in the American sitcom *Ellen* would be announcing that she was gay, in a special edition of the programme on the ABC network. As the *Guardian* journalist Veronica Lee (1997) reported in her piece on the issue, even in advance of the crucial episode the religious right was already on the rampage, with the Reverend Jerry Falwell renaming Ms DeGeneres 'Ms DeGenerate', Pat Robertson calling the decision to have Ellen 'come out' a 'slap in the face for American family values' and the

American Family Association organizing a boycott of companies that advertised during the show. As the *Independent* journalist John Carlin reports, matters were complicated by the fact that Disney, the network's owners, had also given the show's star (Ms DeGeneres) 'the go-ahead to give *Time* magazine an exclusive interview revealing that she is a lesbian in real life'. As Carlin goes on to report:

> Compounding the confusion still further is Oprah Winfrey, who will be making a cameo appearance in the *Ellen* special as the tortured heroine's psychological counsellor, which happens to be the same function she exercises on behalf of the nation as a whole when she interviews real people in her spectacularly popular TV talk show. And then, as if to lay bare proof that television is indeed more real than the tangible world, she will be interviewing Ms. DeGeneres on her show a week before the special is aired. On ABC, of course.
>
> (Carlin 1997)

In conclusion, Carlin offers the view that such is the confusion of fiction and reality in this story that it seems as if the recognition of a social phenomenon as important and widespread, in reality, as homosexuality can only be 'believed to exist by the population at large once it has been fictionally certified on a national network'. Clearly, the 'fictional certification' of reality is a complex process, and one further compounded, in this case, by President Clinton's much publicized decision to make a point of being photographed with Ellen and her real-life lover, Anne Heche, at the 1997 White House annual correspondents' dinner (see Walker 1997).

POLYSEMY, AMBIGUITY AND CONTRADICTION

Returning to the earlier analysis of *The Cosby Show*, I want to suggest that this also has a further significance for my argument here, in connection with the question of the polysemy, ambiguity or otherwise of media texts. I have argued elsewhere (see Morley 1992) that the concept of the 'preferred reading' seems to have, regretfully, disappeared from many recent (mis)applications of the encoding–decoding model in audience studies, and that (correspondingly) the potential polysemy of media texts has been badly exaggerated in many studies of popular culture. I do want to hold on to that position, but I also want to recognize that ambiguity does have a central role to play in these matters. Jhally and Lewis (1992) argue convincingly that the success of *The Cosby Show* is, in one sense, built on layers of ambiguity. It is precisely the fact that the symbols of black culture are strong enough (e.g. the anti-apartheid poster on the Huxtable kids' bedroom door etc.) to incorporate a black audience, but not so strong as to put off a white audience, that makes the programme such a ratings success. The fact that different satisfactions/readings can be set up for different sections of the audience, thus maximizing the show's overall popularity, is crucial to the programme's strategy (cf. James Curran's (1996) commentary on what Jhally and Lewis call 'enlightened racism' in relation to the more traditional mass-communications model of the media's role in the 'selective reinforcement' of stereotypes). This is to argue that the hegemonic power of *The Cosby Show* actually depends on its ambiguity (cf. Fiske 1986) and on its ability to resonate with different audiences in different ways (hegemony as dialogic process connecting/articulating the 'margins' to the 'centre'); that is to say, that we should avoid the trap of equating the ambiguity of television with the empowerment of the audience (as some current versions of 'active audience theory' would seem to do). Popular culture does not have to be univocal or unambiguous in order to be powerful or hegemonic. Conversely, an ambiguous (or polysemic) message is by no means necessarily an empowering one.

However, it is perhaps also worth reminding ourselves just how centralized a system of storytelling television is (insofar as it does still dominate our symbolic environment), and just what a stable and coherent world of predictable images and messages it brings into most people's homes, in most places, on most channels, most of the time. As Michael Morgan (1989) notes, the assumption that news and information programmes are the major source of people's beliefs and opinions may well be quite misplaced. From the perspective of 'cultivation analysis', Morgan argues cogently that as 'most people, most of the time watch dramatic fictional entertainment, which teaches them many basic lessons, facts and values about social and political reality...[and]...tells [them] over and over, what different social types can and should do...what fate has in store for them'. It thus follows that 'regular everyday entertainment may be a tremendously powerful means for expressing and sustaining cultural beliefs and values' (*ibid.*: 245), and, indeed, a rather more important one than news and current affairs media. Certainly, in Britain this tendency has been exacerbated by the growing competitive pressures which have led the commercial television channels to rely more and more heavily on soap operas and drama to bolster their audience ratings at the expense of current affairs and documentaries – which, in Britain, fell by 33 per cent on ITV between 1995 and 1996 (cf. 'ITV is told to stop the rot of soap opera', Paul McCann, *Independent*, 24 April 1997).

As Morgan further notes, if storytelling depends on repetition, then the extent to which mainstream fictional television feeds us repetitive lessons (who are we, what is good and bad, etc.) is historically unprecedented. If repetition is the point, and if recent ethnographic work on how television is actually watched (my own included; see Morley 1992) is correct, then the unit of television consumption is more likely to be a 'segment' (or segments) of televisual 'flow' (cf. Williams 1974) across a period of viewing, rather than a single, discrete programme. If that is the case, the kind of 'single-text' models of media analysis, derived from literary and film studies, that have been largely taken up in cultural studies work on television may, in fact, be of limited applicability to the television audience – except in the case of the viewing of particular 'special' programmes on specifically demarcated 'occasions' (cf. Curran 1976 for a defence of traditional content-analysis procedures against 'structuralist' criticisms). In that case the key point, as Morgan notes, may be the question of 'what cuts across most programmes, what is largely inescapable, whatever content type is selected' (Morgan 1989: 244). Despite all the problems of the 'post hoc ergo propter hoc' fallacy commonly associated with cultivation-analysis perspectives, what may be crucial here is the process Morgan describes as 'mainstreaming' in his analysis of the consequences of 'heavy-viewing' patterns. By 'mainstreaming', Morgan means the process whereby the more time people spend watching television, the less they claim to be either liberal or conservative and the more they describe themselves as 'moderate/middle of the road'. However, to stretch Morgan's metaphor, the problem here is that the 'mainstream' does not run down the middle of an already built road. Rather, the media are simultaneously building the road, the middle of which they then claim to steer down. What we may have here is another instance of what Stuart Hall, in another context, called 'The Great Moving Right Show' (Hall 1988), in which the centre of the political universe – the road down the middle of which the centre line is being drawn – is gradually being shifted to the Right – in which case that shift must then become the crucial focus of our analysis.

This may perhaps be exactly the kind of long-term, across-the-board shift to which George Gerbner et al.'s (1986) 'cultivation studies' may be most sensitive. In his account of the findings of the long-term Annenberg cultivation studies conducted by Gerbner and his colleagues, Michael Morgan (1989) paints a particularly depressing portrait of those characterized in the studies as 'heavy viewers'. In Morgan's account, such people 'spend more time "living" in the world of television, absorb its lessons and apply them to the real world' (ibid.: 248). Thus 'the more people watch television, the more they are fearful and afraid. They are more willing to accept repressive measures in the name of security, and to approve of more extreme ways to punish those who break the rules of the system. They are alienated, depoliticised and afraid of both crime in the streets and of world war' (ibid.: 251). Thus, according to this analysis, Morgan argues that heavy television viewing inculcates a set of paradoxical currents. As he puts it:

> Heavy viewers think like conservatives, want like liberals and yet call themselves moderates. They are less likely to vote, but quicker to turn against an incumbent....They think elected officials do not care about what happens to them, but are more interested in their [politicians'] personal lives than in their policies. They want to cut taxes but improve education, medical care, social security. They distrust 'big Government', but want it to fix things for them to protect them at home and from foreign threats.
>
> (Morgan 1989: 251)

In her contribution to a collection of essays on cultivation analysis, Signorielli

(1990) observes that television's presentation of a 'mean and dangerous world tends to cultivate a sense of…danger, mistrust, insecurity, vulnerability, dependence and despite its supposedly "entertaining" nature – alienation and gloom' (ibid.: 88). The further issue, she continues, is that 'fearful people are more dependent, more easily manipulated and controlled, more susceptible to deceptively simple, strong, tough measures and hard-line postures – both political and religious. They may accept and even welcome repression if it promises to relieve their insecurities' (ibid.: 102).

This bundle of attributes is clearly not a million miles away from the characteristics of the supporters of (in the UK) Thatcher's and (in the USA) Reagan's brand of what Hall aptly dubbed 'Authoritarian Populism' (cf. Hall 1988). However, Morgan goes on to note one last contradictory characteristic of the 'heavy viewers' on whom his analysis focuses, and it is on this that I wish to focus in the conclusion of my argument. This issue concerns the finding that heavy viewers 'are losing confidence in people who run virtually all institutions…but…express trust in God, America – and television' (Morgan 1989: 252). In his book *The Culture of Cynicism* Richard Stivers offers an analysis of television very much in parallel with Morgan's. Stivers claims that 'television describes reality for us, but leaves us with no understanding of it' (Stivers 1994: 141), and that television tends to portray the external world as a 'place of ever-escalating disasters' (ibid.: 143) which are largely incomprehensible, so that 'the more television one watches, the more life appears absurd, but interesting' (ibid.: 141). The question here concerns the fact that even those who, unlike Morgan's heavy viewers, express little or no 'trust' in television – and in television news in particular – are nonetheless vulnerable to its stories. There is evidence to suggest that it is perfectly possible that high levels of explicit viewer cynicism are themselves no barrier to media effects. Thus, during the war in Bosnia, one study of viewers' beliefs concerning what had or had not, in fact, happened there concluded that 'a high level of scepticism about the accuracy and reliability of controlled media can run alongside both extraordinary ignorance and, worse, the absorption of the basic stereotypes being peddled' (Woollacot 1994). It does seem that, as Joshua Meyrowitz puts it in this connection, 'thus we live with a relatively new, basic distrust of power, but also with a seemingly powerless dependence on these in whom we have little trust' (Meyrowitz 1992: 473).

Such 'trust' as we have of the media may well be mixed in with all kinds of postmodern sophistication, cynicism and disclaimers, but the fact remains that, however differentially we decode its stories, both factual and fictional (insofar as we are able to distinguish these genres), television is still there, telling the most widely dispersed stories that go together to make up the culture we live in. To return to Lippman's metaphor, with which I began, the clock may well be unreliable, or even (possibly) running at the wrong speed; we may even know it to be unreliable; but it remains the clock by which most of us tell the time – even if it is a fictional, rather than a factual time, by which we live.

POSTSCRIPT

In conclusion, and at the risk of undermining some part of my own previous argument, I will return briefly to the semi-autobiographical mode in which I began. I wrote the first section of this article in the spring of 1997, during what turned out to be the last few months of an eighteen-year period of Conservative Party rule in Britain. I write this conclusion two months into the period of a new Labour government. Although the initial excitement of a new political regime is now beginning to wear off and some disillusionment has set in, these have been an astounding few weeks for those, such as myself, in Britain whose political sympathies lie to the Left and who have thus had to endure eighteen years of (seemingly interminable) oppression and derision under first Margaret Thatcher's and then John Major's Conservative governments. One of the things that I and others have had to come to terms with in the last few weeks is that the change of government has also, in effect, transformed our relationship to the news. It now seems, retrospectively, that my own long-established lack of interest in TV news could perhaps be at least partly rephrased as a lack of interest in eighteen years of TV Bad News – which is what, from my point of view, was being reported most of the time from 1979, when Mrs Thatcher was first elected to government. Indeed, on the night of the Labour Party's election victory in May 1997 I, like many others, stayed up most of the night, glued to the television set, revelling in the images of distraught Conservative politicians losing their constituency seats. What I wanted was to *see*, live, in real time, the expression on their (previously smug) faces as they were publicly humiliated by the scale of their defeat. For once, I found that I could not get enough of the TV news, and I spent almost the whole of the first day after Labour's election victory still riveted to the images on television, following each detail of the installation of the new regime, with complete fascination and considerable gratification.

I have clearly not been alone in this experience; for some people, their whole relation to the world of politics, rather than simply to political news, has also been transformed. Amy Jenkins, the creator of the 'me-generation' British TV series *This Life* (whose portrait of the apolitical culture of a set of urban, thoroughly cynical, professional, young people has been a major ratings success, striking a chord with many viewers of her generation) announced the end of her 'career ...of political apathy'. In the wake of the election result, she explained:

> I find myself reading the political pages of the newspaper....I eschew my usual diet of 'lifestyle' pieces. I have cut out and pinned up a list of the new cabinet ministers and attempted to memorise their names. I am agog to know what will happen next...all those years I couldn't be bothered with the news – I'd put them down to an unfortunate frivolity in my nature, when all along it was despair. Now I see I was in denial. I simply had not allowed myself to hate them [the Conservative govern-

ment] because hating them would have made my life an angry, miserable place for eighteen years.

(Jenkins 1997)

How often, we must ask, does disengagement with the 'world of news' simply function, principally, as an index of one or another form of alienation – a sense that being on the 'losing side', having no stake in events, means that there is no point in being 'informed' (cf. Merton and Lazarsfeld 1948)? As Jenkins points out, in such a situation more information may simply mean more misery. Jenkins feels that she is now 'living with hope...a new and astonishing experience' (Jenkins 1997) and, precisely because of that, is re-engaged with the world of political news, on television and elsewhere. If my own perception of change, in these respects, is rather less dramatic, it is still noticeable. While my television news-viewing binge did not extend beyond the immediate election aftermath, there was, at least for twenty-four hours, a period when, Walter Lippman notwithstanding, I too was gripped by the progress of the second hand of the 'clock' of TV news.

REFERENCES

Abercrombie, N., Hill, S. and Turner, B. (1984) *The Dominant Ideology Thesis*, London: Allen & Unwin.

Baudrillard, J. (1988) *Selected Writings*, Cambridge: Polity Press.

—— (1995) *The Gulf War Did Not Take Place*, Sydney: Power Publications.

Bodroghkozy, A. (1992) 'Is this what you mean by colour TV?', in L. Spigel and D. Mann (eds) *Private Screenings*, Minneapolis, MN: University of Minnesota Press.

Bourdieu, P. (1984) *Distinction*, London: Routledge.

Branston, G. (1993) 'Infotainment: a twilight zone', unpublished paper.

Carlin, John (1995) 'Black and white in America', *Independent on Sunday*, 28 May.

—— (1997) 'Ellen', *Independent on Sunday*, 13 April.

Corner, J. (1980) 'Codes and cultural analysis', *Media, Culture and Society*, 1980(z).

Curran, J. (1976) 'Content and structuralist analysis of mass communication', Course Unit: D305 *Social Psychology*, Milton Keynes: Open University Press.

—— (1996) 'Rethinking mass communications', in J. Curran, D. Morley and V. Walkerdine (eds) *Cultural Studies and Communications*, London: Edward Arnold.

Davis, M. (1990) *City of Quartz*, London: Verso Books.

De Lillo, D. (1985) *White Noise*, London: Picador.

Dyson, M. (1989) 'Bill Cosby and the politics of race', *Z Magazine*, September.

Fielding, Helen (1995) 'What in the world is going on?', *Independent on Sunday*, 29 January.

Fiske, J. (1986) 'Television: polysemy and popularity', *Critical Studies in Mass Communications* 3.

—— (1992) 'Popularity and the politics of information', in P. Dahlgren and C. Sparks (eds) *Journalism and Popular Culture*, London: Sage.

—— (1996) *Media Matters: Race and Gender in US Politics*, Minneapolis, MN: University of Minnesota Press.

Gates, H. L. (1996) 'TV's black world turns – but stays unreal', *New York Times*, 12 November.

Gerbner, G., Gross, L., Morgan, M. and Signorielli, N. (1986) 'The dynamics of the cultivation process', in J. Bryant and D. Zillman (eds) *Perspectives on Media Effects*, Hillsdale, NJ: Erlbaum Books.

Gray, H. (1995) *Watching Race: TV and the struggle for 'Blackness'*, Minneapolis, MN: University of Minnesota Press.

Gripsrud, J. (1992) 'The aesthetics and politics of melodrama', in P. Dahlgren and C. Sparks (eds) *Journalism and Popular Culture*, London: Sage Publications.

Groombridge, B. (1972) *Television and the People*, Harmondsworth: Penguin.

Hagen, I. (1992) *News Viewing: Ideals and Everyday Practices*, Report no. 15, Bergen: Department of Mass Communications, University of Bergen.

Hall, S. (1972) 'Deviancy, politics and the media', in P. Rock and M. McIntosh (eds) *Deviance and Social Control*, London: Tavistock.

—— (1980) 'Encoding/Decoding', in S. Hall, D. Hobson and A. Lowe (eds) *Culture, Media, Language*, London: Hutchinson.

—— (1988) *The Hard Road to Renewal*, London: Verso Books.

Hartmann, P. and Husband, C. (1972) 'The mass media and racial conflict', in D. McQuail (ed.) *The Sociology of Mass Communication*, Harmondsworth: Penguin.

Jenkins, Amy (1997) 'My life as a political airhead (is over)', *Independent on Sunday*, 11 May.

Jhally, S. and Lewis, J. (1992) *Enlightened Racism*, Boulder, CO: Westview Press.

Lee, Veronica (1997) 'The hate that came out with Ellen', *Guardian*, 24 April.

Lewis, J. (1991) *The Ideological Octopus*, London: Routledge.

Mann, M. (1973) *Consciousness and Action among the Western Working Class*, London: Macmillan.

Martin, G. (1973) 'The press', in D. Thompson (ed.) *Discrimination and Popular Culture*, Harmondsworth: Penguin.

Merton, R. and Lazarsfeld, P. (1948) 'Communication, taste and social action', in L. Bryan (ed.) *The Communication of Ideas*, New York: Harpers.

Meyrowitz, J. (1992) 'The power of television news', *The World and I*, June.

Morgan, M. (1989) 'Television and democracy', in I. Angus and S. Jhally (eds) *Cultural Politics in Contemporary America*, New York and London: Routledge.

Morley, D. (1986) *Family Television*, London: Comedia.

—— (1992) *Television Audiences and Cultural Studies*, London: Routledge.

Parkin, F. (1973) *Class Inequality and Political Order*, London: Paladin.

Patton, P. (1995) 'Introduction', in J. Baudrillard *The Gulf War Did Not Take Place*, Sydney: Power Publications.

Sibley, D. (1996) *Geographies of Exclusion*, London: Routledge.

Signorielli, N. (1990) 'Television's mean and dangerous world', in Signorielli and Morgan (eds) *Cultivation Analysis: New Directions in Media Effects Research*, London: Sage Publications.

Signorielli, N. and Morgan, M. (eds) (1990) *Cultivation Analysis: New Directions in Media Effects Research*, London: Sage Publications.

Sparks, C. (1988) 'The popular press and political democracy', *Media, Culture and Society*, 10 (2): 209–23.

Stivers, R. (1994) *The Culture of Cynicism*, Cambridge, MA: Blackwell.

Walker, Martin (1997) 'Ellen high water', *Guardian*, 30 April.

Walkowitz, R. (1997) 'Reproducing reality: Murphy Brown and illegitimate politics', in C. Brunsdon, J. D'Acci and L. Spigel (eds) *Feminist Television Criticism*, Oxford: Oxford University Press.

Williams, R. (1974) *Television, Technology and Cultural Form*, London: Fontana.

—— (1977) *Marxism and Literature*, Oxford: Oxford University Press.

Woollacot, Martin (1994) 'Forging war: the media in Serbia, Croatia and Bosnia-Herzegovina', *Guardian*, 6 June.

10

CREDIBILITY AND MEDIA DEVELOPMENT

Anders Johansen

On TV the most charismatic among Norway's top politicians is – or has been until recently – the leader of the Socialist Left Party, Erik Solheim. In front of the camera he is the most awkward, hence the most credible. The first time he appeared on TV he was confronted with statistical figures showing that the unemployment problem was not as grave as he had tried to make out. His reply was an account of a shocking experience. Recently, he had seen a man, possibly unemployed, searching for something in a garbage can, probably out of want. Commenting not on the subject for discussion, but on his emotions concerning that subject, he distinguished himself by understanding what the interview was all about.

Media coverage of election campaigns is, above all, concerned with uncovering disagreement between statements put forward on different occasions, or between principles and actual decisions, i.e. it is concerned with the candidates' credibility. This is precisely what the viewers have the impression of being able to judge for themselves. In the intimacy of the close-up everything seems to come into the open. Details and nuances that escape the control of the participants hit the viewers in the eye. The lack of crow's feet at the corners of Michael Dukakis's eyes, transforming his attempt at smiling into an aggressive exposition of teeth, is a well-known example of this effect. The discrepancy between eyes and mouth, more obvious even than in ordinary face-to-face communication, seemed to expose the sneer behind the smiling mask. Norwegian readers probably remember the artery pulsating under our prime minister's pendant when a TV reporter, during the election campaign some years ago, posed the ominous question of whether a politician should stick to the truth. That pulsation showed – and the remarkable thing is that many newspapers commented on this – how she was fighting to keep her confident look, betraying a discrepancy between the inner and the outer, making her transparent, as it were, so that we could sense what was really going on inside her.

This kind of problem may be overcome by deliberately presenting oneself as transparent. This has been Erik Solheim's strategy. Frankly admitting his ignorance of certain subjects, declaring himself in disagreement with his own party programme and with prominent party members, he has impressed the public with an extraordinary degree of honesty. Having mentioned this strategy shortly before his first appearance on TV in 1987, he was asked about its possible gains. 'I don't know if honesty pays', he answered. 'When it comes to honesty, I have no choice. I am not able to lie without everyone seeing it. For me, there is no use trying.'

Since then he has kept repeating this point on every occasion. The campaign of the Socialist Left has been the most honest – this was the main point of his final appeal to the viewers in 1991. When the first results became known, he was interviewed about the possibility of seeing him smile during the night. 'I smile when I am happy,' he answered, 'and I look depressed when I am depressed, and that is something I can do nothing about.'

What is remarkable about this way of handling a public appearance is that it is related not only to the world of social problems, but to the private person behind the appearance as well. When it comes to the crunch, this latter relationship takes priority. In this way a lack of knowledge or principledness may be transformed into a resource of emotional appeal. This is possible only on the condition of a certain criterion of validity: a statement is true if it is in accordance, not with the realities of the outside world, but with the inner world of psychological ones. Solheim was telling the truth about himself – without premeditation, apparently, and with no thought for the consequences.

Figure 10.1 gives an idea of the first seconds of his great TV debut. By not even trying to control his facial expressions, as if he did not care about making a favourable impression at all, he is adding credibility to the demonstration of sincerity implied in his disavowal of the party programme.

In the main, politicians are not suspected of lying. Normally, they are accepted

Figure 10.1 (We'll try to leave as many decisions as possible to local authorities) '...but ah ...we...can't...can't say...ah...once and for all that everything should... everything should...be left... to...' (interruption)

'After all, we can't let people die, and let sick people wait (for treatment), because of the party's principles!'

as sincere. But they may seem to have grown into their public roles, so that when telling the truth about themselves they are simply demonstrating their 'estrangement', i.e. their inability to 'be themselves'. Hence it is not primarily by the value of *sincerity* that Solheim is able to distinguish himself, but by his *authenticity*. It is not enough that the public appearance seems to correspond with the private person behind it; the latter also seems to be in accordance with something more originally and naturally human. Referring to the distinction developed by Trilling (1971), between sincerity and authenticity, credibility may be seen to depend, partly, on the impression of one's not intentionally deceiving the public – and partly, but more decisively, on one's not giving the impression of unwittingly deceiving oneself.

Carl I. Hagen, the leader of the right-wing Progress Party, has a certain renown for sincerity. In populist fashion, he is 'saying aloud what everyone's really thinking'. But his speech is too fluent, and the liveliness and distinctness of his facial expressions seem studied. He may remind one of a clever salesman. One may get the impression that he has taken a course in eloquence. His style was refreshing at first sight, but it soon proved to be a style. His limitation as a TV personality consists in his giving the impression of not really being himself. Strangely, he still has a reputation for handling the TV medium better that anyone else; on each occasion his failure comes as a surprise to political commentators handicapped by outdated concepts of oratory.

In Figure 10.2 Hagen is making a speech, not conversing, as Solheim did, thus disregarding the shift that has taken place in broadcast communication generally, as well as in the contexts of education and management, towards forms of talk characterized by equality and reciprocity, presenting themselves not simply as means of transferring a message, but as interaction as well, thus guarding some sense of the coming together and the affirmation of the personal relationships so vital to everyday private communication. In addition, by looking directly into the camera, Hagen is usurping a position reserved for the TV hosts and reporters and, apart from them, for no one but the king and the prime minister addressing the nation on New Year's Eve, i.e. he is, in a way easily seen through, striking a pose of authority.

How, in a public setting, does one give the impression of being oneself? Confessions of private matters do not, by themselves, add to one's political appeal.

Figure 10.2 'The point is that we wanted to break the cinema monopoly, out of principle, and we want to demonstrate and to show that if Oslo, together with other cities in this country, moved money away from cinema, we might be able to build more nursing homes and homes for the aged, and...'

Rather, charisma is gained by systematically mixing politics and psychology so that one's very political statements take the form of a private confession. A political statement has the air of authenticity if the standpoints do not seem to be absorbed from the outside, but to grow out of one's very personality – and if the commitment not only seems to be in accordance with the importance of the subject of discussion, but also gives evidence that one is 'in touch with one's own emotions'. This is the quality the newspaper commentators saw in Solheim's performance: 'he was himself', in the most 'human', 'spontaneous', 'genuine', 'everyday' way. It is all a question of form – it did not seem to be form at all.

The secret of the authentic expression, then, is a lack of style and form in the traditional sense. Talk that is elegant and striking is used to hide oneself or make an impression on others. Fluency is regarded as sleekness. Poetic turns are empty phrases. Dramatic shifts in emotional investment give the impression of theatricality. As was pointed out by a former minister of culture and education, 'fluency and confident mastery of form is almost offensive, especially when elaborate....In order to be believed, a speaker has to stutter and grope for words – that makes us see that they come from his heart' (Langslet 1988).

This is the meaning of Solheim's hesitations, his incomplete words and self-interruptions. They give the impression, to borrow a phrase from Adorno, that 'the existence of the speaker has communicated itself simultaneously with his subject matter' (Adorno 1986: 8). When connections between words are lost, Adorno observed, 'the whole man, and not thought, speaks' (ibid.: 9). Non-fluency is a sign that the words have 'come from the depth of the speaking subject', adding a sense of human presence, making the speaker 'invulnerable to de-humanized mass communication' (ibid.: 14–15).

This was Solheim's great strength. He did not seem to have complete control over, or to be fully conscious of, the way he presented himself. Signs of eagerness appeared, impulsively but in a suggestive rather than demonstrative way, as if they were not meant for us. He did not smile precisely when it was fitting to smile, i.e. he seemed to smile when he felt the impulse to do so himself. He was nervous and shy, but he made no obvious effort to hide it. He refrained from everything we recognize as impression management and rhetorical devices, and that is modern rhetoric at its very best.

Norway's most efficient orator of the interwar period, Martin Tranmæl, practised a style that was the diametrical opposite to Solheim's. At the speaker's platform 'he was the devil himself', according to eye witnesses. 'He shouted his accusations and he enlarged them and intensified them – the more vigorously, the better.' The same violence was apparent in his bodily appearance. His listeners were impressed by his 'distorted face', by his 'dark, shining eyes' – and by the 'remarkable agitation of his body'. He was 'a jumping jack, unable to stand still, constantly stamping the floor with his feet, gesticulating violently with his arms' (C. Lie 1935: 13–15; cf. H. Lie 1988: 11–13).

Expressions as forceful as these are no longer in evidence. They are not to be trusted. In the 1930s, they were. Most great orators of the early part of the century exhibited a comparable temperament and expressiveness. Tranmæl seemed to be entirely at the mercy of his emotions, and that, I believe, precluded any suspicion of sham acting and rhetorical manipulation. As one eyewitness asked, 'how is it possible to doubt the seriousness and sincerity of a man who is trembling and shaking as if on the brink of a convulsive fit?' (C. Lie 1935: 60).

Tranmæl did not pretend to be himself. Anyone applying the criterion of authenticity to his performance would have had to conclude that he was raving mad. The dramatic form of the speech was in agreement with its *content*, not with the personality performing it. The greatness of the cause justified the effects of the performance; in giving expression to the need for world revolution, it is almost impossible to overdo it. In Tranmæl's case the very lack of agreement between the extravagance of the public speaker and the modesty of the private person was a demonstration of unconditional commitment to the cause he was speaking about. On stage he was an incarnation of that cause, hence the picture of sincerity.

Tranmæl, then, was sincere according to a concept that is almost incomprehensible today: Sincerity, in this sense, does not mean telling the truth about oneself, if necessary at the expense of the cause, but acting as an impersonal instrument through which the idea of that cause can take shape and come alive, committing oneself to the content of one's words to the point of being overwhelmed, or even possessed, by it. A speaker could be seen to be pretending, and stand in danger of being interpreted as unreliable, only if the public got a glimpse of something else behind the standardized language of emotions – another, private self that could be suspected of caution or ulterior motives.

Television has contributed to changing the conditions of political rhetoric. More than anyone else, Ronald Reagan has contributed to the understanding of the medium's possibilities. He was known as 'the great communicator'. Still, he was almost completely inexpressive, seldom changing his facial expression, never gesticulating. In his way of speaking there was a marked absence of intonational and rhythmic shifts. The impression of human presence was created by some very fine nuances – a certain catch in the voice, something almost undefinably relaxed and vulnerable in his bearing.

By avoiding any kind of marked expression, Reagan was acting that he was not acting. Even when presenting a speech, he did nothing to underline his words or charge them with specific emotions. When delivering what has been called the first conversational acceptance speech, he 'might have been talking across the garden fence or maybe chatting in the kitchen with the kids', according to *Time*; 'The entire speech sounded as though it was delivered off the top of Reagan's head, that the thoughts had just occurred to him and, darn it, he was going to share them with his friends all over America' (quoted in Atkinson 1984: 167).

This is not the method to captivate a huge live audience. Repetitions, marked variations in rhythm, intonation and volume of voice, coordinated with expansive non-verbal actions, are needed, not only to overcome the distance between the rostrum and the floor, but also to control the applause, by which the audience convinces itself. Reagan was not able to elicit spontaneous applause. The audience normally reacted only after a more or less embarrassing delay. His expressions were far too sparse and discreet for the audience to recognize them and know with certainty when to applaud. It hesitated, and was never carried away by enthusiasm.

Reagan, giving priority to television coverage, observed the following conditions:

- The extensive use of close-ups means that everything but the most low-key appearance is in danger of appearing to be an exaggeration. If you gesticulate on TV you are, in the best of cases, regarded as an eccentric. Rhetorical devices that greatly impress a mass audience will seem grossly unnatural, even oppressive, on TV. A booming voice, expansive non-verbal actions, etc. will make the speaker appear highly strung, unduly intense, perhaps shifty (cf. Atkinson 1984).
- On TV politicians are seen often, and in a variety of more or less informal situations, so that the viewers have the impression of knowing them as far more than politicians. Against this background, traditional rhetoric will seem highly artificial. According to Meyrowitz (1985), the distinction between two markedly different ways of behaving cannot be maintained when the situations they belong to are not kept strictly apart. If, in this same context of the TV experience, you act as a flamboyant tribune of the people one moment, and as a relaxed conversational partner the next, you are suspiciously inconsistent.
- The audience is typically composed of family groups, in their homes, accustomed to television permitting them to eavesdrop on conversations within comparable groups. Treating them as a mass audience is almost as shocking as if the neighbour did so over a cup of coffee.

Occasionally the cultures of expression of the rostrum and the TV screen conflict in instructive ways. My first example of this kind of conflict (see Figure 10.3) is given by Jan P. Syse, the former leader of the Norwegian Conservative Party, who is committed to some old-fashioned ideals of culture and to the traditional art of oratory, even referring, in his textbook on the subject, to the instructions of the authorities of classical antiquity. The polished surface of his talk, the strangely modulated and insistent voice production, and the emphatic

Figure 10.3 '…and I must say that the way in which this has been presented today, in the press for instance, is entirely wrong and quite off the mark. We were the first to be sceptical about that development; we had already prepared plans for privatisation; we wanted to go further and…' (interruption: 'Please answer the question.')

gestures – which once made a commentator think of a 'wind-up pillar of salt' – are all contrary to the demands of credibility of the TV screen.

My second example (see Figure 10.4) is also a remnant from a bygone political culture, Martin Tranmæl's brother-in-arms Håkon Lie. On the screen he appears with the intensity of a mad fanatic. In this case he is making a propaganda speech – in front of a close circle of conversational partners.

Figure 10.4 'Our task is to create a new Europe – the United States of Europe, where all borders will be removed, and chauvinism will be gone, and youth may travel across the old borders back and forth – opinions will be free, and ideas, and goods, commodities; it's the dream of that day when swords shall be forged into ploughs...ploughs, you see!'

Thorbjørn Berntsen, former minister of environmental affairs, is probably Norway's one remaining tribune of the people. On television, however, his most efficient techniques seem clownish. In fact, combined with bombastic music, his speeches have proved successful as Saturday night entertainment. (See Figure 10.5.)

The privacy of the reception, and the sense of intimacy, is characteristic of broadcast communication generally. Hence, much the same conditions obtain on the radio. Franklin D. Roosevelt was probably the first to exploit this insight. When appearing at the Democratic Party Convention in 1928, he knew that the battle for

Figure 10.5 (TV sound – symphonic grande finale)

nomination was lost. Still, Republicans and independents listening to the radio transmission could be won over to the party's candidate. 'I tried to write and perform this speech for the radio audience exclusively', he commented, 'and in the conviction that the art of rhetoric as we know it would be of no use at all' (Roosevelt; quoted in Freidel 1952: 243). Rather, he pretended to be natural. 'There was nothing strained or fantastic or extravagant about what he said', according to the *New York Times*. 'He escaped all the oratorical pitfalls of the mass meeting....The whole speech was clear and unaffected, without the slightest trace of demagogy' (quoted in *ibid*.: 243–4).

The properties of the medium were not self-evident at the time, and the readaptation of public speakers was far from unproblematic. Hitler, for instance, was never satisfied with his radio speeches. Treating the microphone as a huge mass meeting, occasionally causing the listeners to think something was wrong with their receivers, he even made extensive use of rhetorical pauses, lasting for a minute or more, allowing the listeners to resume housework or conversation, or setting them to work on retuning (Hale 1975: 7).

The body language of public speakers even made it difficult to relate to a microphone. In the American presidential campaign of 1924, when radio transmission of the candidates' speeches was introduced, someone had to sketch a square in chalk on the platform and instruct the speakers not to leave it. According to the *New York Times*, the trick did not work. The candidates simply

> could not be trained to direct their speeches toward the microphone when they got excited. They dashed this way or that, hanging over the speaker's rail, gesticulating at their hearers, causing the radio to lose large portions of the address....To avoid further trouble of this kind, a narrow enclosure has been designed that keeps orators from leaping to the right or left and compels them to face the microphone at all times.
>
> (*New York Times*; quoted in Becker and Lower 1962: 29)

Against this background, Roosevelt, treating the public familiarly, can be evaluated as the first late-modern speaker. By means of a remarkable emotional flatness, he communicated the qualities of intimate relationships. In his 'fireside chats' this style was cultivated, until the speech, while openly declamatory to us, sounded like an improvisation of informal remarks in strict confidence.

The contrast between the platform and the TV image corresponds to the contrast between the theatre stage and the cinema screen.

'Being not acting' is the slogan of 'Method acting', repeated in various versions in all the centres of film production. The will to abstain from acting, or to restrain and subdue it to something imperceptible, is motivated by the properties of the medium. In the close-up, fleeting, ambiguous and inadvertent expressions are far more conspicuous and significant than in any stage performance. Hence the close-up works in the same way as the microphone: The more sensitively it registers the nuances of the actor's talk, the more he can abstain from using his voice as an instrument or practising voice production as a special art.

The microphone, then, has worked to subdue or flatten the actor's speech, relieving it of its theatricality. Similarly, the close-up, according to Balàzs, has given rise to a 'completely new sense of micro physiognomy'. On the stage, the soliloquy is almost the only means of clarifying what is 'really' going on 'inside' the characters. Aiming at naturalness, the theatre has to forego this possibility. Cinema, on the other hand, by drawing attention to the details of inadvertent 'body language', seems to 'uncover what is really happening under the surfaces' in a 'mute soliloquy' that is at once 'more subjective, more subtle and more candid than any spoken soliloquy' (Balàzs 1985: 289).

A new style of acting seems to correspond to these possibilities of interpretation. In the theatre the actor can not possibly display his emotions. He must evoke a mental image of them, by means of language, and language-like non-verbal expressions. In order to communicate with the floor the actor must amplify and underline them. A certain degree of stylization and exaggeration is the condition of even the most naturalistic style of acting. The film actor's performance, however, distinguishes itself by what Hitchcock termed 'negative play', i.e. by 'the ability to express oneself by doing nothing' (quoted in Kracauer 1960: 94). The actor's face and body vaguely suggest a personality that is too complex and too unique to be adequately expressed. These suggestions cannot possibly be construed. They have to be one's own unpremeditated responses, or at least be developed from them. Hence it is not enough that the actor is good at acting. His or her appearance has to fit the character that the director has in mind – a look and a bearing that inadvertently betray the character's nature.

In the theatre, then, the parts endure. Various actors disappear into them, the best ones amazing the public with their versatility as they play one part after the other. While they all play Hamlet in their own distinctive way, Hamlet remains Hamlet. In the cinema, on the other hand, it is the image of the star that endures. James Dean in Rebel Without a Cause is, above all, James Dean. James Dean is still James Dean in The Giant and in East of Eden (who remembers Jett Rink or Cal Trask?), and in various scenes from so-called real life – an insoluble mixture of actor and part.

In this way the film actor resembles the late-modern politician. He obeys and propagates the very same norms of credibility. In order to understand Reagan it is not sufficient to remember that he was an actor. He was a film actor.

Modern media – television, radio, cinema (and photography, I would have added, if time allowed) – have the effect of blurring the distinctions between the private and the public, between the speaker and the subject of the speech, between the personality and the social role. They contribute to a redefinition of personal expressions, conventional signs being replaced by psychological symptoms, and they create new conditions for the communication of credibility, favouring the subtly suggestive at the expense of the demonstratively telling.

On the other hand, the emphasis on media characteristics must not be exaggerated. It is not a question of technological determination, but of more or less obvious possibilities, and of rather flexible limitations. Attempts to realize the values of authenticity were made before the age of the photographic and electronic media. In searching for a naturally muted style of acting, the theatre was ahead of the cinema. The silent movie was full of grimacing and gesticulation, even pantomime; Stanislavsky outlined the principles of Method acting before the screening of the first film. Comparable tendencies can be detected in the field of political oratory long before the advent of television.

'The more high strung and pathetic the delivery, and the more bombastic the words, the better the speech'. This is how Schnitler, the historian of 'the generation of 1814', described the speakers of the Norwegian constitutional assembly. 'Simplicity and straightforwardness were quite simply impossible'; they always favoured 'the strongest, the highest, the most tense and exaggerated expressions'. Their vehemence and pomposity made him think of an Italian opera. 'The language of our great-grandfathers is so strange and remote that it seems to belong to a foreign race', he wrote. Starting in the 1840s a profound 'change in the ideals of form' was to have taken place. The new sense of the inner life, Schnitler wrote at the turn of the century is satisfied only with 'modest and muted expressions' (Schnitler 1911: 430–8).

Hence television, cinema, radio and photography are culturally determining – *insofar as they are also culturally symptomatic.* A protracted process of cultural change may be said to overdetermine the media's conditioning of political rhetoric.

Following Sennett (1974), this change may be characterized as the replacement of a culture of presentation by a culture of representation. Colourful and passionate expression is possible as long as it is conceived as a self-sufficient presentation not as a representation of emotions 'inside'. This is so for at least three reasons:

1   On these premises one may, in good faith, make use of a vocabulary of conventional signs – an impersonal and richly developed language of gestures permitting the emotions to take visible shape.
2   Language – and this is a key to the notion of credibility in classical rhetoric, language constitutes reality. Signs of emotion produce emotions in the audience and in the speaker himself. Hence, someone who is able to move an assembly is necessarily moved by his own expressions. In the political cultures of the eighteenth and nineteenth centuries, as well as in those of classical antiquity, a great orator was, by definition, always sincere (cf. Cicero 1968, vol. I: 333–5; Quintillian 1961, vol. 4: 277–9).
3   If expression is impersonal, if it does not bear witness to or betray one's inner life, one does not run the risk of compromising oneself by making use of it.

This is why only the most traditional and ritualized institutions – La Scala, or the British Parliament – are able to keep up the temperature of communication in public.

In the culture of representations or indices, on the other hand, the 'impersonal' and 'superficial' language of emotions must be reduced as much as possible. In addition, it has to be performed with utter restraint. Impetuousness, elaboration and emphatic distinctness all seems to lack credibility as indications of one's personality and emotional state. In particular, they betray one's intention of making an impression. Hence it is far more convincing if I bite my lip and turn away, as if trying not to communicate my feelings, than if I tear at my hair and beat my chest (Frønes 1984).

From this one may draw the conclusion that nothing but a completely inexpressive appearance may indicate emotions of the really deep and genuine sort in a fully authentic way. In this perspective, Liv Ullman is a great actor.

Rousseau was one of the first philosophers of authenticity. Distrusting everything superficial and conventional – all acting, even language itself – he went to the point of maintaining that putting one's emotions into words is to betray them (Rousseau 1967: 201–2). In the field of politics, his best disciple was Robespierre.

'Patriotism comes from the heart', according to Robespierre. This psychologizing of politics goes together with a drastic simplification of oratorical style. Those who saw and heard him emphasize his 'reserve', his 'dull and monotonous voice', his 'inscrutable face', etc. (Taine, 1880: 57). 'He is almost motionless', according to one of them.

> The only thing that brings life to this inexpressive face is a nervous twitch, sometimes at the corner of the eyes, sometimes at the corner of the mouth. He speaks slowly and with a penetrating but never seductive voice. His delivery is without conventional elegance and oratorical tricks of any kind.
>
> (quoted in Sieburg 1936: 74)

Robespierre's remarkable lack of recognizable form seems to have inspired trust, even at his age. He was interpreted not only as saying but as actually showing 'the purity of his heart'. His speeches seem to have had a violent effect on the audience, which is described as 'collapsing in convulsive sobbing', or as 'shouting and stamping with their feet, so that one feared the building of the Jacobean club would tumble down' (ibid.: 75–6).

Robespierre's form can be read as a political programme. The genuine feelings of the heart are, in eighteenth-century understanding, natural. With regard to them, all men are equal. To be able to show them, men have to liberate themselves from oppressive cultural forms. When not hiding emotions but sharing them, they all unite. To be inexpressive, then, is to celebrate the values of liberty, equality and fraternity.

Fascism is normally associated with theatricality. This is the only form of political aesthetics readily recognized as such. Conversely, democracy is seen to be anti-theatrical. This is what the Danish author Herman Bang (1907–8) realized when, at the turn of the century, he deplored the decline of the art of acting, and the restraining of all forms of personal expression in everyday life, as part of the striving for equality and democracy.

Santayana's (1961: 85–7) concept of 'the aesthetics of democracy' may be useful in this context. It consists of a 'love of uniformity' – a sense of materials, for instance, as they show to advantage when form is reduced to a minimum. The simplicity of the form gives prominence to the substance – the beauty of fabrics is best appreciated when they are plain; the qualities of the stone are emphasized by the long, undecorated wall – and this goes for social and psychological qualities as well. To be authentic is to 'be oneself', just like everyone else, and that impression is best conveyed by inexpressiveness and inarticulateness. This aesthetics is democratic because the substance uncovered behind the surface variations is uniform and common – like the 'humanness' that makes a person 'one of us'.

Most people are quite unprepared for this kind of aestheticization of politics. Its effectiveness always comes as a surprise. Before the Norwegian election campaign of 1989 a study was conducted to find out which political leader was thought to make the best show on TV. Hagen was ranked number one, far ahead of everyone else; Solheim was at the very bottom of the list. After the interviews and the debates, however, the list was turned upside down.

To sum up, modern media put a premium on 'negative acting'. This is what Solheim has understood. 'For me it is a question of learning to relax', he explains, 'so that I can be myself in front of the camera. I don't believe in studying mimicry and body language and pretending to be something that is not me. That would have undermined my credibility'.

Being himself means, in the first place, telling the truth in such a way that the newspaper journalists, who would never dream of ranking other political leaders as more or less honest, have described him as 'profoundly', 'enormously' or 'exaggeratedly' honest. In the second place it means being awkward to such a degree that they wonder at his 'openness', his 'sensitivity', his 'unprotected nakedness'.

In this way, I think, Solheim has been able to rise above the role of the politician. Because of him being himself – in the way that James Dean was himself, actor and part in one – the political values he administers have simply appeared to rise to the surface and become visible on the outside. 'There has to be agreement between the form and the content', he explained at the occasion of receiving a marketing prize for his election campaign some years ago. 'Hagen's personality is not suited to marketing the values of human care and warmth and responsibility for nature, whereas mine is unsuited to marketing the survival of the fittest'.

His inarticulateness has been a guarantee of the unity between politics and psychology. This is an advanced variant of the aesthetics of democracy: 'The simplicity of the form gives prominence to the substance' (see Figure 10.6).

Today, almost ten years after his sensational debut, Solheim has lost some of his old appeal. First, his lack of style has, by at least part of the public, come to be perceived as a style. Second, as he has become more experienced, and gained in verbal fluency and control over his facial expressions, he has little by little come to resemble the other politicians. Also, in the setting of a political rally, with a huge studio audience making itself very much heard, which is what Norwegian TV now

Figure 10.6 'I can guarantee you this, that no one can force me into saying something I don't mean. And the reason why I say I regret this (statement) is that it was … it was … stupid of me.'

seems to prefer, Solheim's particular strength may not show to advantage as it did in the intimate interview situation more common in the late 1980s.

Finally, a man who takes politics personally the way Solheim does is vulnerable. When his party suffered a serious setback two years ago he completely disappeared from the scene for six months, brooding, I guess, over his own failure. When he returned, he seemed frozen, protected by his appearance as by armour, fixing his eyes on his opponent, for instance, not listening attentively, as in his former conversational attitude, but turning towards him in a defiant manner, staring aggressively. Even if he now seems to be more relaxed, he may never again be able to project the impression of spontaneity and transparency characteristic of the early days of his political career.

In this context, however, psychological explanations are out of place. Let me simply take note of this loss of credibility and conclude that signs of authenticity are not only subtle but also very fragile things.

REFERENCES

Adorno, T. (1986) *The Jargon of Authenticity*, London: Routledge.

Atkinson, Max (1984) *Our Master's Voices*, London: Methuen.

Balàzs, Béla (1985) 'The close-up', in G. Mast and M. Cohen (eds) *Film Theory and Criticism*, New York: Oxford University Press.

Bang, Herman (1907–8) 'Skuespilkunstens nedgang', *Det ny Aarhundrede*, vol. 5.

Becker, S.L. and Lower, E.W. (1962) 'Broadcasting in presidential campaigns', in Sidney Kraus (ed.) *The Great Debates*, Bloomington, IN, and London: Indiana University Press.

Cicero (1968) *De oratore*, Cambridge, MA: Harvard University Press.

Freidel, Frank (1952) *Franklin D. Roosevelt*, vol. 2, Boston, MA: Little, Brown.

Frønes, Ivor (1984) *Om historiske fortolkningsformer*, Oslo: Department of Sociology, University of Oslo.

Hale, Julian (1975) *Radio Power: Propaganda and International Broadcasting*, London: Paul Elek.

Kracauer, Siegfried (1960) *Theory of Film*, London: Oxford University Press.

Langslet, Lars Roar (1988) *Mennesker og milepoeler*, Oslo: Cappelen.

Lie, Carl (1935) *Martin Tranmæl. En psykologisk studie*, Bergen.

Lie, Håkon (1988) *Martin Tranmæl – et bål av vilje*, Oslo: Tiden.

Meyrowitz, Joshua (1985) *No Sense of Place. The Impact of Electronic Media on Social Behavior*, New York: Oxford University Press.

Quintillian (1961) *Institutio oratoria*, Cambridge, MA: Harvard University Press.

Rousseau, Jean-Jacques (1967) *Lettre à M. d'Alembert*, Paris: Garnier-Flanmarion.

Santayana, George (1961) *The Sense of Beauty*, New York: Collier.

Schnitler, Carl W. (1911) *Slegten fra 1814*, Oslo: Aschehong.

Sennet, Richard (1974) *The Fall of Public Man*, New York: Vintage.

Sieburg, Friedrich (1936) *Robespierre*, Copenhagen: Aschehong.

Taine, Hippolyte (1880) *Jacobinismens ledere*, Copenhagen: Hauberg & Gjellerup.

Trilling, Lionel (1971) *Sincerity and Authenticity*, Cambridge, MA: Harvard University Press.

DOCUMENTARY

The transformation of a social aesthetic

John Corner

INTRODUCTION

In this article I want to raise some questions about the changing character of television documentary in Britain, developing further some questions which I raised in a recent critical study of documentary film and television (Corner 1996a). Many of these questions have broader international dimensions. I want to work towards making some comments on specific shifts in format and style, but these shifts can best be understood if they are related to the broader debate about documentary functions and documentary forms. This debate has recently intensified, for different reasons, both within the television industry and within media scholarship. I have suggested (Corner 1995) that it is useful to regard it as a debate about 'documentarism' as much as 'documentary', because some of the transformations around which discussion has gathered concern programmes not self-identified as 'documentary' even though their use of image and speech often derives directly from the tradition of documentary work. Of course, precisely what is and what is not 'documentary' has always been a matter of argument. John Grierson's seminal essays on the matter (Hardy 1979) recognized this in the 1930s, but the intensive hybridization which has occurred in factual television since the early 1990s has produced a situation in which the whole matter of generic boundaries has become more problematic.

Before turning my attention to the specific questions raised by the shifts, however, I want to establish two rather distinct if related theoretical contexts for reading their significance. The first of these concerns the current general circumstances of television as public communication; the second, as I indicated above, is that broader debate about the status and future of documentary which precedes the new developments by many years but which has been considerably reinvigorated by them and which has also been provided with many new instances for critical assessment.

PUBLIC TELEVISION IN THE 1990s

A number of books and articles published since the early 1990s have variously 'taken stock' of the state of television as a public medium. Their diagnoses have varied not only in accordance with authorial views, but also in relation to the specific national television systems about which their principal comments are made. So, for instance, writers in the United States have generally (and not surprisingly) indicated a more comprehensively gloomy judgement than writers in Europe. Writers in Britain, while generally aware of the dangers of that nervously celebratory populism which has afflicted a wide range of commentary on popular culture, have nevertheless found more to be positive about in the range of programme developments, and in the relationship between the forms of national television and democratic public values.

Such national differences notwithstanding, however (and it is worth noting that the collapsing of these differences is the source of a potentially dangerous transnational essentialism in some recent writing on the media), the broad framing from which few television systems are free is that provided by an increasingly competitive, commercialized audiovisual environment. Against the virtually global backdrop of this deregulation and re-regulation of television into a more (in some cases one should say 'even more') intensively commodified medium[1], the sense that the possibilities for public culture are reduced, that we are facing a general crisis in the relationship between politics, culture and mediation, seems well founded. Television is increasingly subject to 'dispersal', a dispersal across channels, across genres, across national boundaries, and increasingly across and into other forms of audiovisual product and electronic cultural technology. The scale and velocity of these developments are escaping the (often very limited) forms of 'public' containment which in some countries served to require of television a measure of accountability and public-service function. In those countries with no such tradition the possibilities of ever developing one are becoming minimal.

Of course, not everyone would respond pessimistically to this dynamic. In a number of countries there have been enough imposed unities and repressively regulated aesthetics at work under the banner of 'public television' to provoke a measure of reaction against the very idea of 'publicness', and to induce a hope in the anti-elitist and pluralizing tendencies of the market. Given the way in which international media research is currently positioned uneasily between modernist and postmodernist perspectives – or, to put it differently, is made insecure by their concurrent and even combined application – it is also not surprising that the concept of a dispersed, anti-public aesthetic for television, an aesthetic of difference, possible self-contradiction and multiple identity-pleasures – in short, an aesthetic of committed irresponsibility – can be actively welcomed. I shall return to this playoff between defensive versions of the 'public' and burgeoning versions of 'privatization' at the end of this chapter.

DOCUMENTARY: A FLAWED GENRE?

Documentary has, over the years, attracted a good deal of epistemological critique both from within the ranks of its most thoughtful practitioners and from media scholarship. Some of this is derived from the largely American perspective on television itself as epistemologically flawed, particularly in its supposed 'factual' genres (thus it is often denounced *tout court* as a gigantic distraction machine, a misinformation device, an ideological apparatus). However, some critique is more generically specific, regarding documentary formats – in their subtle, illusory realisms and modes of sustained, narrativized referentiality – as more suspect and dangerous than perhaps most other kinds of output.[2] I have noted in my recent work (Corner 1996a) what I consider to be an important difference between criticism of documentary as generically flawed beyond repair by its epistemological claims and criticism which focuses on its current forms of institutionalization and practice, thereby admitting the possibility of its rehabilitation. As we shall see, this difference figures in assessment of the shifts in form to which I will shortly turn, sometimes causing a degree of ambivalence which I take to be symptomatic of deeper tensions in media research.

Three very recent books on documentary issues, Bill Nichols's *Blurred Boundaries* (Nichols 1994), Mary Ann Rabinowitz's *They Must Be Represented* (Rabinowitz 1994) and Brian Winston's *Claiming the Real* (Winston 1995) all serve in various ways to thicken the texture of contemporary documentary criticism. All sound strongly pessimistic notes too, but the form this pessimism takes, as well as its implications, differs according to that division in opinion about the sources of documentary inadequacy which I noted just above.

Nichols offers a sustained, calculatedly intemperate critique of the fashion for 'reality television', which he sees as a 'perversion' of documentary responsibilities. Without committing him to self-contradiction, it is interesting how this stance reactively pushes him towards a certain upholding of the kinds of implicit criteria for making 'proper' documentaries which his work has elsewhere been interested in critically undercutting (see, for instance, Nichols 1991). Indeed, one might see something rather paradoxical in Nichols getting upset about *any* kind of 'blurred boundaries' after so many years in which the main gist of his scholarship (a good deal more circumspect here than that of many other critics, nevertheless) has precisely been to question conventional exercises in boundary maintenance and to encourage ambitious boundary-crossing, especially across into dramatic form.

Very early on in her book, Rabinowitz airs her view that documentary may well be an obsolete form, one entirely predicated on the 'mechanics of sight and sound' of monopoly capitalism. 'Our present moment of post-industrial late capitalism perhaps requires another mode of postmodern representation', she muses (Rabinowitz 1994: ix). There is not much ground here, it would seem, upon which to carry out reconstruction work. It is interesting to contrast her assessment with that of John Thornton Caldwell, who, in his impressively ambitious account of new trends away from 'transparency' and towards an opaque 'videography' in

American television, says this of documentary: 'Since postmodern practice also privileges endless recombinations and assemblage, documentary can arguably be seen as postmodernism's most privileged mode of production' (Caldwell 1995: 244). However, this difference in the kind of postmodern/documentary relationship posited (here appropriation not displacement) still leads to a negative assessment of the political and cultural consequences following from documentary's current 'restyling' of the real.

Winston (1995), in an account which matches historical scholarship with critical acuity, is nevertheless sceptical about the survival of documentary's referential claims in a postmodern world, and (a rather different kind of point, this) a world in which digital image-processing is steadily undermining whatever degree of reliability photographic and electronic images might once have been thought to have. On the whole, he seems to find the waning of the genre to be no more than it deserves, given its history of fraudulent and pretentious realisms (the idealist realism of John Grierson in the 1930s and the resounding empiricist naturalism of vérité over three decades being his two chief targets). He sees one line of possible development to offer itself if documentaries, instead of making truth claims themselves, somehow give up on the realist project entirely and allow greater space for audiences to generate their own 'truths' from what they see and hear:

> Grounding the documentary idea in reception rather than in representation is exactly the way to preserve its validity. It allows for the audience to make the truth claim for the documentary rather than the documentary implicitly making the claim for itself.
>
> (Winston 1995: 253)

This is a preservation formula which raises problems about the grounding of truth claims and criteria of 'validity' which are, if anything, even larger than the ones which have apparently made representational claims untenable.

So around documentary at present there exists a dense but overall rather ambivalent climate of opinion. To take Nichols's (1994) phrase, it is clear that, particularly through a number of developments in infotainment, the old epistemic and discursive boundaries are being regularly and heavily blurred (though not, we should note, being *collapsed entirely* – it is hard to imagine a declassifying move of such a radical nature being brought about by television's generic mixing alone, particularly when other parts of the schedule reinforce the separateness of 'fact' and 'fiction'). But the blurring of boundaries, which sounds like it should be a matter for celebration among the deconstructors of convention, is not seen to be such a good thing at all, connected as it is with a further commodification of television and often with political conservatism. A gap has opened up between discursive innovation and the particular historical forms of its socialization – indeed, it looks as though some boundaries are in urgent need of a vigorous *re-establishing!*[3] This awkwardness over the new political opportunity-costs of representational boundaries is compounded by the continuation of a deeper uncertainty over whether the very idea of documentary is worth saving anyway. Is it a *possible* category of representation for progressive use? Or is it in effect a category mistake, a pseudo-genre constructed out of various forms of cognitive and affective repression whose disappearance from the public arena, no matter what the cause, cannot but be in some way emancipatory? A frequently offered remedy for documentary rehabilitation in the 1980s was, of course, increased reflexivity – the more a documentary showed itself to be aware of its own devices and of its own contingencies of being, the more progressive a public function it would perform. But the kind of confidently modernist prescriptivism behind this recipe does not appear to be quite so available in the 1990s.

DOCUMENTARY MODALITY: FOUR PRIMARY INGREDIENTS

Typologies of documentary discourse have been drafted by a number of writers, perhaps most influentially by Nichols (1991). In my own work (Corner 1995, 1996a) I have used typologies to varying purpose, identifying different documentary strands in broadcast television and attempting to plot future developments. Here I want to suggest that there are four discursive ingredients out of which a very large number of programme types are currently constructed, even though there are clearly other discourses too. These are observationalism, interview, narratives of enquiry and the implicatory plane. A brief examination of what is entailed in each will provide a good basis for looking at the newer points of shift.

Observationalism

This is strong in indexicality and relatively weak in its transformations. There is a whole set of conventions about the viewing distances and devices of continuity used in rendering action and behaviour as unseen, ongoing actuality. At one end of the scale there is the 'purism' of certain kinds of vérité programme-making, seeking often to work selectively with real-time segments and keeping to a minimum any directorial intervention in what is filmed. But there is now a whole range of possibilities for presenting viewers with sounds and images which they are supposed to relate to in the role of vicarious witnesses of reality, rather than as observers of an 'illustration' secondary to truths rendered by another discourse. Elsewhere (Corner 1996a) I have noted the difference between 'reactive' and 'proactive' forms of observationalism, the latter occurring where forms of direction and staging are employed but where the basic diegetic conventions of there being a plane of directly observed action 'relayed' to the viewer are maintained. At the far end of proactive observationalism is full-scale dramatic reconstruction, now widely used in a range of television formats, though the scopic mobility and interplay of image with speech which this usually allows itself through its procedures of construction are more akin to fictional narrative form than to vérité style.

Interview speech

The interview of variously accessed speakers remains a central and powerful feature of much documentarism. Testimony of different kinds – expositional, descriptive and personal – forms a means both of securing authority of account but also, in many radical projects, of subverting the 'official', of contradicting the established. Of course, there are a number of ways apart from synchronized shooting in which interview speech can be recorded and then used against visuals within a programme, and these have been fully explored in film and television practice (they include the strongly subjective/reflective effect gained by using speech as voiceover across images of the speaker). When compared with the testimony speech to be found in the proliferating varieties of talk show, two factors distinguish much documentary usage of interview material. First of all, there is the tighter framing around speaker and topic gained by not having to work within the discursive relations and modes of address of programmes as studio events. The availability of location setting and its opportunities for *mise en scène* are additional factors here. Then there is the significance which is introduced by interview speech being placed into communicatively strategic relationships (variously confirmatory, elaborative or contradictory) with other interview material and with the main strand of visually established or visually underwritten exposition (Corner (1996a) explores this in relation to a number of examples). As I note below, however, an emphasis on 'experience' and 'feeling', similar to that of the new chat shows, is becoming more obvious across the documentary range.

Narratives of enquiry and exposition

Journalistic enquiry has produced its own documentary logics, within whose terms many regular television documentary series work to achieve a viewable coherence and to honour their requirement to show 'fairness'. These logics comprise both vertical relations, between image and speech within a shot, and horizontal relations, between shots and then between sequences. Such combinatory logics, almost always narrativized to some degree, allow for a wide movement across space and time, and for the specific mixing of evidence and argument, the matching of claim to counter-claim etc. When compared, for instance, to the aesthetics of independent cinema documentary, there is also a constraining tendency towards 'literalism' in the use of images. Typically, such expositional logics are grounded in the regular appearance of an on-screen presenter or the regular use of voiceover commentary. There are variations in the schemes by which things are seen to 'unfold' over time and the extent to which the act of enquiry itself is narrativized as an observed process (e.g. visits to interviewees, public records offices, *in situ* reportorial address). A contrast can be made here with the classic public informational mode of documentary, stretching from 1930s cinema through to contemporary arts and science programmes, where the exposition is grounded in the presentation of *established* knowledge rather than the production of new knowledge (although the pretence of 'discovery' may be used as a device for building an attractive exposition).

The implicatory plane

Although the documentary image usually has a strong literalist force (this person in this situation saying these things or involved in this action), it also often has a developed implicatory level. This can be organized both pro-filmically (in terms of what the camera depicts) and filmically (by means of the kinds of shot and forms of editing through which the depiction is rendered). The associative, sometimes self-consciously metaphoric, level of meaning generated here constitutes a plane of the implicit, which often figures in debates about documentary 'fairness' and often, therefore, also about the presence of directorial viewpoints (seen as legitimate or otherwise) working about the primary level of depiction. It is, of course, quite open to directors, as well as editing shots to make 'points' (in the form of visual commentary), to introduce shots having little or no directly referential content whatsoever, shots working self-evidently and exclusively at the level of the metaphoric. But, not surprisingly, there is still some reluctance by documentarists seeking a wide, popular audience to move to such explicitly authorial modes, interrupting (perhaps fatally) the primary depictive development. Movements of meaning at a secondary, associative level serve to connect the narratives of many television documentaries more firmly, more deeply, to the dynamics of the 'mythic'. Quests, problems, solutions, individuals, specific places can be made to resonate with a cultural significance that more literalist approaches would not produce.

Having outlined some of the principal modes at work in television documentary, I want to turn now to the points of shift. Such points, as I indicated earlier, may constitute a gradual 'resocialization' (and repoliticization too) of the documentary aesthetic, gradually establishing new kinds of mediated seeing and hearing (and in the process, perhaps, marginalizing others) in a way which will change both the cognitive and affective profile of the genre as a whole, and its relationship with other kinds of television.

FOUR TRENDS IN RECENT BRITISH DOCUMENTARY

Extension of access

No one could survey documentary television in Britain since 1993 without noting a further extension in the range of people who appear on the screen and in the range of topics considered suitable for documentary treatment. 'Testimony' has become a familiar mode, one which has retained its power to engage and disturb.

In particular, there has been an interest in getting beyond 'official' versions, whether these are of the current political and social order or of historical events and conditions. The most striking work has occurred at the interface between the 'public' and the 'private' – there have been projects on crime, drug abuse, parenthood, education, various aspects of the changing role of women and of family life, career insecurity, experiences of work and of illness (with some productively shocking new approaches here). The best of these projects have had an edge of critical inquiry and sometimes an ethnographic depth, which must be regarded as significant developments in the potential of the medium. Historical series have often used archive film against interview testimony to 'revisit' issues in national history and popular memory, in the process generating a steady, troubling pressure on the mythic and the 'taken for granted'. Perhaps the BBC's *Video Diaries* series, in which members of the public use camcorders to record aspects of their own lives for eventual screening in a thirty-minute programme, has been the innovation with the largest impact, giving rise to a wide range of other formats combining 'access' functions with the conventions and appeal of mainstream documentary programming (see Corner 1994 for a more detailed discussion of this development).

The 'reality TV' factor

Largely as a result of the intensification of competition between channels and the influence of US models, there has undoubtedly been an intensification of narrative and immediacy values, and a certain fetishization of certain kinds of 'true-life witness' viewing. In the light of my comments above, it is interesting that a distinctive kind of experiential, action-related 'testimony' also features as a key ingredient in several successful formats. The BBC's 'emergency services' series *999*, based on a highly successful US precedent, CBS's *Rescue 911*, was the breakthrough programme in British 'reality TV', although *Crimewatch UK*, reconstructing crimes in the declared interest of enlisting police/public cooperation, has been running for over ten years (for reviews of this strand of programming, see Corner 1995, 1996a, 1996b; Kilborn 1994). Around *999*'s mix of dramatizations and 'ultra-vérité' sequences a critical argument has developed about the loss of documentary integrity and the slide towards the provision of a scopic experience and narrative framing (often accompanied by music) which replaces concern for referential complexity with purely representational values, trading directly off other aspects of entertainment culture. *The Living Soap* (1993), a BBC series about a group of students living in a flat in Manchester, was interesting here. Though cast primarily within the terms of the classic observationalist approach, it involved significant directorial intervention to produce that generic correspondence to soap viewing which its title promised (e.g. fully projected characterization, developing interpersonal relations, episodic structures, the approximation of overheard speech to 'dialogue'). It also drew on the tradition of 'access' television by having a room in the house with a fixed camera, allowing participants to register their own feelings and judgements in direct address. Its indebtedness to the self-commentaries and the calculated use of the grotesque and the farcical in Paul Watson's *Sylvania Waters* (BBC, 1992), a 'neo-vérité' series about an Australian family living in a wealthy suburb, is clear. The sustained use of police surveillance material, again combining action values with public-service credentials, is one of the very latest recipes to find a large audience. It seems to me that, whatever the judgement as to the quality and social influence of this work, the range of documentary address has been significantly reconfigured by the looks, sounds, intensities, rhythms and moods (often musically cued) of the newer programmes.

Symbolic density

Many productions, pitched at different levels of seriousness and targeted at different audiences, have employed an increased symbolic density in their visualizations. They have developed what I earlier called the 'implicatory' level. A more allusive, richer documentary language has resulted, one in which beautiful images and pleasing compositions and *mises en scène* have become more frequently incorporated into the overall depictive design, including that of interview settings. This can give a fashionably 'cool' toning to productions, in contrast with the 'hot' values to which the factors noted earlier can contribute, although both can be seen as serving to constitute documentary as 'spectacle' more strongly than in the past.

Some examples of this aestheticization carry echoes of the lyrical, essayistic realism to be found in the 'classic' cinema documentaries of the 1930s; other examples hold their subjects at a densely stylized distance, which connects them more directly to concurrent developments in advertising and promotional imaging. It is precisely an 'excessive' concern with the figurative, serving to de-referentialize image and sound into mere expressions of videographic creativity, which Caldwell (1995) notes in US television. This 'excess' has not yet established itself in British programming, but it well might.

Most of the qualities I have noted under this heading are linked to an authorialism of approach, in which the director openly projects the work as 'creative' and perhaps even distinctively personal in perspective, in contrast to the conventions of current affairs and mainstream broadcast reportage, and also those of the new 'reality shows'.

Comedy and irony

An as yet marginal, but potentially significant, trend I would like to identify here is a movement, across different formats and topic fields, towards comic or variously ironic treatments, either in whole or in part. This is a difficult area in which to make judgements, with so little work upon which to base generalization, but, while fears have been expressed about a kind of 'postmodernization' of documentary in which witty and sardonic stylizations replace sustained enquiry, there has also been some work which has used comic methods to strongly critical effect. Here Michael Moore's *TV Nation* (in Britain, on Channel 4 from 1994), basing itself on the kinds of persona, audience address and subversive theatricality which he employed in his successful feature documentary *Roger and Me* (1989, distributed by Warner), is exemplary. The latter is discussed in detail in Corner 1996a. Irony is here used penetratively rather than – as so often elsewhere in the schedules – evasively. This linking of documentary purposes to comic and sometimes farcical devices can generate an affective power which the more committedly 'sober' tradition of programme-making (see Nichols 1991) is hard put to achieve. Perhaps the possibilities here offer some of the most interesting lines of current development for documentarists wanting to retain a radical, questioning edge in their work while attracting large audiences within an increasingly competitive television marketplace.

Clearly, these shifts are the result of rather different sets of imperatives and intentions, even if they are all at the moment finding a place in the changing ecology of British television. One dynamic is certainly towards the documentary as 'attractive viewing', a dynamic in which the re-imagining of treatment is a market requirement more than a directorial enthusiasm for discursive renewal (though often it is both). But other developments show the continuation of close thematic engagement together with a remarkable widening of the topics about which documentary can be inquisitive and critical. A relatively new exploration of the subjective world in documentary, a concern with taking the viewer on 'inner journeys' (often the project of *Video Diaries*), has not yet displaced address to the 'outer' realms of the political and the social. Preoccupation with the novelty of immediate witness (the 'ultra-vérité' formats) and perhaps with the personally revelatory (testimony/confessional formats), has not (yet) significantly reduced the amount of enquiry and exposition in the documentary schedules.

The threat of a 'narrowing' and 'thinning' of documentary as a result of economic changes in the funding of broadcasting remains strong (one concisely explored in Kilborn 1996), but there is evidence to suggest that documentarism has never been more imaginative and various than it is at the present, never more aware of both its discursive limitations and its distinctive potential.

Let me finally return to that broader context of television and knowledge from which I began. The older forms of 'unitary' public address, often grounded in class assumptions and paternalist condescension, have all but disappeared from British television news and current affairs. As we have seen, however, this has been achieved less by a reappraisal of documentary's social function and social address in changed times than by the new market imperatives of the television industry. These imperatives will doubtless have the frequent effect of resituating documentary programming as 'entertainment' and of generating novel formats by which to do this. But, as I hope to have indicated, the break-up of the old model has also shown new kinds of 'social sightline' being offered by documentary, new renditions of the personal within the public, of interior life within the exterior world. Many of those assumptions about the rationality and seriousness of public life which guided the format and tone of earlier television documentary have been exchanged for new uncertainties, for scepticism, for irony, and often for the fascinations of testimony and vicarious witness.

But this is not all loss. For the old assumptions often worked comfortably with strong elements of national mythology (about, for instance, unities of character, sentiment and custom) and with the articulation of class privilege. Within the range of the new work, alongside artful complacency I find much that renders 'real conditions of living' with an intensity and provocativeness at least equal to that of the work of the past. Whether these new discourses can survive the conditions of a more marketized and fragmented television system and somehow achieve a degree of progressive 'civic' coherence remains to be seen. Certainly, it is right to be wary and sceptical at the moment. A new fluidity of representational boundaries in documentary has appeared both in the form of a refusal to honour older unities and in response to the market need to hybridize across genres in the search for competitively attractive new recipes. However, refusal and transgression on their own are not enough – it is in the staking out of new boundaries, differences and distinctions (implicit and tentative though this will often be), and then in the newer forms of projected boundary relationship (e.g. between the real and the imaginary, between depictions of agency in the context of structure, between distance and involvement, between present actuality and both the frightening and the inspiring possibilities) that the real social and political future of documentary television lies.

ACKNOWLEDGEMENT

I am grateful to Elihu Katz at the Annenberg School of Communication, University of Pennsylvania, Brian Winston at the University of Wales, Cardiff, and Bjorn Sorennsen at the University of Trondheim for organizing events where I was able to debate further the ideas contained in this article following their first airing at the Bergen seminar.

NOTES

1 The nature of 'commodification' in respect of cultural production needs much closer attention than it usually gets when used as a term of blanket denunciation. This attention would need to pay regard not only to the different levels at which, say, a television programme can be seen as a 'commodity', but also to the different kinds of commodity function and their possible coexistence with other functions. A useful recent discussion is to be found in Mosco (1996).

2 The dominance of 'suspicion/critique' as the principle of academic engagement with documentary has recently been vigorously criticized by Carroll (1996), who gives particular attention to what he regards as lapses in some of the (highly influential) arguments advanced by Bill Nichols (1991).

3 In her suggestive and subtle essay on contemporary US television, Margaret Morse uses 'distraction' as a key term, indicating by it a degree of boundary collapse, a temporary inability to differentiate between different levels of reality (Morse 1990: 193–5). She notes an 'attenuated fiction effect' – 'partial loss of touch with the here and now' – behind this cognitive state (ibid.: 193).

REFERENCES

Caldwell, J. T. (1995) *Televisuality: Style, Crisis and Authority in American Television*, New Brunswick, NJ: Rutgers University Press.

Carroll, N. (1996) 'Nonfiction film and postmodernist skepticism', in D. Bordwell and N. Carroll (eds) *Post Theory: Reconstructing Film Studies*, Madison, WI: University of Wisconsin Press.

Corner, J. (1994) 'Mediating the ordinary', in M. Aldridge and N. Hewitt (eds) *Controlling Broadcasting*, Manchester: Manchester University Press.

—— (1995) *Television Form and Public Address*, London: Arnold.

—— (1996a) *The Art of Record*, Manchester: Manchester University Press.

—— (ed.) (1996b) 'Changing forms of actuality', special issue of *Media, Culture and Society* 18(1).

Hardy, F. (1979) *Grierson on Documentary*, London: Faber.

Kilborn, R. (1994) 'How real can you get? Recent developments in reality television', *European Journal of Communication* 9(4): 421–39.

—— (1996) 'New contexts for documentary production in Britain', *Media, Culture and Society* 18(1): 141–50.

Morse, M. (1990) 'An ontology of everyday distraction', in P. Mellencamp (ed.) *Logics of Television*, London: British Film Institute.

Mosco, V. (1996) *The Political Economy of Communication*, London: Sage Publications.

Nichols, W. (1991) *Representing Reality*, Bloomington and Indianapolis, IN: Indiana University Press.

—— (1994) *Blurred Boundaries*, Bloomington and Indianapolis, IN: Indiana University Press.

Rabinowitz, M. A. (1994) *They Must Be Represented*, London and New York: Verso.

Winston, B. (1995) *Claiming the Real*, London: British Film Institute.

12

SCIENCE ON TV

Forms and reception of science programmes on French television

Suzanne de Cheveigné

INTRODUCTION

Science on television is a problem in France. Science programmes appear and disappear, official reports are written, Britain is regularly quoted as a example, scientists blame journalists, journalists blame TV programmers, and so on. And yet the French read large numbers of science magazines and books – so they are apparently not particularly allergic to science. Then what's wrong? To try to answer this question we carried out an extensive reception study of science programmes broadcast on French television, interviewing adults, children, scientists and producers. The part concerning adults will be reported here, but, before that, let us describe the theoretical model it was based on.

One of the authors' (Véron) has long been preoccupied by production of meaning by the media. Media are the focal point of a number of constraints, both on the production side and on the reception side (Véron 1988a). They are certainly not simply a transparent technical set-up. They do not only 'transport' information; they propose a complex relation to their readers or viewers – what he called a 'reading contract', a concept originally developed to understand how readers choose between magazines of very similar content on a very competitive market (Véron 1988b, 1992). Applied to television, we could call it a 'viewing contract'. This contract is proposed in the text, linguistically and in image, through the way in which enunciator and addressee are constructed, and the relation set up between the two. The work of the French linguist Antoine Culioli, whose enunciation theory specifically takes into account the construction of the addressee (or co-enunciator as he calls it, illustrating its equal importance), provides the basic linguistic tools for this analysis (Fisher and Frankel 1983; Fisher and Véron 1986).

The relation set up in the text between addressee and enunciator, discursive beings, is in fact a proposal by the media of a relationship with the 'real' reader. If it is accepted, he or she will buy and read the paper or watch the channel. If not, the reader will turn to a competitor. The notion of addressee developed differs significantly from those of model (Eco 1979) or implied (Iser 1978) reader developed in reader-oriented criticism, because it concerns relationship and form, not just content. It is not a question of competence required of the reader, but rather a meta-discourse on the mode of address of the reader or viewer, on shared world visions, on the role of the media, etc. Here the approaches taken by Gregory Bateson or Erving Goffman allow a close analysis of a situation that is similar in many ways to interpersonal interaction.

To put things briefly, we consider that the manner in which things are said, the way in which the viewer is addressed, counts at least as much as the content of what is said. Only if the relationship proposed to the viewers is felt to be satisfactory will they watch a given programme – as we shall see in this study.

The study was carried out between March 1993 and September 1994, and covered both science programmes and general-interest programmes with a scientific theme.[1] Two years later half of the science programmes had disappeared, which just goes to illustrate the extreme instability of the field. Commercial television was introduced in France in 1982, the Franco-German cultural channel Arte appeared in 1988 and a more educational one, La Cinquième, at the end of 1994. All these events affected television in general and popularization programmes in particular.

IDENTIFYING THE FORMS

By television forms, we mean types of organization of time and space within a programme, i.e. a documentary sequence filmed in a laboratory, a discussion in a studio, in the presence of an audience or not, etc. In France, ten or fifteen years ago a programme would be purely of one form or another. Today television programmes in general, and those used in science popularization in particular, have changed. Shorter ones have appeared, down to five-minute 'clips'. The longer ones often have a hybrid structure, combining successively various forms: a short documentary, then a discussion in the studio, a game, etc. This evolution is said to be related to the zapping habits that viewers have acquired. Whatever the reasons, we have chosen to work on the fairly 'microscopic' scale of single forms rather than that of a whole programme.

We needed to elaborate criteria for comparing and classifying these forms, to allow us to define as wide a range as possible for the tests. We considered that two institutions face each other in science programmes, the television institution and the scientific institution, and that traces of the negotiation between the two are visible in the different forms. Of the two institutions, television, via its members, is the one in charge of the 'contact' with the viewer; normally, only they address him or her directly, looking into the camera. And this element of 'contact' is one of the main characteristics of television.[2] One means of classifying the microforms is to compare the relative presence of one institution or the other. We 'measured' the hold of each institution through the presence of its members (reporters, hosts or scientists) or its equipment (visible cameras, screens, microphones or scientific apparatus), and whose 'territory' (studio or laboratory) the sequence was filmed on.

A tape was made of five sequences of about 2–3 minutes each (plus one edited in inverse order) around the general theme of brain, memory, etc. Three excerpts of talk shows were chosen, one with no studio audience, one with a distant audience and one with the audience close behind the guests. Two reports in laboratories were also shown, one a demonstration of a PET camera by a reporter, the other a scientist at work in her laboratory.[3] Twenty interviewees were selected from as wide a spectrum as possible, in terms of age, sex and socio-professional categories. The interviews were semi-directive, carried out roughly half in focus groups of four to five people and half individually, in their homes. They lasted 1.5–2 hours and had the following structure:

1   The interview began with questions on the person's a priori vision of science, of popularization and of television as a source of knowledge.
2   A first excerpt was shown, then the form, the behaviour of the different participants, the relations between them, etc. were discussed. The five excerpts were shown successively, each followed by the same discussion.
3   A comparative conclusion was requested – best and worst sequence, or ideal programme.

Of course, asking people to express their opinions on television sequences is somewhat artificial – as any reception study inevitably is. The advantage of the set-up which we used is that it allows comparisons, both between people and between one person's reactions to different sequences. The hypothesis underlying this is that the perturbation due to the interview situation is roughly the same for all sequences and for all interviewees, and can in a sense be subtracted out. During long discussions such as these the interviewees developed coherent and systematic positions[4] and we believe that comparing their discourses allows valid conclusions to be drawn.

TWO ESSENTIAL VARIABLES

Television was a familiar institution for all of the adults interviewed, who had clearly structured reactions towards it. We made a first classification of the interviews according to whether they were favourable or not to television and, in particular, whether television was considered a legitimate source of scientific knowledge.

The scientific institution appears less clearly to the general public. It was often perceived as distant and even mysterious. People had very different visions of the accessibility of the knowledge it produces. Those visions strongly depended on their appreciation of the limits of their own knowledge, of their capacity to learn and understand, and on the memories that school has left them. Again, two categories appeared: interviews of people for whom the learning process did not seem problematic and ones that expressed very painful associations.

The two criteria, attitude towards television and attitude towards acquiring knowledge, are independent; taken together they give four possible positions or readings. Within each one, we found a coherent set of reactions, remarkably similar from one person to another. There are not as many readings of this material as individuals; in other words, it is not infinitely polysemic, which is fortunate because otherwise no further analysis could be carried out. Nor does everyone react in the same way; there are several general publics for science programmes, not just one. We shall describe these reactions below. It is important, however, to bear in mind that these are readings of a specific object, science programmes, not a classification of people. If the same people were presented, say, with books on architecture their reactions might well have to be grouped completely differently.

THE INTELLECTUAL READING

This position is very critical of television in general:

> One follows this programme after another programme, it follows on. You become an alienated viewer. You *are* an alienated viewer.

It is particularly critical of television as a source of knowledge:

> I am not persuaded that it brings us knowledge. Because knowledge is something that has to be thought about, and that one has to ask for. I don't think television brings us knowledge.

The intellectual wants a direct view of scientists, their environment and their work, with no apparent mediation.

The intellectuals differentiate him or herself from other viewers:

> That's what I have gathered, because what *people* have gathered…

They can dissociate their personal tastes and the evaluation they make of a given performance, for instance dislike the reporter in the PET camera and yet admit that his explanations are clear – clear for the 'others'. For this group, television is not a legitimate source of knowledge, only a window that should be as transparent as possible onto the scientific world.

THE BENEFICIARY READING

In this constellation television is definitely considered a legitimate source of knowledge, and scientific knowledge is thought to be accessible. In general, the beneficiaries have less than university-level education. They are not troubled by their ignorance: they recognize and accept it. They are curious, and optimistic about their capacity to collect information as long as they make an effort. Note, however, their aggregative model of knowledge:

> Science doesn't necessarily address a minority of people, it's easy to understand the basics of science.

To watch this kind of programme you must concentrate. But anyhow, however little you retain, it is always worthwhile.

The mediation of the journalist is not only accepted but requested:

> He's the intermediary between the scientist and the viewer, so he has to put the scientific discourse on the viewer's level...to aim the questions at what can interest the viewer in his daily life.

The beneficiary in fact identifies with the journalist:

> The host asks questions in place of the viewer [Q: Is that a good thing?] Of course, he doesn't necessarily ask all the questions that we ask ourselves, but at least...in fact, he is the viewer, he represents the viewer. Anyhow, that's what he should do.

The beneficiary reading does not reject spectacular aspects:

> [The very dramatized sequence in the PET camera] is all set up in a manner that makes us very interested.

In other words, the television institution is completely accepted, even if a given performance may be criticized. There is no rejection of any elements that remind the beneficiary of school, an important difference from other positions, as we shall see.

> For me, it is not entertainment. It is like school; we were taught theory. Well there, TV is an intermediary. The scientist teaches us a number of things.

Nevertheless, the possibility of identifying with the teacher is appreciated:

They aren't all seated at the same table, it's less like a conversation. It's more like questioning. It can give the viewer the impression that he's the one who put the guest on the bench and that he is asking him the questions. Whereas when the people are seated around a table, they give the impression of being on their own. And we are here, looking through the keyhole.

The world of science is very distant for these people. Scientists seem to have a way of thinking of their own:

Scientists are people who are confronted with a problem and...they go round and round it until they find a solution, not one solution but several solutions, and they never finish circling around the same subject. That is not the usual way people do things. So they are people who may have a way of thinking that is different from others, it has to be.

So they find it reassuring if the scientist seems accessible:

He doesn't have the physical aspect, the way of dressing that a scientist can have...with glasses, completely dishevelled, on his own planet, so to speak...We feel closer.

Whereas intellectuals did not mention the practical applications of science, the optimism of the beneficiaries goes along with pragmatic requirements of science; they are ready to learn about things that concern everyday life. A certain evolution has taken place since a previous study (Fouquier and Véron 1985), where more interest in great 'themata' such as the origins of life, of the universe, etc. was expressed by the corresponding group.

DISAPPOINTED BENEFICIARIES

One of the focus groups, basically close to the beneficiaries, had very strong reactions, as often happens in focus groups. This type of effect can be interesting since it brings out more sharply the cognitive and affective mechanisms underlying the position. The group members became extremely critical of television, expressing both distrust in the journalists and distress when they were not felt to be filling their mediating role. The response to the sequence in the PET camera where the reporter received an injection of radioactive water was as follows:

I don't believe it....You see him, he gets into it, he talks, and then it's not him. It's someone else's arm [laughter]. Frankly, it's clear, you don't hesitate a second. He shows how you are placed. You can see that it's not him. It's obvious to me. Well, I don't mind at all, he's not there for that, he's there to explain.

In contrast to the beneficiaries and even more so to the intimists, our next reading, this group violently rejected a sequence from which they felt completely excluded, an interview of a scientist by a journalist (who at the time was also anchorman on one of the main evening news bulletins) in a studio with no audience present:

You get the impression you are a little mouse, they aren't talking to us.

Before [another sequence, in a TV studio, with an audience], you had the impression you were invited to the programme and here you feel you are bothering them. You want to go away and leave them.

These disappointed beneficiaries find the host 'stressed', 'uncomfortable', think he has not played his role, that the camera 'surprised them while they were preparing the programme':

What the scientist says is interesting too, but you get the impression that in the studio, the words fly and there is no one to stop them, no reporter, no camera, nothing.

The host in the excerpt they liked always underscores the fact that his programme was well prepared; he looks at his notes, recalls statements made during preparation, etc. The one in the sequence they criticize so bitterly is seen to be learning something new himself from the person he is interviewing. He was not filling the function of mediator – in a literal sense, standing between them and the strange world of science.

THE INTIMISTIC READING

The people in this category expressed a positive attitude towards television, similar to that of the beneficiaries, though a little more critical. They were less curious, more passive, less prepared to make an effort than the beneficiaries:

It is true that I have an appetite, a desire to learn certain things. But, all the same, I won't make the effort to go and find out about them. But if I happen onto an interesting programme or an interesting book that discusses scientific things, I can easily be interested.

For the intimists, the journalists are not intermediaries, the shield between the scientist and the viewer, as they are for the beneficiaries. They engage in a conversation with the scientists and should allow them to speak without 'translating' their words. The host they praise here is the same one that just received such strong criticism from the 'disappointed beneficiaries', the one alone in the studio with a scientist:

> The host was playing his proper role. He was asking questions, they were being answered, he didn't have to rewrite the answers.

The host should step in, though, 'if the scientist's discourse gets off the course', he should 'bring the debate back'. The intimist can identify with the journalist:

> He is the one who guides the debate where he wants it to go. He asks the questions that everyone can ask.

The intimists, like the beneficiaries, are very attentive to the journalist's perfor-mance, but their requirements are different: he or she should not get in between them and the scientist, as happened here:

> You get the impression that he is there to make us understand, a sort of translator for us, when in fact he doesn't answer the questions. It goes via his mind and his thought and I think he transforms things. He interprets what he feels like interpreting.

A very important point that distinguishes intimists from beneficiaries is that they are far more sensitive about their ignorance and often feel that it is being under-scored:

> [Science] makes me think of something I am very interested in but that makes me feel tiny....It makes me think of 'Science et Vie Junior' because the normal 'Science et Vie' is too tough for me.[5]

> [A host started out saying that the aim of the programme was to popu-larize science.] Saying so at the beginning maybe means: 'anyhow, we can't speak like we do among ourselves because you wouldn't under-stand'. I don't know if it is very positive to say so.

> [A sequence with a scientist in her lab started with her driving up in her car.] I don't like the cliché 'look, she's a woman just like you' and then no, in fact, she's much more intelligent than you are. And you say 'Shucks'. You almost end up saying 'I've got a nicer car.'

This sensitivity to the limits of their knowledge makes intimists reject anything that reminds them of school. A talk show with the host seated at a desk at the centre of a semicircle of guests with an audience just behind them gets most criti-cism from that point of view.

[The host] is a little like an inspector in the amphitheatre, handing out trophies at the end of the school year.

It gives me the impression that they're going back over what I didn't revise when I was at school, but that their telling me, well, there are people who do research on those subjects.

The audience seated just behind the guests bothers the intimist (hence the name we gave them – another sequence where the audience was seated much further away from the guests did not cause the same reactions).

I, personally, prefer intimacy in science to having things spread out in front of a lot of people, so the audience behind bothers me.

Intimists oppose public situations to intimate ones. What they want is a personal, face-to-face conversation with the scientist – the type of set-up that G. Bateson (1973) would have called symmetric (as opposed to a complementary, knowledgeable teacher/ignorant pupil type of situation).[6] The excerpt with the host alone with his guest, listening to him carefully – the one that was so bitterly criticized by the 'disappointed beneficiaries' – comes closest to satisfying these expectations.

You could have been his pal, if he'd been here, and you could have asked him questions.

You could perfectly well be there. I think you could even take part in the discussion if you had things to add.

For the intimists, it does not matter if the vocabulary isn't clear. In fact, over-simplification is interpreted again as a suggestion of their ignorance:

Clear, while still using scientific terms. Which means that they don't take the viewer for a fool by trying to replace one word by another. Because there are words that can't be replaced. And even if we don't know them off hand, we are quite capable of understanding them. It's a manner of respect for the viewer to say a simple sentence using scientific words.

Unlike the beneficiaries, the intimists dislike what they consider to be artificial and spectacular set-ups in the programmes filmed outside the studio. The television institution should not be too visible.

As long as they let her talk, explain, as long as they let her work and that the journalists are at a distance and film her, it's interesting. As soon as they make her get out of her car, take the scene a second time, it's like a school video. I find it afflicting.

They do not appreciate debates, which they consider sterile.

What we want to know is why they got there and not the final point of divergence that means that there are different schools.

The intimists dislike what they consider to be a lack of respect for the scientists. Contrary to the intellectuals, they do not want too direct a view into the world of science. Television should be discrete.

I don't see how they can send such badly behaved people to interview people like that.

The demonstration of the PET camera was particularly criticized:

Science isn't a game, a box of magic tricks, you don't do tricks like that.

If intimists are so sensitive to the border between ignorance and knowledge, it is because they know, through their own experience, the effort and investment that it requires to cross it. Most of the people who took this position are on an ascendant social trajectory. During the past thirty to forty years a large proportion of the French population has gained access to higher education, an opportunity that their parents did not have. Children on such ascendant social trajectories were no doubt often under strong pressure to succeed. Moreover, the French school system is very selective, and selection is mainly based on mathematics and science. These people know that it is not easy to acquire knowledge, or to master the stakes of a new professional or a scientific domain. That may be why, although they are not hostile to television, they are not as optimistic about the knowledge it can bring as beneficiaries are.

At any rate, for them the only genuine situation is direct contact with a scientist, with the person who knows what he or she is talking about. Hence their insistence that the mediator should not be an obstacle between them and the scientist. Their strong valorization of knowledge and competence requires that the limit between what is scientific and what is not should not be erased, that scientists be shown respect. That is also why difficult technical terms are not a problem for them – the difficulty only serves better to underscore the limit between knowledge and ignorance.

This group clearly preferred an intimate conversation between host and guest. Nevertheless, the talk show with the host in the centre and an audience close behind the semicircle of guests still managed to let them relate to the scientist – in spite of the audience and what they described as a classroom set-up. In fact, this programme was quite well accepted by all the categories, but for different reasons! This may be due to the studio set-up, which could be interpreted in a number of ways. It is interesting to note that the interviewees (including professionals) sometimes had trouble describing it and explaining who was talking to whom, since the studio audience is behind the guests and the cameras are, of course, in front of them:

> [The scientist] wants to be direct with the viewer, not with the journalist. He answers the viewer. And yet, paradoxically, he turns his back. [silence] The viewers, that's us. It's television. It's the listeners.

Perhaps this is a case of a high degree of polysemia cleverly built into the programme?

THE EXCLUDED POSITION

One person in this study (and one in the 1984 one; see Fouquier and Véron 1985) adopted the last of the four possible positions: against television and uncomfortable about knowledge acquisition. First, she expressed a negative judgement of television, which was accused of generating false beliefs:

> I don't think people are more interested in science than before. But because of the media and of popularisation, they think they are interested. They think that what television or magazines explain to them is science....It's not a square approach, it's popularisation.

Popularization fails, in spite of the efforts made:

> [The scientist] seems to take himself terribly seriously. That's typically the kind of fellow I really don't want to hear making theories. He seems to thinks he's very superior. He annoys me. The other one [the host] is always playing his role, trying to put things within people's reach with his comparisons and his explanations.

A characteristic way of reasoning, in a sort of logical loop, appears in this reading, as though the person were saying: 'I can't understand science, so if ever I do understand, it's not really science.' If something is simple, it will be denied all pertinence − a hopeless situation. This happened with the sequence that the intimists had liked so much, host and scientist alone in the studio. The host rapidly summarized the proceedings at the end of the interview:

> It's hyper-complicated, you really don't know what they are exactly talking about....The conclusion he made to introduce the next part, I

think it in no way summarised what I heard before. I find it so general that you get the impression that he's not talking about anything.

The studio audience is of some help: science was found less haughty when the audience was close to the guests. In a show where the audience was seated way back in a sort of alcove it was thought to have been badly treated:

> Something bothered me there too, it's the people in the back in that sort of window, there. You wonder, they're just four miserable-looking [people]....If they're there to look pretty, they could have done without them....They look bored stiff too.

The spectacular side of things also helped. The sequence in the PET camera was the one this person preferred – 'interactive between the studio and elsewhere'. But this spectacular aspect was appreciated in itself, with no relation to discourse about science. No possible applications of science were mentioned in this reading, which mainly expressed the impossibility of any relationship to the world of science.

CONCLUSION

There are different ways of reading science programmes, of interpreting the situations – as school-like or not, for instance. Different roles required of the mediator were to provide a protecting shield between the viewer and a strange scientist or to be literally a host who brings the two together, who allows them to meet. There were different conceptions of knowledge, too. What we have explored here are different relational demands on media. In the intimistic reading the main requirement was for a symmetric relationship, one which put the viewer on the same plane as the scientists, the mediator only facilitating their meeting. In the beneficiary reading the downside of a complementary relationship was happily accepted, but with a strong demand for the mediation – or, more precisely, the interposition – of a journalist. Neither type of mediation is necessary in the intellectual reading, which is confident in its own capacity of interpretation. Neither is of any help to the excluded.

This means that there is no single, ideal way of presenting science. For some people the mediating role of a television host or reporter is essential; for others it is unacceptable. A clearly defined didactic situation where the knowledge differential between the viewer and the scientist or the TV host is underscored can be happily accepted by one category, but will be rejected by another. Behind these differing reactions to form we can see different relationships to the media, different expectations of science and even different ideas about what the popularization of science can mean: transmission of practical knowledge or the chance to meet a scientist.

NOTES

1 A more complete description can be found in de Cheveigné and Véron (1996).
2 On French television the only exception to this rule used to be official election campaigns, where politicians spoke into the camera, or solemn announcements from the President of the Republic. A new one has appeared, mainly in the news, with distant interviews where the screen is divided into two halves, one for the anchor person and one for the interviewee, who looks at the viewer as well as at the interviewer. On the indexical dimension of contact, see Véron (1983). R. C. Allen (1992) calls this mode rhetorical address.
3 Respectively, *Connaissance de la Science* (TV5), *Savoir Plus* (F2), *La Marche du siècle* (F3), *Savoir Plus* again, *Envoyé Spécial* (F2).
4 For brevity, we 'personify' the positions. It must be remembered, though, that we are talking about the meeting of given objects with given people.
5 *Science et Vie Junior* is the version for children (from about age 10 up) of *Science et vie*, a popular science magazine.
6 Bateson (1973) considered real exchanges, but the same distinction can be applied to the relationship between enunciator and addressee in the media.

REFERENCES

Allen, R. C. (ed.) (1992) *Channels of Discourse, Reassembled: Television and Contemporary Criticism*, London: Routledge.

Bateson, G. (1973) *Steps to an Ecology of Mind*, London: Paladin Granada.

de Cheveigné, S. and Véron, E. (1996) 'Science on TV: forms and reception of science programmes on French television', *Public Understanding of Science* 5: 231.

Eco, U. (1979) *Lector in Fabula*, Milan: Bompiani.

Fisher, S. and Frankel, J.-J. (eds) (1983) 'Linguistique, énonciation: aspects et détermination', *Connaissance et Langage* 7.

Fisher, S. and Véron, E. (1986) 'Théorie de l'énonciation et discours sociaux', *Études de Lettres* 71–92.

Fouquier, E. and Véron, E. (1985) *Les Spectacles scientifiques télévisés. Figures de la production et de la réception*, Paris: La Documentation Française.

Iser, W. (1978) *The Act of Reading*, Baltimore, MD: Johns Hopkins University Press.

Véron, E. (1983) 'Il est là, je le vois, il me parle', *Communications* 38: 98–120.

—— (1988a) *La Sémiosis sociale. Fragments d'une sociosémiotique*, Paris: Presses Universitaires de Vincennes.

—— (1988b) 'Presse écrite et théorie des discours sociaux: production, réception régulation', in P. Charaudeau (ed.) *La Presse. Produit, production, réception*, Paris: Didier Érudition.

—— (1992) 'Reading is doing: enunciation in the discourse of the print media', *Marketing Signs* 14–15.

INDEX

Abercrombie, N. 140
academia *see* scholars
access television 179–80
acting styles 166–7, 168, 169, 170
address, modes of 74
Adorno, Theodor 162
advertising 38, 67, 70n8
aesthetic: democratic 169–70;
    documentary 178, 180
agon 80, 86n7
alea 80, 86n7
alienation of viewers 137, 142, 143, 156,
    188
Allen, R. C. 101
Allor, M. 102
ambiguity 151, 152
American Family Association 151
Anderson, Benedict 29–30
Ang, I. 102
anthropology 19, 87n13; *see also*
    ethnography
anti-authoritarianism 46
anxiety, family/work 96
apartheid, television 145
Appadurai, Arjun 19, 21, 30–1
architecture, demolished 7
archive film 179
areté 46
Aristotle 1, 77
Arlen, Michael 26
Arte 186
arts on television 48
Atkinson, Max 163, 164
audience 38, 91; as communities 29;
    documentary 175; gender 97;
    home/studio 91, 93, 163–4;
    identification 82, 84; mediated

knowledge 3, 91, 92, 94–5, 104n8;
    news 128–9, 137, 140–1, 152;
    public-service broadcasting 38; race
    25, 28; rhetoric 163–4; and text 3,
    74, 75; *see also* viewers
audience discussion programmes 101,
    104n12
audience participation programmes 91–2
audience research 101–2, 103n5, 151
Austin, J. L. 88n14
authenticity 93, 117, 161, 162, 171
'Authoritarian Populism' (Hall) 154

Balàzs, Béla 167
Bang, Herman 169
Baran, S. 127
Bateson, Gregory 186, 193
Baudrillard, Jean: end of real 144; Gulf
    War 35; hyper-real 147;
    selfworld/system world 100; virtual
    media events 143
Bauman, Zygmunt 50–1
BBC sport 64
Becker, S. L. 166
Benamou, Michael 83, 84
Bergen, Candice 148, 150
Berger, John 49
Bernsten, Thorbjørn 165
Bierig, J. 91
Bildungsroman 22
Billig, Michael 77–8, 86n6
black entertainment television 25
black public sphere 28
Bodroghkozy, A. 145
body language 167
books 104n9
Bordwell, David 69n7, 73

Bosnian war 154
boundaries: blurred 99, 167, 173, 176; collapsing 184n3; genres 173; transgressed 145
Bourdieu, Pierre: fields 2, 40; *habitus* 41–2, 45; *Homo Academicus* 40; knowledge/ignorance 138; professional recognition 43; *Sur la Télévision* 35, 40–1, 43, 44–5
Boyd-Barrett, O. 126
Branston, G. 139
Brecht, Bertolt 140
Breckenridge, Carole 19, 21, 31
Brémond, Paul 73
Brennan, Susan E. 75
Britain: current affairs 138; documentary 173, 179–83; racism 145; television news 137
British Midland chairman 57
broadcasting as metaphor 37
Brookside 60, 61
BSS cable system 112–13
Bull, Francis 48
Bulmer, Martin 7
Burgess, Robert G. 43
Burke, Kenneth 77
Butler, Judith 83, 88n15

cable subscribers 112–13
cable television 113–15
Caillois, Roger 80, 86n7, 87n8 and n9
Caldwell, J.T. 175–6, 181
capital punishment 9, 58
Carey, J.W. 29, 95–6, 98
Carlin, John 145, 151
Carroll, N. 183n2
Casualty 66
celebrities 59
centre/periphery image 19
certainty, narrative 69n6
Certeau, Michel de 3, 23, 75, 77, 110–12, 119
Chamberlain, Neville 56
Channel 5 137
channels: BSS 112–13; cable system 113–15; choice 15; programmes 116; site 115–16
charisma 161–2
chat shows 59, 60
Cheveigné, Suzanne de 4, 49
childhood space 110
Cicero 1, 77, 86n6, 168

cinema 55, 109–10, 115, 167; *see also* films
La Cinquième 186
citizenship 7–8; audience 38, 91; as community 20; cultural rights 11–13, 16; Enlightenment 37; identity 7, 9; information 11, 58; knowledge 12; loyalties 15; news 4; representation 12, 13; rights 9, 10; simple/complex 8–10, 13; voting 9
civic virtues 8
civil society 10
Civilisation (Clark) 49
Clark, Herbert H. 75
Clark, Kenneth 49
class: alienation 142; documentary 182; ideology 140; interests 139; news watching 137–8; viewing 133–4
Clinton, Bill 151
close-up: cinema 55; politicians on television 159, 164, 168; television 45, 46, 55
closure 57–8, 64, 66, 69n6
cognition, and recognition 77–8
Cohen, A. 128
colonialism 126
comedy: documentary 180–1; situation comedy 96, 98
commentators 56–7
commodification, cultural production 183n1
common ground 75–6, 84, 86n5
common knowledge *see* knowledge
communication: elite 95; international 126; knowledge 93–4; media 77, 102–3, 103n3; public access 126; ritual model 3, 96; television's dominance 42–3; transmission model 3, 95, 98
communication studies 18, 52
communicative ethos 74
communitarianism 8, 23
communities: audiences 29; citizenship 20; construction 18; genres 23; imagined 29, 30, 99; minority 20–2; national 29; religious 23
competition 8
computer-mediated interaction 75
conservatives 8; *see also* right wing
consumerism 10
consumption, culture of 23
content-analysis 127, 153

Corner, John 4, 13, 61, 62, 91, 97, 140, 173, 175, 177, 178, 180, 182
corporate power 11, 16
Cosby Show, The 145–7, 151–2
cosmopolitanism 19
Cosmos (Sagan) 49
Crimewatch UK 180
Crossroads 61
Cruz, J. 95
Culioli, Antoine 185
cultivation research 103n7, 153–4
cultural capital 41, 139
cultural objects 30
cultural production 183n1
cultural representation 168–9
cultural rights 11–13, 16
culture: consumption 23; folk 22–3; fragmentation 10; homogenization 18; imperialism 128–9; media 1, 100; narrative 73; oppression 169; popular 47, 152; shared 10
Curran, J. 95, 102, 152, 153
current affairs 62, 138, 152
cynicism 142, 154

Daguerre, L. J. M. 108
Dahlgren, Peter 16, 28–9
Dahrendorf, Ralf 8
Davis, M. 144, 145
Day After, The 147
Dayan, Daniel 2, 27
De Lillo, Don 144
Dean, James 167, 170
decentring of subject 110
decoding, comprehension 140–1; *see also* encoding–decoding model
DeGeneres, Ellen 150–1
democracy: aesthetics 169–70; anti-theatrical 169; television 2, 4, 173
demolition, modern architecture 7
Denmark 125, 132, 133
dependency, media-systems 105n14, 144–7
Derrida, Jacques 36
desequestration 99, 104n11
Diamond, Elin 83
diasporas 19, 22, 24, 30
difference 7, 10
digital television 15, 175
Dimmick, J. 91
disciplines, scholars 48
discontinuity 67–8, 70n8

discourse 9–10, 13–14, 72; *see also* discursive space; public discourse
discovery 97, 98, 102
discursive space: common ground 86n5; rhetoric 76–8; television 84, 85; text/audience 3, 74–5, 85
discussion programmes 92, 101, 104n12
distraction 183n3
documentaries 4; aesthetic 178, 181; audiences 176; changes 173, 179–80; class privilege 183; criticisms 61, 183n2; epistemology 175; integrity 180; lack of closure 64; narrative in 62; national myths 183; persuasion 77; pessimism 175; postmodernism 175–6, 181–2; pressures 152; public discourse 61; realism 176, 180–1; reception/representation 176–7; symbolic density 181; truth 176
documentaries, types 62; comedy/irony 181–2; drama 104n12; ethnographical study 71–2, 73–4, 180; implication 179; informational 98, 178; interview speech 178; investigative 14; narrative of enquiry 178; observationalism 162–3, 177; performative 83, 87n12; testimony 179–80, 182; video diaries 14
Donahue 91
drama 59, 66–7, 104n12, 147–51
Drotner, K. 98
Dukakis, Michael 159
Dyson, M. 146

Eastman, George 108
Eco, Umberto 118, 186
educational television 49
Ehrmann, Jacques 83
Eisenstein, Elizabeth 29
elites 19, 95
Elliott, P. 128
Ellis, John 3, 13
emic/etic categories 130, 132–3
emigration 21–2
encoding–decoding model 95, 140, 151
Enlightenment project 37, 39
entertainment 45, 69, 78
enunciation theory 185
episode 67–8
epistemology 103n2; documentary 175; lay 92; mediated knowledge 97;

postmodernism 35; structuralism 36; viewing 86
ER 66
essentialism 173
ethnic television 25, 26
ethnic videos 22–3
ethnicity 20
ethnography: changing sites 30–1; documentary 71–2, 73–4, 179; pilgrimage 26
ethos 46, 74
Euclidean space 110, 115
eunoia 46
European Union, Denmark 125
evaluation, screen personality 46
exclusion 15, 80, 145
executions 58
exilic television 25, 26
experience: desequestrated 99, 104n11; knowledge 47; mapping 119; meaning 77; personal/through television 144–5; representation 11–12; rights to 11–12; working through 57
experts 92, 93
explanation 55, 63

fact/fiction, television 139–40
Falwell, Jerry 150
familiar: media research 102; prior knowledge 105n16; recognition 96–7; situation comedy 98
family, anxiety 96
family values 147, 148, 150
Family, The 63
fan/non-fan readings 101
fascism 169
female audiences 97
fiction 12, 139–40, 141
Fielding, Helen 138
fields (Bourdieu) 2, 40
filiation 20
filming, influence on filmed 62
films 67, 180; *see also* cinema
Fiore, Q. 95
Fisher, S. 185
Fishing Party, The 63
Fiske, John 69n5, 64, 139, 147–8, 149, 150, 152
folk culture 22–3
formalism, narrative 69n7, 73
Foucault, Michel 36–7

Fouquier, E. 190, 195
fragmentation: culture 10; knowledge 12, 109; postmodernism 12, 83, 84; public sphere 38; textuality 84
framing 68
Framing Science 78, 82, 85
France: commercial television 186; community-oriented genres 23; French Revolution 7–8; science on television 185–96
Frankel, J.-J. 185
Freeth, Martin 76
Freidel, Frank 166
French Revolution 7–8
Freud, Sigmund 69n1
funding for institutions 43

Galbraith, John Kenneth 11
Galtung, J. 127
Gans, H. 128
Garfinkel, Harold 87n13
Garnham, Nicholas 39, 40, 95, 102
Gates, H. L. 146
gay press 28
gays, coming out 150–1
Gellner, Ernest 69n6, 69
gender: audience 97; knowledge 139
Genini, Isa 26
genres: boundaries 173; community-oriented 23; documentary 62; televison 13; US network television 38
Geraldo 59
Gerbner, George 47, 91, 98, 142, 153
Giddens, Anthony 98, 99, 104n9, 127
Gillespie, Marie 23, 24
Gitlin, Todd 20
globalization 19
Goffman, Erving 45, 87n13, 98, 186
Golding, P. 128
Gray, Herman 146
Greimas, A. J. 73
Grierson, John 173, 176
Gripsrud, Jostein 2, 37, 69n5, 137, 139
Groombridge, Brian 137
Gross, Larry 28, 91
Grossberg, L. 95, 99
group: dispersed 22; identity 18, 20–1; marginalized 15
Guardian 150
Guiding Light 60
Gulf War 35, 57
Gutenberg, J. G. 108, 109

Habermas, Jürgen 2, 37, 43, 45, 100, 102, 129
habitus 41–2, 45, 96
Hagen, Carl I. 161, 170
Hagen, I. 136, 137–8
Hale, Julian 166
Hall, Stuart: 'Authoritarian Populism' 154; encoding–decoding model 95, 140; 'The Great Moving Right Show' 153; media dependence 144; sharing of culture 10
Hardy, F. 173
Hartmann, P. 145
Hawkins, R. P. 103n7
Heche, Anne 151
Hello magazine 137
Herbst, Susan 28
Hill, Anita 147
Himmelfarb, Gertrude 8
Hitchcock, Alfred 167
Hjarvard, S. 127
Hobson, D. 96
Hoffman, Eva 26
home 110, 115, 116
Home and Away 60–1
home videos 24
homogenization of culture 18
Horizon 76
Horton, D. 99
hospitals as drama 66
housebreaking 60
Huizinga, Jan 79
human relationships 61
human rights 7
Husband, C. 145
hyper-reality 147

identification 82, 84
identity: citizenship 7, 9; constructed 20, 30; group 18, 20–1; interaction 132; media 28; national 19–20, 38; public/private sphere 21–2
identity politics 9, 99
ideology 37, 140
ignorance 138–9
ilinx 80
image: association 14; cinema 167; knowledge 14; literalism 177; and message 46, 47–8; moving 108; stabilised 55
imaginary space 118, 119–20
imagined communities 29, 30, 99

imperialism, cultural 128–9
implication, documentary 179
Independent 139, 151, 152
Independent on Sunday 150
information: citizenship 11, 58; explanation 55; flow 125; and knowledge 3, 51, 97; narcotic effect 137; television/newspaper 136–7
information processing 55
infotainment 92
Inhelder, Bärbel 110
insecurity 153–4
institutions 8, 11, 20, 43, 103n6, 168–9, 189–90
integrity of documentary 180
intellectuals: legislators/interpreters 50–1; media 51, 52; and technicians of knowledge 49–50; *see also* scholars
intention 77
interaction: computer-mediated 75; identity 132; mediated 99; space 75–6; technology 84
interests, class 139
International Associaton for Mass Communication Research 129
International Channel Network 25
international news 126–9; *see also* news; News of the World project
interpretation 50–1, 57–8
intertextuality 84
interview speech 178
intimacy 45, 68, 165–6, 193
invention 77
Iranian television, Los Angeles 25, 28
irony, documentary 181–2
Iser, W. 100, 186

Jakobson, Roman 73
Jary, D. 98
Jencks, Charles 7
Jenkins, Amy 155–6
Jensen, Klaus Bruhn 4, 129, 133
Jhally, S. 145–7, 151–2
Johansen, Anders 4, 44
Johnson, Mark 77, 118, 119, 133
Jokelin, R. 127
Jones, Bridget (Fielding) 139
journalism: autonomy/market pressures 40–1; enquiry 178; financial constraints 128
journalists: *habitus* 41–2; professional

recognition 40; representing viewers 189, 191; and scholars 2, 34, 39
journey/situation 109–10
Julia 145

Kabul 58
Kahn, Joel S. 7
Katz, Elihu 21, 23, 26
Kilborn, R. 180, 182
Kilroy 57, 59, 91
knowledge 1–2; citizenship 12; communicated 93–4; conflicting forms 39; established/new 178–9; experience 47; familiar 105n16; fragmented 12, 109; gendered 139; and ignorance 138–9; images 14; and information 3, 51, 97; media 1, 100, 101; mediated 3, 91, 92, 94–5, 97, 98, 100, 103, 104n8; popular culture 47, 152; rational argument 14; re-contextualized 94, 99–100; reproduction 94; scholars 35; and subjectivity 37; technicians of 49–50; and television 35–7, 104n12, 188, 189; transmission 93; and truth 35, 36
Kodak camera 108
Korean Television Enterprises 25
KULT programme 1
Kvale, S. 131

labour division 144
Labour government 4, 155
Labov, William 111
Laidi, Zaki 19
Lakoff, George 77, 118, 119
language 1
Lapierre, Nicole 20
Larsen, Peter 3, 120
Lasswell, H. D. 77, 95
Laurel, Brenda 75–6
Lazarsfeld, P. 137, 156
Lee, Veronica 150
legitimacy: media 40; news 129
lesbianism 150–1
Lévi-Strauss, Claude 71, 73
Lewis, Justin 95, 141, 142, 143, 144, 145–7, 151–2
liberalism 8, 37
Libération 24
Lie, C. 162, 163

Lie, Håkon 162, 165
Liebes, Tamar 23
lifestyles 41; see also habitus
Linde, Charlotte 111
linguistics 73
Lippman, Walter 136, 154, 156
literary figures, Norway 48–9
Living Soap, The 180–1
Livingstone, Sonia 3, 57, 91, 92, 93, 95, 100, 101, 102, 103n4
local/global dichotomy 19
local news 4, 138
logic 88n14
Los Angeles, Iranian television 25, 28
Los Angeles riots 147, 148
Lower, E. W. 166
ludus 80, 82, 84, 87n9
Lunt, P. K. 57, 91, 101, 103n4
Lyotard, Jean-François: narrative collapsing 7, 72; play 75; postmodernism 35

MacBride, Sean 126
McCann, Paul 152
McCombs, M. E. 91
McKeon, Richard 77
McLuhan, M. 95
Mann, M. 140
map: cable subscribers 113; experience 119; internalised 114; metaphor 118–19; verbal 111, 112, 117; viewing 117–20
marginalization of groups 15
marketplace 10
Martin, Graham 137
me-generation 155
Mead, George Herbert 132
meaning: and experience 77; linguistics 73; and media 185; mediated 100; structuralists 73; television 64; text 73
media: communication 77, 102–3, 103n3; community construction 18; identity 28; interdiasporic 22–4; knowledge/culture 1, 100, 101; legitimacy 40; local/global 19; meaning 184; and minorities 20–1; narcotic effect 137; particularistic 22, 28; public sphere 95; and scholars 39, 44–5; social sciences 48; social structure 127; trust 154
media dependency 105n14, 144–7
media research 43, 102, 174; audience

101–2, 103n5, 151; communication studies 18, 52; cultivation research 103n7, 153–4; ethnographic study 71–2, 73–4, 180; News of the World project 125, 129–34; reception studies 100, 133, 176–7, 186–7, 190; Rhetoric, Knowledge, Mediation 1; viewing studies 152
mediated knowledge 103, 104n8; audience 3, 91, 92, 94–5, 104n8; discovery 97, 98; epistemology 97; representation 94–5; television 71–2
Mehl, Dominique 57
Melucci, Alberto 9
memory 20
Mepham, John 12
Merton, R. 137, 156
message 46, 47–8, 77–8, 96, 140
metaphor 37, 77, 118–19
Metz, Christian 73
Meyrowitz, Joshua 45, 46, 95, 98, 143, 144, 147, 154, 164
micro public spheres 2, 18, 28–9
microphone 166
migrant workers 19
mimicry 80, 87n8
mini series 66
minority communities 20–2
minority television 10, 25–6
mnemonics 118
modernity, architecture 7
Modleski, T. 97
Mohammadi, Annabelle Sreberny 28
Moi, Toril 40
Moore, Michael 182
Morgan, Michael 142, 143, 152, 153, 154
Morgenstern, S. 104n8
Morley, David 4, 74, 77, 129, 137, 138, 151, 152
Morse, Margaret 184n3
Mosco, V. 183n1
Mulhall, Stephen 8
Murdock, Graham 2, 44
Murphy Brown 147–50
music and time 44
mutual aid 8
myth-making, television 71
myths, national 183

Naficy, Hamid 24, 25, 26–7, 29
narcotization, news media 137

narrative 66–7; and certainty 69n6; classical 67; collapse of 7, 72; culture 73; documentaries 62; enquiry 177; episodic 67–8; formalist theories 69n7, 73; news 141; soap operas 141; sport 65–6; television 71–2
narrowcasting 10
national communities 29
national identity 19–20, 38
negative acting 167, 170
Neighbours 60, 61
neoliberalism 8
neo-vérité 180
New Green Revolution, A 76, 82
New Right 8
New York Times 166
news 4; alienation 143, 156; audience interpretation 128–9, 137, 140–1, 152; class 137–8; commentators 56–7; content analyses 127–8; disorder/control 56; flow 126–9; global 4; images 55; immediacy 56; information 136–7; legitimacy 129; local 4, 138; narrative structure 141; national 138; personalizing stories 137, 143–4; politicians 143–4; psychological perspective 59; selection 127, 128; standards 128; stories without endings 57–8; talk shows 56–7; working-through 3
news anchorperson 56
News of the World project 125, 129–34
newsletters 22
Newsnight 59
newspapers 127, 136–7
Nichols, Bill 61, 82–3, 84, 87n12, 175, 176, 177, 182, 183n2
Niepce, J. N. 108
999 180
Noelle-Neumann, E. 91
normativity 96–8, 104n8, 144
Norway: BSS cable system 112–13; constitutional assembly 168; literary/scientific scholars 48–9; news 137–8; orators 162–3, 164; politicians 159–62
Norwegian Research Council 1
nostalgia 26, 98
NYPD Blue 62

observational documentary 62–3, 177
Ong, Walter 29

oppression, cultural forms 169
OprahWinfrey 59, 91, 151
oral histories 22
orators, Norway 162–3, 164
Ottosen, Rune 42, 43

paidia 80
Panorama 138
Parkin, F. 142
parody 83
participation rights 12
particularism 19, 22, 28
pastiche 83
paternalism 14–15
Patton, P. 143
Peirce, C. S. 118, 119
performance 75, 82–5, 87n13
performativity: documentary 83, 87n12;
    television 84–5
personalizing of news stories 137, 143–4
persuasion, documentary 77
Peters, Hans Peter 43
phenomenology, space–time 98
Philo, C. 100, 104n8
photography 108
phronesis 46
Piaget, Jean 110
Pike, Kenneth 130, 132–3
pilgrimages 22, 23, 26–7
Pingree, S. 103n7
place, and space 3, 110–12
Plato 86n6
play 75, 79–82, 86n7, 87n10
police as drama 66
politicians: close-ups 159, 164, 167;
    credibility 159, 160–1; news 143–4;
    Norway 159–62
politics: aestheticized 170; end of apathy
    155–6; of identity 9, 99; rhetoric 4,
    162–3, 164; on television 4
polysemy 151
popular culture, knowledge 47, 152
popularization 34, 72, 195
populism 173
postmodernism: consumerism 10;
    documentary 175–6, 181–2;
    epistemology 35; fragmentation 12,
    83, 84; interpretation 50–1; Lyotard
    35; narratives collapsing 7; public
    discourse 51; simulacra 150–1
power relations 23, 132
presentation, and representation 168

Price, Monroe E. 8, 15
printing press 108
production, cultural 183n1
professional recognition,
    scholars/journalists 40, 43
programme scheduling 69
programmes: formation 13; sequence
    flow 116; time/space organization
    186–7
projective space 110, 116–17
Propp, Vladimir 73
Pruitt-Igoe housing development 7
psychoanalysis, working through 55,
    69n1
psychology: documentaries 63; news 59;
    play 81–2, 87n10
Public Culture 19
public discourse: distorted 46;
    documentaries 61; as entertainment
    45; postmodern 51; representation
    15–16; responsibility 40; television
    9–10
public interest, state intervention 11
public-service broadcasting: audience as
    citizens 38; critics 16; depth of
    treatment 51; as home 115;
    participation 12; paternalism 14;
    representation 12
public sphere: black 28; fragmented 38;
    Habermas 2, 102; liberal 37; media
    95; micro 2, 18, 28–9; mimicry/*ilinx*
    80; studio debates 92
public/private sphere: boundaries
    blurred 99, 167; documentary 180;
    home videos 24; identity 21–2
publicity 41, 43, 59
Punjabis, home videos 24

Quayle, Dan 147–50
Quintilian 1, 168

Rabinowitz, Mary Ann 175
Racine, Jean Luc 19
racism 145, 152
radio, intimacy 165–6
rational argument 14
readings: beneficiary 189–91; fan/non-
    fan 101; intellectual 188–9; intimistic
    191–5; negotiated 140; preferred
    151; soap opera 101
Reagan, Ronald 144, 163–4, 167

real-time, news broadcasts 56
reality: cultivation research 103n7;
     documentary 176, 180–1; and drama
     147–51; embodied 83; hyper-reality
     147; play 81
reality television 175, 180–81
reception theory 100, 133, 176–7,
     186–7, 190
recognition: and cognition 77–8; familiar
     96–7, 98; professional 40, 43; public
     43
Rees, Anthony M. 7
Reith, John 78
religious communities 23
religious right wingers 150–1
Renov, Michael 72, 77
repetition 88n15
representation: citizenship 12, 13;
     cultural 168–9; documentary 176–7;
     experience 11–12; free markets 16;
     mediated knowledge 94–5; and
     presentation 168; public discourse
     15–16; public-service broadcasting
     12; and reception 176–7; semiotic
     118, 120; symbolic 91
reproduction, knowledge 94
Rescue 911 179
research see media research
rhetoric: audience 163–4; classical 1;
     close-up 46; discursive space 75,
     76–8, 82; mnemonics 118; Norway
     162–3, 164; politics 4; style 162–3,
     164–5; truth 75
Rhetoric Knowledge Mediation research
     project 1
Ricoeur, Paul 77
right wing 8, 150–1
rights: citizenship 9, 10; cultural 11–13,
     16; human 7; participation 12
ritual: communication 3, 96; play 79;
     viewing 80
Robertson, Pat 150
Robespierre, Maximilien 169
Roger and Me 182
Roosevelt, Franklin D. 165–6
Roots 147
Rorty, Richard 36
Rose, B. G. 91
Rousseau, Jean-Jacques 169
Rubin, A. M. 91
Ruge, M. 127
Ryle, Gilbert 69n6

Sagan, Carl 49
Sanders, Claire 10
Santayana, George 170
Sarajevo, siege of 58
Sartre, Jean-Paul 49–50
Saussure, Ferdinand de 126
Scannell, Paddy 74
Schiller, H. 129
Schlesinger, Philip 29, 95, 97
Schnapper, Dominique 20
Schnitler, Carl W. 168
scholars: communication studies 52;
     funding 43; habitus 41–2, 45;
     intellectuals/technicians of
     knowledge 49–50; and journalists 2,
     34, 39; knowledge 35; and media 39,
     44–5; professional recognition 40,
     43; public function 34; public
     recognition 43; stereotypes 46–7; on
     television 34, 42, 46, 51
Schramm, Wilbur 127
Schroeder, K. C. 96, 100
Schudson, Michael 30
Schutz, Alfred 98
science documentary, revised 71, 72, 78,
     82, 85–6
science on television 4, 48, 185–6;
     beneficiary reading 189–90;
     disappointed beneficiaries 190–1;
     excluded position 195–6; institutions
     involved 187–8, 190; intellectual
     reading 188–9; intimistic reading
     191–5; reception study 186–7, 196;
     socially constructed 86n2
scientists 49, 85
screen: as place 119; television 116;
     window pane metaphor 117
screen personality 46
segregation 144
Seiter, E. 96
self 41, 100; see also identity
semiotics 73, 118, 120, 126
Sennett, Richard 45
serial drama 66–7
Shaw, D. 91
Short Stories 62
Sibley, D. 144
Sieburg, Friedrich 169
Signorielli, N. 142, 153
signs, emic/etic categories 130, 132–3
Silverstone, Roger 3, 71, 72, 76, 77, 78,
     79, 82, 85, 129

simulacra 150–1; *see also* hyper-reality
simultaneity 120
situation/journey 109–10
situation comedies 96, 98
Sky TV 64
soap opera: chat shows 59, 60; message 96; narrative 141; nostalgia 98; readings 101; social issues 60–1; teenage viewers 61; textual rhythm 97; time lags in showing 60–1
social cohesion 38
social construction: science 86n2; style 46
social responsibility 9
social sciences, media 48
social settings, time–space 98–9
sociocultural functions 3, 127
sociologists 48
Solheim, Erik 159–60, 160–2, 170–1
Sorlin, Pierre 29, 68
space: centred 110; de Certeau 110–11; Euclidean 110, 115; flow 116; imaginary 118, 119–20; individual conception 110; interaction 75–6; literal 74; mental/social 131; mnemonics 118; and place 3, 110–12; as practised space 111–12; projective 110, 116–17; symbolic 74; topological 110, 114, 116
space–time distanciation *see* time–space
Sparks, C. 139
speculation 58
sport 64–6
Squire, C. 96
St Elsewhere 66
Stand and Deliver 47
Stanislavsky 168
stars, cinema 167
state: citizenship 9, 10–11; and identity 21; intervention 11
Steiner, George 79
stereotypes 2, 46–7, 152
Stivers, Richard 154
storytelling 152; *see also* narrative
structuralism 36, 73, 153
studio audience 91, 93
studio debates 92, 98
style: rhetoric 162–3, 164; social production 46
subject, decentred 110
subjectivity 37
surveillance 9

Swift, Adam 8
Sylvania Waters 63, 181
symbolic density, documentary 181
symbolic representation 91
symbolic space 74
Syse, Jan P. 164

Taine, Hippolyte 169
talk shows 14, 56–7, 59, 96
Tamil Ozhi 23–4
Taylor, E. 96
technicians of knowledge 49–50
technology 76, 108–9
teenagers, soap operas 61
television: anti-authoritarian 46; authenticity 117; close-up 45, 46, 55, 159, 164, 167; communication 42–3; and democracy 2, 4; discourse 9–10, 72; discursive space 84, 85; dispersal of 173; fact/fiction 139–40; films 67; function 3, 78; genres 4, 13, 186–7; ignorance of technology 108–9; as institution 187–91; interruptions 67–8, 70n8; knowledge 35–7, 104n12, 188, 189; meaning-making 64; mediation 71–2; models of 55; mythopoeic 71; narrative 21–2; and newspapers 136–7; normativity 144; performativity 84–5; play 81; politics 4; rhetoric 163–4; rules 69; and scholars 34, 42, 46, 51; scientists 85; storytelling 152; text 82; as tour 113–14; viewing 109–10, 115; working through 55, 57–60, 64, 68
television, types: access 180–1; diasporic 24; digital 15, 176; educational 49; ethnic 25, 26; exilic 25, 26; minority 10, 25–6; transnational 25–6
television apartheid 145
television documentary *see* documentaries
Television and Everyday Life 82
television news *see* news
television sport 64–6
testimony 179–80, 182
text: and audience 3, 74, 75; authenticity 117; discursive space 3, 74–5, 85; fragmentation 84; meaning 73; rhythm 97; television 82
This Life 155
Thomas, Clarence 143–4, 147
Thompson, J. B. 93, 97, 99, 100, 127
Thussu, D. 126

Time 150, 151, 163
time 44, 94, 120; real-time 56; soap
    opera showings 60–1
Time, The Place, The 91
time–space distanciation 98, 99, 100–1,
    102, 104n9
Tocqueville, Alexis de 8
topological space 110, 114, 116
tour 111, 112, 113–14, 117
tradition 22–3
Tranmæl, Martin 162–3
transnational television 25–6
travelling 23; and watching 114, 117
Trilling, Lionel 161
True Stories 62
trust, media 154
truth: documentary 176, 177; and
    knowledge 35, 36; logic 88n14;
    performance 75; play 75; rhetoric 75
Tuchman, G. 128
Tumber, H. 95
Turner, Victor 20, 87n13
TV Nation 182

Ullman, Liv 169
uncertainty 69, 69n6
UNESCO: New World Information and
    Communication Order 127; News of
    the World project 129–31
universalism, rejected 20
Urry, J. 99
US television 38, 145–6

Valensi, Lucette 20
validity 176
values, particular/universal 18
Varis, T. 127, 128
Vattimo, Gianni 85
vérité programme-making 177
Véron, Eliséo 185, 190, 195
Video Diaries 94, 180, 182
videos, home 14, 22–3, 24

viewer subscription 15
viewers: alienated 137, 142, 143, 156,
    188; attention 68; cynicism 154;
    light/heavy 105n15, 153, 154; news
    137, 138, 141–2; social background
    133–4; *see also* audience
viewing 109–10; epistemology 86; heavy
    153, 154; map 117–20; ritual 80;
    studies of 152; television/cinema
    109–10, 115; and travelling 114, 117
viewing contract 185
violence 44, 97, 104n13
virtual media events 143
voting, rights/requirements 9

Walker, Martin 151
Walkowitz, R. 147, 149–50
Wallis, R. 127
watching television *see* viewing
Watkins, B. 105n15
Watkins, John 69n6, 69
Watson, Paul 63, 181
Ways of Seeing (Berger) 49
White, D. 128
Williams, Raymond 37–8, 83, 116, 137,
    148, 152
Wilson, Tony 74
Winfrey, Oprah 59, 91, 151
Winnicott, D. W. 81, 87n10
Winston, Brian 175, 176
Wohl, R. R. 99
women: celebrated 96; domestic rhythm
    97; male-dominated 103n7; violence
    104n13
Woollacot, Martin 154
working through process 3, 55, 57–60,
    69n1, 64, 68
World in Action 138
written text, authenticity 117

zapping 3, 114, 186